T. S. Eliot

T. S. Eliot 1938. (*Copyright E. McKnight Kauffer*)

T. S. ELIOT

A symposium from Conrad Aiken, Luciano Anceschi,
G. B. Angioletti, W. H. Auden, George Barker, Mont-
gomery Belgion, Clive Bell, John Betjeman, Amalendu
Bose, Ronald Bottrall, E. Martin Browne, Emilio Cecchi,
Nevill Coghill, Ernst Robert Curtius, Bishnu Dey, Ashley
Dukes, Lawrence Durrell, William Empson, George
Every, G. S. Fraser, Henri Fluchère, Michael Hamburger,
Desmond Hawkins, John Heath-Stubbs, Pierre Jean
Jouve, Wyndham Lewis, E. F. C. Ludowyk, Louis
MacNeice, Claude Edmonde Magny, Richard March,
Eugenio Montale, Marianne Moore, Nicholas Moore,
F. V. Morley, Edwin Muir, Norman Nicholson,
Hugh Gordon Porteus, Mario Praz, Kath-
leen Raine, James Reeves, Anne Rid-
ler, George Seferis, Edith Sitwell,
Stephen Spender, Tambi-
muttu, Ruthven Todd,
Vernon Watkins

Compiled by Richard March and Tambimuttu

𝒫𝓛

Editions Poetry London

1948

First Published September, 1948
by PL Editions Poetry London Limited, 26 Manchester
Square, London, W1
Second Edition, December, 1948

Typography
by Anthony Froshaug MSIA

Setting
by Monotyping Service Limited, 10 Gough Square, London,
EC4

Printed in Great Britain
by Henry Ling Limited, The Dorset Press, Dorchester

Contents

Foreword

This book was conceived as a tribute to T. S. Eliot, on his sixtieth birthday, from his friends, critics and admirers in many parts of the world. The idea for it first arose from a suggestion by Professor E. F. C. Ludowyk, the director of English studies in the University of Ceylon, who wrote to us in a letter: 'It is T. S. Eliot's sixtieth birthday on September the 26th. Are you going to do anything to celebrate the event?'

Accordingly, invitations to join in on a celebration proper to the occasion were sent out, especially to the younger writers, as well as to those of Mr Eliot's own generation. The response, with one or two exceptions, has exceeded all expectations. Our only regret is that there was not time enough for many others to decorate his cake, who were keen to do so. But though this book was meant as a birthday book, it is apparent that in scope and interest it has far outgrown its original function. The material ranges over a whole historical epoch, and casts many revealing sidelights on the literary scene as it has unfolded itself during more than thirty years.

It has been our aim to present a picture of T. S. Eliot, the man, in the particular setting in which he has been active as poet and man of letters, against a background of poems in homage, and critical essays on his work. Pure criticism has been kept down to a minimum, since this predominates among the vast mass of writing that has already appeared about Mr Eliot. It was felt that a more useful and unusual book would result, if we asked for reminiscences from those who were intimately associated with Mr Eliot at various times, and for personal statements describing the writers' first reaction to his poetry, or the manner in which they became acquainted with it or were influenced by it. And one important aspect of this book that has emerged, is the account it gives of the deepening of a sense of their native tradition, and of the relation of

11

tradition to the living present, that has resulted from a study of Mr Eliot's work in many countries.

The Editors take the opportunity of thanking contributors for the prompt way in which contributions were delivered, in some cases at very short notice indeed. In particular, they would like to express their thanks to Mr John Hayward for his interest and valuable advice, and for his assistance in revising the manuscript. The plates have been reproduced by kind permission of the Houghton Library at Harvard, and of Mr John Hayward from whose private collection we obtained the MS pages. And a special word of thanks goes to the printers and binders, without whose ready co-operation, in difficult circumstances, this book would not have been produced at the appropriate time.

R. M.
T. T.

T. S. Eliot

Clive Bell

How Pleasant to know Mr Eliot

It would be better, of course, if he were to record his encounters with me, for in that way students, besides enjoying
a bit of prose by our greatest living poet, might learn the
exact truth: the author of *Mr Apollinax* is surely one to remember dates and details. So far as I can remember, it was in
the summer of 1916 that first we met. Bertrand Russell asked
me to look out for a man called 'Eliot' who had just come, or
was just coming, to England, and had been his best pupil at
Harvard: he may have said 'My only good pupil', but if so,
doubtless he exaggerated as philosophers will. Eliot came to
dinner at 46 Gordon Square, where I was living with Maynard
Keynes; however, I was alone that night, and so after dinner
the poet and I sat in my room at the top of the house and
talked about books. I was not sure that he altogether liked my
enthusiasm for Merimée's stories and Horace Walpole's letters; but for my part I liked him so much that I determined,
there and then, to make him acquainted with some of my
friends. Soon afterwards I introduced him to Roger Fry and
Virginia Woolf, both of whom were to play parts in later encounters.

Virginia liked Tom from the first and appreciated his poetry: also she teased him. Roger was excited and enthusiastic,
and, as usual when excited, constructive. He it was who urged
Eliot to elucidate the text of *The Waste Land* with explanatory notes. Eliot met him half way: he supplied notes, but
whether they are explanatory is for others to decide. Between
Virginia and myself somehow the poet became a sort of 'family joke': it is not easy to say why. To some people the combination of human frailties with supernatural powers will always appear preposterous, which is, I suppose, a roundabout
way of saying that a genius is an oddity. To us at any rate this
mixture, genius, in its rarest form, combined with studied

15

primness of manner and speech, seemed deliciously comic. Besides, Virginia was a born and infectious mocker. I would receive a post-card, for in those happy days (the middle 'twenties maybe) there was no telephone at Charleston, my summer refuge: 'Come to lunch on Sunday. Tom is coming, and, what is more, is coming with a four-piece suit'. This came from Rodmell, five or six miles away, where Leonard Woolf still lives, where Eliot was a frequent visitor, and whence frequently he was brought to Charleston for a meal. One of these meals, a dinner-party, he will hardly have forgotten.

He will remember it not so much for what was said as for what was done. We had been sent a brace of grouse. My wife, who takes my opinion on sporting matters and on no others, enquired whether this would be enough for a party of eight. I said it would not, and that a bird between two was a fair allowance. She thinks she may have confused this estimate with something I had once said about snipe – two a mouth. Anyhow more grouse were ordered, and, when the soup-plates had been cleared away, entered three platters supporting sixteen birds – ten on table and six on the sideboard. Even the inventor of Sweeney appeared to think this unusual. The evening was not to end, however, without its contribution to scholarship; for somebody wondered whether anything was known of Mrs Porter and her daughter beyond the fact that they wash their feet in soda water. 'These characters are known', said the master, 'only from an Ayrian camp-fire song of which one other line has been preserved:
And so they oughter.
Of such pieces, epic or didactic', he continued, 'most have been lost, wholly or in part, in the mists of antiquity; but I recall one that is generally admitted to be complete:
Some say the Dutch ain't no style, ain't no style,
But they have all the while, all the while.'
And this reminds me of a poem I once wrote, on T. S. Eliot, in French, and sent to Mrs Woolf on the back of a post-card. It is unlikely to have been saved: it was called *Sur Le tombeau de Tom.*

I am getting a little out of date. If I met Eliot in 1916, it

16

must have been in '17 that I went to Garsington for an Easter party taking with me some ten or dozen copies of the last, and perhaps the first, publication of the Egoist Press, *The Love Song of J. Alfred Prufrock*. Anyone with a taste for research can fix the date, for the book, or brochure rather, had just appeared and I distributed my copies hot from the press like so many Good Friday buns. Who were the recipients? Our host and hostess, Philip and Lady Ottoline Morell, of course. Mrs St John Hutchinson, Katherine Mansfield, Aldous Huxley, Middleton Murry, Lytton Strachey perhaps, and, I think, Gertler. Were there others? Maria Balthus for instance (later Mrs Aldous Huxley). I cannot tell: but of this I am sure, it was Katherine Mansfield who read the poem aloud. As you may suppose, it caused a stir, much discussion, some perplexity. I wonder how many of us have kept our copies. Mine I have stowed in some secret place where I cannot now lay hands on it. Already it must be worth a deal of money; for, not only is it the first edition of a fine poem by a fine poet, of one of his earliest works too, but, unless I mistake, the brochure itself is bound in a trashy yellow jacket and is badly printed on bad paper. Misprints, if I remember right, and letters turned upside-down are discoverable. In a word, it is the sort of thing for which bibliophiles give hundreds. But though it must be amongst my most valuable mislaid possessions, I esteem it less than certain envelopes addressed, after the manner of Mallarmé, in verse, and addressed to me. Of these I own several, which, by taking pains, I could bring to light; but happily I may spare myself a dusty search since only the other morning arrived what will serve to give a taste of my correspondent's mettle.

O stalwart SUSSEX postman, who is
Delivering the post from LEWES,
Cycle apace to CHARLESTON, FIRLE,
While knitting at your plain and purl,
Deliver there to good CLIVE BELL,
(You know the man, you know him well,
He plays the virginals and spinet),
This note – there's almost nothing in it.

17

For the benefit of the author I may say that this pleasantry gave satisfaction to the postman invoked. He considered it 'clever.' He was not quite sure about the 'spinet,' but knew that I was fond of shooting: it was not true about the 'virginals' he hoped.

At Sunday evening performances, especially those given by the Phoenix Society, I used to admire Mr Eliot's faultless dress, white waistcoat and all: whether at an evening party, or in the country (you will remember the 'four piece suit') or in the city, always the poet made himself inconspicuous by the appropriateness of his costume.

> *Flowed up the hill and down King William Street*
> *To where Saint Mary Woolnoth kept the hours*
> *With a dead sound on the final stroke of nine.*

> *There I saw one I knew, and stopped him, crying:* 'Stetson!'
I might have cried 'Tom: cry you mercy, I took you for a banker.' And a banker he was in these early days; at least he worked in a bank. How characteristic! And how wise! Instead of doing as most young poets of promise do, eking out a living with journalism, which slacks the sacred strings, thus too often belying the promise, Eliot stuck to his desk – in King William Street or thereabouts, and found time of an evening to say all that he deemed worth saying. I doubt whether he has written a slovenly or an otiose line. He has kept his honour as bright as La Bruyère kept his.

If T. S. Eliot were not a famous poet, he would be known as a remarkably clever man. This cleverness comes out delightfully in conversation, and it came out rather unexpectedly one night at a birthday party given in her riverside house by Mrs St John Hutchinson. She had invited, so she said, the ten cleverest men in London to meet the ten most beautiful women: those who were not invited are not obliged to consider her judgment infallible. After supper we pulled crackers; and Lady Diana Cooper, having surreptitiously collected the riddles in which, along with caps and whistles, crackers used to abound, mounted a chair and announced that she would now put our wits to the test. She read the riddles aloud, and almost before the question was propounded pat came the answer from

At Garsington in the early nineteen-twenties. Left to right: Lord
David Cecil, Leslie Hartley, Anthony Asquith, T. S. Eliot, Edward
Sackville West.

two of the guests: Maynard Keynes and T. S. Eliot. You might have supposed that a certain sedate primness of speech, inherited maybe from a line of New England ancestors, would have put Eliot at a disadvantage. It did. Luckily, Maynard Keynes, when excited, sometimes developed a slight stutter. He stuttered ever so little on this occasion; he stuttered sufficiently; the handicaps were equal, and the two cleverest of the clever ran neck and neck all the way. It is only fair to add that Aldous Huxley might have come in a better third had not righteous indignation, provoked by the imbecility of the conundrums, in some measure balked the stride of his lofty intellect.

If in this paper I have not done much to explain the nature of Eliot's genius, I shall not apologize. Anyone who cares enough about poetry to read tittle-tattle about a poet needs no help from a tattler.

Conrad Aiken

King Bolo and Others

Forty years ago Cambridge, Massachusetts, or that part of
it adjacent to Harvard College, was not at all the ugly manu-
facturing city it has become: it was still in many senses a village. Lilacs and white picket fences under elms, horse-drawn
watering-carts to lay the dust in the blindingly dusty streets
of summer, board-walks put down on the pavements every
winter and taken up again every spring, sleighs and pungs in
the snow, and the dreadful college bell reverberant over all.
Were we gayer as undergraduates than those of today? At all
events we were gay, and my earliest single recollection of our
sixty-year-old hero is of a singularly attractive, tall, and rather
dapper young man, with a somewhat Lamian smile, who reeled out of the door of the Lampoon on a spring evening, and,
catching sight of me, threw his arms about me – from the
open windows above came the unmistakable uproar of a punch
in progress. 'And that,' observed my astonished companion,
'if Tom remembers it tomorrow, will cause him to suffer
agonies of shyness.' And no doubt it did: for he *was* shy. Not
that this by any means kept him out of social circulation. For
if we met to begin with as fellow editors of the Harvard Advocate (*diaboli Advocati*), whether at board meetings on the top
floor of the Union, or at initiations, or punches, or even at tea
(with rum in it), we also met at Buckingham and Brattle Hall
dances and at the Signet, a club with vaguely literary preten-
sions, and an excellent small library, which was said to have
been founded by a scion of the Bonaparte family. He was
early explicit, too, about the necessity, if one was shy, of dis-
ciplining oneself, lest one miss certain varieties of experience
which one did not naturally 'take' to. The dances, and the
parties, were a part of this discipline, as later on – after a year
at the Sorbonne, at the end of which we met in Paris for *sirop
de fraises* – was his taking of boxing-lessons. He had returned

20

to Cambridge and Harvard to work for his doctorate in philosophy, returning already perceptibly Europeanized: he made
a point, for a while, a conspicuously un-American point, of
carrying a cane – was it a malacca? – a little self-conscious
about it, and complaining that its 'nice conduct' was no such
easy matter. He had taken a room in Ash Street, installing in
it a small stove – 'something to point the chairs at' – and a
Gauguin *Crucifixion*, brought from Paris. The suggestion that
the latter was a kind of sophisticated primitivism brought the
reply, with a waspishness that was characteristic, that there
'was nothing primitive about it.' (A waspishness, let us say
parenthetically, that has now and then got him into trouble:
'Shelley was a fool,' for example, or, of Chekhov, 'I prefer my
Ibsen straight.') The boxing lessons, meanwhile, took place at
a toughish gymnasium in Boston's South End, where, under
the tutelage of an ex-pugilist with some such monicker as
Steve O'Donnell, he learned not only the rudiments of boxing, but also, as he put it, 'how to swarm with passion up a
rope' – his delight in this attainment was manifest. Was Steve
O'Donnell the prototype of Sweeney, as some have suggested?
Anyway, it was our habit to dine together after these gym-
nastic afternoons, usually at the Greek restaurant in Stuart
Street, a small, dirty, and wonderfully inexpensive establishment which was in fact half restaurant and half pool-room;
and it was here on one unfortunate occasion, when he had
accidentally hit Steve too hard, that he turned up with a magnificent black eye, a shiner that did Steve great credit: it was
really iridescent.

What did we talk about? or what didn't we? It was the
first 'great' era of the comic strip, of Krazy Kat, and Mutt and
Jeff, and Rube Goldberg's elaborate lunacies: it was also perhaps the most creative period of American slang, and in both
these departments of invention he took enormous pleasure.
How delighted we were with the word 'dinge' for negro! This
rich native creativeness was to be reflected, of course, in his
poetry, notably in Prufrock, just as our dear deplorable friend,
Miss X, the *precieuse ridicule* to end all preciosity, serving tea
so exquisitely among her bric-a-brac, was to be pinned like a

21

butterfly to a page in *Portrait of a Lady*. But more immediately it gave rise to the series of hilariously naughty *parerga* which was devoted spasmodically to that singular and sterling character known as King Bolo, not to mention King Bolo's Queen, 'that airy fairy hairy-'un, who led the dance on Golder's Green with Cardinal Bessarion.' These admirable stanzas, notable at times for their penetrating social criticisms were to continue for years as a sort of cynical counterpoint to the study of Sanskrit and the treatise on epistemology. Their influence on the development of a Style will no doubt come in due course to the attention of Herr Dr Krapp of Wien.

But what did we talk about? What to write, of course, and how to write, and what to read – Charles Louis Philippe and Vildrac, fresh from Paris – but also increasingly, and perhaps more concernedly, where to live, and how. Europe? And if so London, or Paris? Could one successfully lay siege to either, and how should one go about it? A year or so later, letters of introduction took me to London, and to W. H. Davies in Little Russell Street, to Rupert Brooke in Gray's Inn, to Edward Thomas, Harold Monro, and Ezra Pound. With me also was the typescript of *Prufrock*, typed by its author with meticulous care on a Blickensderfer which produced only italics, and *La Figlia che Piange*, neither of which was I able to sell. Monro – though ten years later he was a convert, if this side idolatry – thought *Prufrock* bordered on 'insanity.' But Pound, serving tea not so exquisitely among his beautiful Gaudiers, recognized *Prufrock* instantly, and this was the beginning.

The beginning of the war, too: which was to wash Eliot up in London, back from Marburg, where he had just begun his studies, and myself in Boston. Where to live? The letters are full of the question. England was clearly impossible. 'A people which is satisfied with such disgusting food *is not* civilized.' London is at first detested. But Oxford, and Merton, with its 'Alexandrian verse, nuts and wine,' the professors with pregnant wives and sprawling children, and hideous pictures on their walls, makes him long even for London, perhaps to work in the British Museum. 'Come, let us desert our wives, and

22

fly to a land where there are no Medici prints, nothing but
concubinage and conversation. Oxford is very pretty, but I
don't like to be dead.' Conversation yes – but where to find it?
Well, 'Pound is rather intelligent as a talker: his verse is
touchingly incompetent.' 'O Conversation, the staff of life,
shall I get any at Oxford?' Then follows his *War Poem, for
the $100 prize, entitled UP BOYS AND AT 'EM! Adapted to
the tune of 'C. Columbo lived in Spain,' and within the compass
of the average male or female voice*, and a new stanza of King
Bolo. And he adds 'I am keen on rhymes in -een.'

As for more serious work, he writes: 'I think you criticize
my work too leniently. It still seems to me strained and intellectual.' (This refers to an unfinished poem, never published, called *The Love Song of St Sebastian*.) 'I know the kind of
verse I want, and I know that this isn't it, and I know why. I
shan't do anything that will satisfy me (as some of my old
stuff *does* satisfy me – whether it be good or not) for years. I
feel it more and more. And I don't know whether I want to.
Why should one worry about that? I feel that such matters
take care of themselves, and have no dependence upon our
planning.'

I can't say that I always understand
My own meaning when I would be very fine.
But the fact is that I have nothing planned
Except perhaps to be a moment merry . . .
The prediction is uncanny: for the year is 1915.

Wyndham Lewis

Early London Environment

The end of last month and of this month respectively (March and April namely) have been the dead-line for articles I had agreed to write about two very old friends of mine. The circumstances attending the composition of these articles, in one respect at least, has been dramatic. For one of these friends is confined in a criminal asylum in America: but the other is among us here, a rarely honoured member of his profession, dwelling in the bland atmosphere of general approbation.

As I took up my pen and addressed myself to these tasks, I could not help but wonder what qualities are conducive to one issue, what to the other: which are those that draw A down into such portentous shadows, which that thrust B up into so brilliantly sunlit a position? Need the Freudian machinery be invoked? For me I think the question tends to take no count of the climb up into the sun, but only the problem of what keeps anybody – A B C or D – out of a madhouse.

This is not, however, an excursion into psychology nor psychiatry. What made the description of this rhetorical gesture of wondering enquiry almost essential, or something on similar lines, is the fact that I first met B (the subject of this article) at the home of A. And their two destinies at that early date, again, form so much one indistinguishable pattern – so that you could not speak of B without mentioning A, that their personalities, if not their literary reputations, would of necessity be discussed. A good opportunity presents itself at this point to observe that personalities, the 'scene' not literary reputations, is to be the sole subject-matter.

The task more particularly assigned me, as I understand it, is to say something about the earliest phase of Mr T. S. Eliot's life in London, or what I recall of it. There is, naturally, a scarcity of witnesses – it was a long time ago, and his movements as yet private and unprominent. So, on this most solemn occasion, I shall do my best.

I am much more of an authority on Mr Eliot at a later date. The earlier Mr Eliot about whom I am to write is a figure entering the portals – seated in the parlour – of Heartbreak House. He and war came together. Preparatory to going into the army I pressed on with the composition of *Tarr* – and also was not able to move about a great deal. What I have to tell will be, perhaps, a little like a portrait which is all accessories and not much figure – that is, if the author of the *Cantos* can be described as an accessory.

Well, Mr Eliot swam into my ken in Ezra Pound's diminutive triangular sitting-room, in which all Ezra's social life was transacted, since, although really absurdly tiny, it was the only room in the Pound flat where there was any daylight.

In the base of the triangle was the door. As I entered the room I discovered an agreeable stranger parked up one of the sides of the triangle. He softly growled at me, as we shook hands. American. A graceful neck I noted, with what elsewhere I have described as 'a Gioconda smile.' Though not feminine – besides being physically large his personality visibly moved within the male pale – there *were* dimples in the warm dark skin; undoubtedly he used his eyes a little like a Leonardo. He was a very attractive fellow then; a sort of looks unusual this side of the Atlantic. I liked him, though I may say not at all connecting him with texts Ezra had shown me about some fictional character dreadfully troubled with old age, in which the lines (for it had been verse) 'I am growing old, I am growing old, I shall wear the bottoms of my trousers rolled' – a feature, apparently, of the humiliations reserved for the superannuated – I was unable to make head or tail of.

Ezra now lay flung back in typical posture of aggressive ease. It resembled extreme exhaustion. (Looking back, I believe he *did* over-fatigue himself, like an excitable dog, use his last ounce of vitality, and that he did in fact become exhausted.) However, he kept steadily beneath his quizzical but self-satisfied observation his latest prize, or discovery – the author of *Prufrock*. The new collector's-piece went on smiling

25

and growling out melodiously his apt and bright answers to promptings from the exhausted figure of his proud captor. His ears did not grow red, or I am sure I should have noticed it. Ezra then gave us all some preserved fruit, of which it was his habit to eat a great deal.

The poem of which this was the author had, I believe, already been published. But Pound had the air of having produced it from his hat a moment before, and its author with it simultaneously, out of the same capacious headpiece. He blinked and winked with contemplative conceit and contentment, chewing a sugared and wonderfully shrunken pear: then removed his glasses to wipe off the film of oily London dust that might have collected – but really to withdraw, as it were, and leave me alone with Mr Prufrock for a moment.

Then, that finished, Ezra would squint quickly, sideways, up at me – 'granpa'-wise, over the rims of his glasses. With chuckles, and much heavy fun, in his screwed-up smiling slits of eyes, he would be as good as saying to me in the Amos and Andy patter of his choice: 'Yor ole uncle Ezz is wise to wot youse thinkin. Waaal Wynd damn I'se tellin *yew*, he's lot better'n he looks!'

Contempt on my part was always assumed, because a mania like Pound's to act as a nursery and lying-in establishment – *bureau de renseignment* and unofficial agency for unknown literary talent did involve the successive presence of numbers of preposterous people. These I would find either groping around in the dark in the large middle-room of the flat – even playing the piano there: or quite often seated where Mr Eliot was now installed. The situation therefore was one for which a regular convention existed, of quizzical dumbshow on the part of the incorrigible host, and stony stares back from me.

This very small room, in which Mr Eliot had alighted, and in which he sat placidly smiling, was, allowance made for the comic side of Ezra's manic herding of talent, a considerable place. Dorothy Shakespeare had become Dorothy Pound and of course was in this dwarf room too, nodding, with a quick jerk of the head, unquestioning approval of Ezra's sallies, or hieratically rigid as she moved delicately to observe the Kensingtonian Tea ritual. (Long habit in the paternal mansion responsible, she was a good turncoat *bourgeoise*, who wore her red cockade with a grim pleasant gaucherie.) In any event, all social transactions were necessarily *intime*. One at a time was their rule for genius.

Mr Eliot would presently be taken to a much larger place – where there would be more than just a crowded little triangle to sit in: not so important, yet an essential part of Ezra's exiguous social machine. For those not familiar with the hills and valleys of London, the event with which I opened took place practically at the foot of Notting Hill. Now almost at the top of that hill stood a squarish Victorian mansion, of no great size but highly respectable, within whose walls Ford Madox Ford (known then as Hueffer) lived and entertained with Violet Hunt. A gate in a tall wall gave access to it, and standing in the centre of a patch of grass, just visible from the pavement, was a large carving of Ezra by Breszka. It was Ezra in the form of a marble phallus. Mr Eliot would have to be taken here.

A number of people were to be met, certainly, belonging to the literary, theatrical, and occasionally monied, world at Hueffers (as it is better to call him, rather than Ford): for he was unspeakably gregarious. But Mr Eliot would be taken around there primarily to be shown to Hueffer. The latter gentleman in all probability thought he wrote poems like *Prufrock* just as well if not better himself. A sort of Wild West turn like Ezra, at whose hyperborean antics he could smile – that would be one thing. But it would be quite another for what was, as he saw it, a kind of Harvardian Rupert Brooke to make claims upon his tolerance. Such I imagine might be the situation arising from such a contact. But by South Lodge Mr Eliot would have to pass, as part of the initiatory proceedings.

There is no exacter manner available to me of dating my first encounter with Mr Eliot than by stating that before the first number of my magazine *Blast* I did not know him, and he was not known I think to others: but that before my second number I knew him. *Blast No 1* was published in June 1914, *Blast No 2* in July 1915. In *No 2* I printed some poems of his – *Preludes* and *Rhapsody on a Windy Night*. The last of the

Preludes (No 4) contains especially fine lines, which I have often seen quoted:

> *I am moved by fancies that are curled*
> *Around these images, and cling:*
> *The notion of some infinitely gentle,*
> *Infinitely suffering thing.*
> *Wipe your hand across your mouth, and laugh;*
> *The worlds revolve like ancient women*
> *Gathering fuel in vacant lots.*

It is no secret that Ezra Pound exercised a very powerful influence upon Mr Eliot. I do not have to define the nature of this influence, of course. Mr Eliot was lifted out of his lunar alley-ways and *fin de siècle* nocturnes, into a massive region of verbal creation in contact with that astonishing didactic intelligence, that is all. *Gerontion* (1920) is a close relative of *Prufrock*, certain matters filtered through an aged mask in both cases, but *Gerontion* technically is 'school of Ezra'.

The didactic vocation was exercised by Ezra, unfortunately, in the void (with the exception of such a happy chance as his association with his fellow-countryman Mr Eliot) – in a triangular box, as we have seen, practically at the foot of Notting Hill. Between Hueffer and himself there was a solid bond. Ezra 'believed in' Ford. Ford, who knew what he was talking about, praised the other's verses to the skies. And Ezra regarded it as typical – and very justly – that Hueffer should find no support in England for the *English Review*.

Degas's often quoted remark, made to another American, with whom publicity was second-nature, 'Whistler, you behave as if you had no talent,' applies to this case. Ezra, the would-be master or teacher, often behaved 'as if he had no talent.'

It occurs to me that to some English ears these remarks and descriptions may appear wanting in reticence. That is not so at all. In the first place, we are public figures. A man becomes that of his own free will – in fact the becoming it entails quite a lot of work, frequently requiring many years of pretty close attention and solid labour. In the arts the personality is engaged; accordingly everything about this figure is public, or

28

one day will be. Indeed, the more *publicity* the better pleased is every *public man*.

This is number one consideration. In the second place, although I bring the scene to life in which Mr Eliot at that stage of his career found himself, it is the scene, and not Mr Eliot, I recreate.

Knowing the principal figures in it still so well does not make the re-creation easier – though you would perhaps suppose it would. Some of these figures do not change much: others do. For instance, in 1938 when I was painting Ezra (the picture is now in the Tate) he swaggered in, coat-tails flying, a malacca cane out of the 'nineties aslant beneath his arm, the lion's head from the Scandinavian North-West thrown back. There was no conversation. He flung himself at full length into my best chair for that pose, closed his eyes and was motionless, just as a dog who has been taxing its strength to the full flings itself down and sleeps. Ezra was not haggard, he looked quite well, but was exhausted. He did not sleep, but he did not move for two hours by the clock.

'Go to it Wyndham!' he gruffled without opening his eyes, as soon as his mane of as yet entirely ungrizzled hair had adjusted itself to the cushioned chair-top. A reference to my portrait of Mr Eliot, painted some months earlier, produced the remark that now I had a 'better subject to work from.' A mild and not unpleasing example of the gasconade. But that was how I always found Ezra, full of bombast, germanic kindness, but *always* in appearance the Westerner in excelsis. On the tips of his toes with aggressive vitality, till he dropped, or as good as. (A note here I should like to add: I have had experience of Ezra for a long time: in some respects he does not forget the teaching of Chinese sages.)

With Mr Eliot it has always been quite the opposite. Appearing at one's front door, or arriving at a dinner-rendezvous (I am thinking of the late 'thirties, not his more vernal years of course) his face would be haggard, he would seem at his last gasp. (Did he know?) To ask *him* to lie down for a short while at once was what I always felt I ought to do. However, when he had taken his place at a table, given his face a dry

29

wash with his hands, and having had a little refreshment, Mr Eliot would rapidly shed all resemblance to the harassed and exhausted refugee, in flight from some Scourge of God. Apparently a modest reserve of power, prudently set aside, would be drawn on. He would be as lively as ever he could be or any one need be – for of course it is not necessary to fly about on the tips of one's toes with one's scarf and coat-tails flying.

Immediately after world war 1 – I had not long left a military hospital and was restarting with a new studio – Mr Eliot himself is, for me, much more distinct. For instance we went to the Loire and Brittany together – that holiday involving a meeting, the first for both of us, with James Joyce in Paris: after that a stay at Saumur, and then the Breton coast in the Golfe de Vannes region. I hope I shall not be destroying some sentimental illusion if I record that to my surprise I remarked that my companion entered most scrupulously in a small note-book the day's expenses. This he would do in the evening at a café table when we had our night-cap. There was not much more he could spend before he got into bed.

The intermediate years – since he first sat in Pound's toy room – had greatly matured Mr Eliot. The 'Gioconda' period seemed a thing of the distant past, the saturnine vein was strongly fed with the harsh spectacle of the times. He was an American who was in flight from the same thing that kept Pound over here, and with what had he been delected, as soon as he had firmly settled himself upon this side of the water? The spectacle of Europe committing suicide – just that.

The Hollow Men (of 1925) is generally considered Mr Eliot's most successful attempt to make the paralysis and decay concrete for his contemporaries, in drained-out cadences and desiccated vocables. *The* date of the *Hollow Men* takes one on to the times when I was often with Mr Eliot at the Schiffs', in Cambridge Square or at Eastbourne, and in the relaxation of a household where we were very much spoiled by our hosts, for my part for the last time I saw Mr Eliot in a mood that was very young. Even in the early 'thirties, however, the haggard and exhausted mask of which I spoke earlier was seen nothing of. I must get back now without delay to the foot of Notting

Hill, in the first 12 months after the 'lights had gone out in Europe.'

Pound possessed, in Miss Harriet Weaver, a very substantial auxiliary indeed. Her little office in Adelphi rather than South Lodge would be a place worth visiting for Mr Eliot. Sympathy, as much as ambition, would cause him to prefer the active Quaker lady, editress, to the ineffectual ex-editor Ford Madox Hueffer.

The Egoist was Miss Weaver's paper, but at the period of which I speak you would rather have supposed that it belonged to Ezra Pound. *The Egoist* also on occasion published books (my novel *Tarr* for instance). And the old files of *The Egoist* contain much work of Mr Eliot's. This, I should suppose, was the first place where his work appeared in England. The way was also smoothed by Pound for *Prufrock's* début in book form. So, for all his queerness at times – ham-publicity of self, misreading of part of poet in society – in spite of anything that may be said Ezra is not only *himself* a great poet, but has been of the most amazing use to other people. Let it not be forgotten for instance that it was he who was responsible for the all-important contact for James Joyce – namely Miss Weaver. It was *his* critical understanding, *his* generosity, involved in the detection and appreciation of the literary genius of James Joyce. It was through him that a very considerable sum of money was put at Joyce's disposal, at the critical moment.

Such is the career-side of Mr Eliot's association with Ezra Pound. But he met in his company Imagists and others, several of those who at a later time wrote for him in *The Criterion* – Gould Fletcher, Aldington, Flint. And when I spoke of Ezra *transacting* his social life, there was nothing social for him that did not have a bearing upon the business of writing. If it had not it would be dull. He was a man of letters, in the marrow of his bones and down to the red rooted follicles of his hair. He breathed Letters, ate Letters, dreamt Letters. A very rare kind of man. To fall into the clutches of this benevolent mentor was not the making of Mr Eliot – for he had already begun *making himself*, after quite a distinct fashion, in *Prufrock* and other pieces. Here was a stiffening. Here were a variety of transformations, technical and otherwise, which it is not my specifically non-critical function to indicate.

Had it not been the very earliest period of Mr Eliot's life in literary circles in England, some account of which was required of me, the background would not have been dominated by one figure, as in this article certainly has been the case. It always seems to be in the little triangular room, practically at the foot of Notting Hill, that I see Mr Eliot. I recall entering it, for example, when on leave (a *bombadier*). Mr Eliot was there – in the same place as the first time (there was nowhere else to sit however). After a little I found him examining me, his head on one side. I asked him what there was about me that puzzled him. He was wondering, he answered, whether the short hair suited me or not. (Before the army it had been thick and long.) My point is forcibly brought out by the fact that I had no idea where Mr Eliot lived. He appeared – he often was to be found – in the triangle, the supreme figure of Ezra a few feet away of course. I am not displeased, nor I am sure will Mr Eliot be, that the dictates of my commission led me perforce to write quite a lot about this old friend of ours.

Edith Sitwell

For T. S. Eliot

Prometheus, nailed to this barren rock, the world,
Above the howling dark, the rising dust,
What eagle suns devour your heart of fire?

Dead as the stone that seals the Sepulchre,
The street musicians with their blind
And empty worlds for eyes
Sound the Marsyas music, and the crowd's onolatries.

Braying, respond. The preacher mounts the stone
That seals the Tomb, and cries 'We must atone!'
The world has changed to rock. Where is the rod
To draw from it tears? Where is the sleeping God?
Yet there is something left. . . . Begin again!

And learn from the philosopher Ammonius
Who took a long-eared almond-furrèd ass
(With a hide like the husk of the sleepy earth) to school:

He sat upon a stool
With Origen and Porphyry, who wore a dunce's cap
That his long ears refused. . . . Why was he there? Mayhap

Within his two sole see-saw syllables
(The freezing Light which makes all objects real,
The yawning Dark to which we must return)

All language lies. The human race began
With but a single word . . .
What was that first word Man
In the beginning heard?

Now, at the end, few words are left
That can mean something to the heart. Only the one word
    'Bread',
Its assonance, the short and fading 'Breath',
And that word's horizontal rhyme, its echo, 'Death'.

But our Prometheus, who is crucified
Upon this rock, the world, above the crowd's onolatries,
Brought us his word of fire.
Then the burden of Atlas' woe, changed into pence
To lay on the innocent eyes,
The crazy hen-coop laughter, and the cries
Of Buyers and Sellers in the Temple, die:
The terrible rolling back of the Dark from the Tomb is heard –
Slain by the deathless, the Promethean word.

William Empson

The Style of the Master

I do not propose here to try to judge or define the achievement of Eliot; indeed I feel, like most other verse writers of
my generation, that I do not know for certain how much of
my own mind he invented, let alone how much of it is a reaction against him or indeed a consequence of misreading him.
He has a very penetrating influence, perhaps not unlike an
east wind. All I can do here is to put down a few reminiscences
of him, from meetings much rarer than I should have wished;
stories greatly in his favour, I should have thought, but you
never know how people will take things. And when I have tried
out my Eliot anecdotes on an anti-Eliot man he has generally
taken them as confirming his worst impressions. So they are
not designed to flatter (and, by the way, I could not have invented them) but they are a sort of witness to the Eliot legend,
and it deserves to be recorded.

My most impressive memory is of walking up Kingsway
with him after some lunch, probably about 1930, when finding myself along with the great man I felt it opportune to
raise a practical question which had been giving me a little
anxiety. 'Do you really think it necessary, Mr Eliot,' I broke
out, 'as you said in the preface to the Pound anthology, for a
poet to write verse at least every week?' He was preparing to
cross into Russell Square, eyeing the traffic both ways, and we
were dodging it as his slow reply proceeded. 'I had in mind
Pound when I wrote that passage' began the deep sad voice,
and there was a considerable pause. 'Taking the question in
general, I should say, in the case of many poets, that the most
important thing for them to do . . . is to write as little as
possible.' The gravity of the last phrase was so pure as to give
it an almost lyrical quality. A reader may be tempted to suppose that this was a snub or at least a joke, but I still do not
believe it was; and at the time it seemed to me not only very

wise but a very satisfactory answer. He had taken quite a weight off my mind.

In this kind of case, indeed, the Johnsonian pessimism was quite practical and helpful; one felt more doubtful about it in generalizations. There was a party (I forget everybody else in the room) where Eliot broke into some chatter about a letter being misunderstood. 'Ah, letters,' he said, rather as if they were some rare kind of bird, 'I had to look into the question of letters at one time. I found that the mistake . . . that most people make . . . about letters, is that after writing their letters, carefully, they go out, and look for a pillar-box. I found that it is very much better, after giving one's attention to composing the letter, to . . . pop it into the fire.' This kind of thing was a little unnerving, because one did not know how tragically it ought to be taken; it was clearly not to be regarded as a flippancy. There was some dinner including a very charming diplomat's wife, who remarked to Eliot that she too was very fond of reading. She didn't get much time, but she was always reading in bed, biographies and things. 'With pen in hand?' inquired Mr Eliot, in a voice which contrived to form a question without leaving its lowest note of gloom. There was a rather fluttered disclaimer, and he went on 'It is the chief penalty of becoming a professional literary man that one can no longer read anything with pleasure.' This went down very well, but it struck me that the Johnsonian manner requires more gusto as a contrast to the pessimism; perhaps after all, looking back, a mistaken complaint, because if untruth is all that is required to justify this sort of quip it was surely quite untrue that he no longer read anything with pleasure.

My earliest memory of Eliot, speaking of untruth, was when he came to Cambridge to give the Clark lectures and was prepared to receive undergraduates after breakfast on Thursdays; this was in the middle 1920's. At the first of these very awed gatherings someone asked him what he thought of Proust. 'I have not read Proust' was the deliberate reply. How the conversation was picked up again is beyond conjecture, but no one cared to plumb into the motives of his abstinence. It was felt to be a rather impressive trait in this powerful character. Next week a new member of the group asked what he thought of the translation of Proust by Scott Moncrieff, and Eliot delivered a very weighty, and rather long, tribute to that work. It was not enough, he said, to say that it was better than the original in many single passages; it was his impression that the translation was at no point inferior to the original (which, to be sure, was often careless French), either in accuracy of detail or in the general impression of the whole. We were startled by so much loquacity from the silent master rather than by any disagreement with what he had said before; in fact it seemed quite clear to me what Eliot meant – he did not consider he had 'read' a book unless he had written copious notes about it and so on. I no longer feel sure that this was what he meant, but I am still quite sure that he was not merely lying to impress the children; maybe at the earlier meeting he hadn't bothered to listen to what they were saying.

Perhaps the most charming case of his peculiar note, which however wilful in its sadness is always at the opposite pole to malice, occurred when a younger poet (long ago now) published a diary. I should explain that Eliot takes cheese rather seriously; as witness the pronouncement, 'I find I can no longer travel except where there is a native cheese. I am therefore bounded, northwards by Yorkshire . . .' and the rest of the points of the compass were all tidy (I think he had a fair run to the south) but I no longer know what they were. The younger poet had recorded a lunch with 'Tom', at which he had told Tom that simplicity and deep feeling were what made good poetry, and Tom had agreed. This was what gave his own poetry its lasting qualities ('Yes' Tom had said) and on the other hand gave good reason to prophecy that the poetry of Tom would only prove a passing fashion. Tom had seemed much struck by this. Meeting Eliot not long after I made bold to mention the diary, and he said 'Very interesting. He did me the kindness . . . to send me the proofs . . . of the parts . . . concerning myself.' I said I hoped he had found them all right. His manner became a trifle severe, though not noticeably sadder. 'I found it necessary,' he said 'in the interests of truth, to correct the name of the cheese.'

37

James Reeves

Cambridge Twenty Years Ago

The stranger who enters an Anglican church at service time is handed two books, *Hymns Ancient and Modern* and *The Book of Common Prayer*. When I went up to Cambridge twenty years ago, I was handed as it were, in much the same spirit, two little books, the one in prose, the other in verse. They were *The Sacred Wood* and *Poems 1909–1925*. Those who played the part of sidesmen were not, it should perhaps be said, my tutors but my fellow-undergraduates. Eliot was not at this time 'officially' recognized. The attitude of the English school varied according to the temperament of the lecturers; the more rebellious were enthusiastic, the more conventional loudly and derisively hostile. The 'centre' were temperately and critically sympathetic towards what they recognized as an important new influence, even though it was hailed with undiscriminating adulation by intellectual undergraduates.

Cautiously received among dons, Eliot was read, learned, discussed and above all imitated by undergraduates with competitive eagerness. It is easy now to laugh at the blind and fanatical enthusiasms of twenty years ago, but we were not altogether uncritical. Whatever may be said now of the influence of *The Waste Land*, *The Hollow Men*, *Gerontion* and those other poems of the 'disillusioned' period, it is certain that it was inescapable, inevitable. To the ordinary freshman like myself with a typical school background in English literature, the Georgians and the Romantics, especially Keats and Rupert Brooke, stood for what was normal, what was essentially poetic, in poetry. From romanticism, gone to seed in the facile beauty-culture of *The London Mercury*, we were looking for some new avenue of departure, new influences which should be exciting, urgent, passionate. The rediscovery of the Metaphysicals and the Elizabethans in *The Sacred Wood* and the nervousness, vitality, intellectual passion of the Poems seemed to offer just what we had been seeking. Two features of these poems made, perhaps, bad masters – their obscurity and their cynicism. But the obscurity was exciting; it made for a toughness of quality which seemed to make poetry once more a worthy subject of study for intelligent minds. As for cynicism – well, what a much more interesting figure was the youthful Jack Donne than the sentimentalized Rupert Brooke!

Two magazines were started in Cambridge about this time. 'This time', by the way, was the beginning of what I think was the last generation of undergraduates to remain more or less indifferent to politics. Few read a daily newspaper; on the rare occasions when one wanted to consult *The Times*, the copy in the Union reading-room was sufficient, and one was sure to find it unclaimed. *Cambridge Left* and undergraduate Communism began, I think, after the national crisis of 1931. *The Venture*, run mainly by Michael Redgrave, and *Experiment*, under J. Bronowski, William Empson and Hugh Sykes Davies – these two contemporaries were pure of all politics; there was scarcely a reference to the world outside, over which lingered the last golden rays of Locarno sunshine. *The Venture*, tastefully produced, adorned with woodcuts and filled with neo-Georgian poems and stories, was in reality an undergraduate heir to Sir John Squire's *London Mercury;* but *Experiment*, claiming to be youthful, rebellious, provocative, and to be concerned with 'all the intellectual interests of undergraduates', contained articles on science as well as literature, stills from modernist films, photographs of surrealistic paintings, much obscure poetry and experimental prose, of which latter our proudest example was a hitherto unpublished extract from Joyce's *Work in Progress*. We published articles on Hemingway, Hopkins, Joyce, Eliot; an attack on Wyndham Lewis; poems influenced by Hopkins, the Metaphysicals, the Imagists, Laura Riding and of course Eliot. Regular contributors, apart from the three editors named above, included Elsie Phare, John Davenport, T. H. White, George Reavey, Humphrey Jennings, Basil Wright, Richard Eberhart, Kathleen Raine, Edward Wilson and myself. Our interests were

39

many, our activities multifarious – or so they seemed. We wrote, we read, we discussed; we went to the Festival and saw Flora Robson and Robert Donat before they became world-famous; Lopokova danced at the A.D.C.; Gerald Noxon and Stuart Legg showed the classical Russian films long before every film society in London was showing them. Narrow, cliquish, self-opiniated it may sound now to some; but it was to us a very full, a very exciting, and a very worth-while world.

Over this world presided the spirit of T. S. Eliot. I say 'the spirit' because so far as I know Eliot made no public appearances in Cambridge at this time. Nor of course do I mean that Eliot's writings had a direct influence on everything that was said or written during these years. Many other writers – those I have mentioned, and I should have added D. H. Lawrence – had their influence. All the same, Eliot's influence was paramount, though not altogether unchallenged. What has persisted most obstinately for me, out of all the intellectual influences of that time, apart from the general direction of interest caused by Eliot's literary criticisms, has been the rhythm and imagery of the *Poems 1909–1925*. I have written of others perhaps too much, as implying an identity of interest which they would deny; but to speak now principally of myself, I must confess that though I have read and continue to read the later poems with admiration and emotion, yet they can never have upon me the effect of the earlier poems. Like many of my contemporaries, I have found the detachment, and at the same time the evidences of a tortured sensibility, which the earlier poems reveal, more to my mind than the religious ardours of the later poems, and certainly much more so than the jocularities of *Old Possum*. In saying this, of course, I can only convict myself, in the eyes of some readers, of a hopeless timidity, even dishonesty, certainly an obtuse failure to accept what Eliot feels to be the only possible outcome of the early poems. All this is known, and discounted, by his later readers. It does not matter much to any but myself and those who feel as I do. Eliot has put *The Waste Land* far behind him and trudged with difficulty and with infinite pain, out

40

into a region where the dry cellars infested by rats, the grimy town streets and the cactus-land are only disturbing memories. But to me these memories remain more intense, more real, and therefore more poetic, and paradoxically more fertile, than the rose-garden and the later landscape. Perhaps this feeling is sentimental, perhaps perverse, but certainly the only possible one for me.

No doubt the rhythm and imagery of the early poems persists most ineffaceably because I subjected myself to it at a particularly impressionable age. At all events there is no denying the persistence. It is as if Eliot wrote too well in these poems for the effect of his later writing to be felt fully by anyone who surrendered to the early spell. What a spell it is! How often is one haunted by the uneasy images of *Prufrock*, *Mr Apollinax*, *Gerontion*, the *Rhapsody on a Windy Night*.

> . . . *a crowd of twisted things;*
> *A twisted branch upon the beach*
> *Eaten smooth, and polished*
> *As if the world gave up*
> *The secret of its skeleton,*
> *Stiff and white.*
> *A broken spring in a factory yard,*
> *Rust that clings to the form that the strength has left*
> *Hard and curled and ready to snap.*

and:

> *Phlebas the Phoenician, a fortnight dead,*
> *Forgot the cry of gulls, and the deep sea swell*
> *And the profit and loss.*
> *A current under sea picked his bones in whispers.*

and, from one of the Ariel Poems:

> *The pain of living and the drug of dreams,*
> *Curl up the small soul in the window seat . . .*

How often do the images I recall from Eliot remind me of the passage in Keats' letters where he says, 'Poetry . . . should strike the reader as a wording of his own highest thoughts, and appear almost a remembrance.' Almost a remembrance – yes, the power of the most intense and evocative poetry is just this, that it seems to arise naturally, out of one's own uncon-

41

scious. So deeply has Eliot's poetic world sunk into my unconscious that I find myself continually remembering his images as if they were my own memories. And yet one's subconscious is selective, it does not yield itself up at random. Comparing the images from Eliot's poems which occur most frequently to my mind, I discover in them a common quality, the quality of pity. The whole of Eliot's early world – its fantastic, hopeless landscape, its wry, satiric figures drifting past, the odd cosmopolitan figures from the half-worlds of London commerce and Continental expatriate society – this whole world is touched with pity. Is the world of the later poems created as an escape from this overwhelming compassion for a helpless and hopelessly corrupted culture? No other poet, except Shakespeare, has the capacity for expressing tenderness without sentimentality and without illusions.

W. H. Auden

For T. S. Eliot

When things began to happen to our favourite spot,
A key missing, a library bust defaced,
    Then on the tennis-court one morning
    Outrageous, the bloody corpse and always,

Day after day, the unheard-of drought, it was you
Who, not speechless with shock but finding the right
    Language for thirst and fear, did most to
    Prevent a panic. It is the crime that

Counts, you will say. We know; but would gratefully add
To-day as we wait for the law to take its course,
    (And which of us shall escape whipping?)
    That your sixty years have not been wasted.

Desmond Hawkins

The Pope of Russell Square

I recall an afternoon tea in the early 1930's. I am the only guest and my host is a 'distinguished literary figure'. He has invited me from kindness and to satisfy the request of a friend. I affect to despise the great man, of course, but am secretly and horribly aware that hitherto I have only read about distinguished literary figures and never met one. So far the conversation has not gone well.

My host puts down his cup, looks at me disapprovingly and remarks 'I don't understand you young men. I have met all the great writers of the present time, and I can think of half a dozen you might have chosen as the god of your generation – but who on earth could have guessed it would be old Tom Eliot? None of us ever took much notice of him.'

I didn't actually throw anything at that point, but the condescension appalled me. There was the awful familiarity of 'Tom', for one thing. I had no idea then of what 'T. S.' stood for, but the very initials had a glamour which was made ridiculous by 'old Tom'. It only remained for my host to dismiss D. H. Lawrence as 'Bert' and I'm certain I should have crowned him with the teapot.

Some months later I went to see Charles Laughton in *Measure for Measure* and after the play I was taken to Laughton's dressing-room. I had never been backstage before and moreover I was full of admiration for Laughton's performance, so I naturally gave all my excited attention to the actor and ignored the ordinary-looking man in conventional city clothes who was lolling peacefully in a chair. Laughton accepted our congratulations and our obvious admiration, and then nodded to the man in the chair. 'I've forgotten to introduce you,' he said. 'This is Mr T. S. Eliot.' No actor ever lost the limelight so suddenly and completely. The play and the player were forgotten. What were they, beside the author of *The Waste Land*?

44

But why recall that one had, if you like, the soul of a gallery-girl? Is the simple response of the usual fan worth mentioning? It is not for me to say, perhaps, but I think it helps to describe the 'climate' of those years. There cannot be many writers of my generation who were not equally intense in their veneration of Eliot, and not many of our seniors who were not astounded by it. Eliot was championed by us, discussed, quoted, idolized (and inevitably imitated) with a partisan fervour which even Shaw or Lawrence might have envied. And yet he had no intoxicating 'message', no angry polemic, no crusading banner. Everything was an incongruity – the Royalism, the incense-swinging, the correct bank-manager look, pervading a High Bohemia of armchair communists. Absurd! But it happened. It happened because the poetry got into your head like a song-hit, because the essays acquired imperceptibly the momentum of authority: the if and buts, the cautious buttressing, are reminders that this was an unpopular popularity. After all, the tide wasn't running that way.

As the 'thirties wore on we got used to 'the Pope of Russell Square'. I suppose every budding poet and critic made his pilgrimage to that small high room and perhaps came away with something to do for *The Criterion*. One learnt by degrees that genius didn't necessarily wear a beard and have neurotic love-affairs, but might be found in a Kensington churchwarden who discussed cheese with the scholarly taste of a connoisseur. Truth mercifully is stranger than fiction.

What, in a phrase, was the nature of the influence he exerted on us? There was the fastidious air of cultural snobbism which came as a timely antidote to the chumminess of the sloppier sort of Romanticism: the landscape needed an ivory tower (but with modern conveniences, of course, windows that opened outwards and situated near the main line). More than that, Eliot restored the position of poetry as a high art and not merely a capricious effusion. The 'twenties had been dominated by the novelists. In the 'thirties the initiative passed to the poets – and the change was due more to Eliot than to anyone else. He rekindled the technical excitement of verse as a medium, making it once more an enchanted country to ex-

45

plore and scramble about in. He was to poetry what Henry James had been to the novel.

And it is as a latter-day James that he remains most vividly in my mind – refining mysteries to the point of certainty that at least no difficulty has escaped his attention, obstinately and admirably rating the *succès d'estime* above all other prizes, haunted by perfection, magnificently obsessed with the trade secrets of his profession, a mandarin whose slightly too gentlemanly air reveals that his England has a tincture still of New England. You might have met him any morning in the Park, elegant, the rolled umbrella in position, the uncommonly handsome head a trifle bowed as if to escape the notice of the Eumenides; on his way perhaps to Lady Ottoline's where Yeats and A. E. would be eloquent, and Ethel Smythe would brandish her ear-trumpet, and the young men who might some day write something would listen with truculent ambitious envy. And Mr Eliot would bow ceremoniously and demonstrate his intellectual invulnerability with the faintly dandified good breeding that made one inquisitive. I remember the comic despair of a deboshed choirboy from Swansea who said, 'He must be a beastly drinker. I bet he locks himself in the bathroom and sops up gin in secret.'

And here I remind myself with joy that this is no obituary, so we may all be spared a final peroration on T. S. E.'s achievements, his kindness to the obscure young, his love of cats, and so on. Instead I will explain why I shall not choose an umbrella as his birthday-present. Some years ago I persuaded him to broadcast to India a reading of *East Coker*. The broadcast was arranged by Z. A. Bokhari, a man of princely impulses who could never allow that anyone else had the largest, most sumptuous and regal specimen of anything at all. When Eliot claimed to be the owner of the biggest umbrella in London, I saw a familiar glint in Bokhari's eye. Within a week sundry Malacca importers were laying enormous handles at Bokhari's feet, and silk workers were commissioned to make appropriately vast tents of umbrella fabric. Bigger and better umbrellas began to rain in on Russell Square. As the climax, Bokhari discovered the most fantastic eighteenth-century carved pipe I have ever seen and had it adapted as the handle of what must always be the world's largest and craziest gamp. Overwhelmed, like the Sorcerer's Apprentice, by this invasion of gargantuan brollies, Eliot wired in true Indian-merchant style. I quote from memory (a slipshod habit of which he will disapprove):

Impossible accept more umbrellas aaa Market saturated aaa Refusing further shipments aaa Send elephants instead.

Well, elephants are always acceptable (so long as they're not white) but they are hard to come by. No, I'd like to send him a wopsical hat, if I knew where to buy one . . .

Nicholas Moore

Three Poems for Mr Eliot
Muse as a Bicyclist

*Plato's ideas gain much of their power and appeal from the
myths which clothe them, for he is indeed the* fabulator maximus
Donald Stauffer: *The Nature of Poetry*

I read of Mr Eliot day and night.
I read of him, I read, I read of him.
And in the street I see dim ghosts that fright,
The dirty, shabby housemaids of his whim.

But Plato lights indeed a darkling candle:
I too, with love, can dream of fish and chips,
And one whose simple impulse I can handle
Better than these abstruse arithmetics.

I write of Mr Eliot in honour,
Knowing I lack all art in chemistry,
But that I yet may shower symbols upon her
Who rides, in daytime too, most beautifully.

Bathcubes

That Mr Eliot always reminds me of bathcubes
May not speak much for him; but bathcubes
Bear much the same relationship to women
As he to me: he mightily pleaseth me.

The tall, strong pines, dark needles all erect
Reflected in these women's baths! The lines
Of tall and elegant verses, and the pursued
Images chasing through my cloudy mind from him!

I recognize his virtue as I speak it,
To cleanse the air with sweet correctitude.
What white breasts in the warming steam of baths!
What fragrant odours! What long circling arms!

And how those pines stand dark on foreign shores!
And how one mocks the pleasures one adores!

Portrait of Mr Eliot *à la Mode*

Beginning with portraits of the disaffected,
Unhappy people older than their age,
He went on next to map whole worlds of sorrow,
With classic contrasts neat on every page:

He seemed himself at one with the rejected,
The feeble women and the cumbrous men,
And everywhere our world, and his, was hollow.
His cynicisms made it whole again.

But suddenly the materials went wild,
The horror grew, he had to find release.
A God appeared, benevolent and mild,
And pitying, and gave his anguish peace.

Yet still the problem nags him; what to say
To keep the Furies of his words at bay.

Irving Babbitt and the Continent

While Eliot is still alive and *compos mentis* somebody else can hardly undertake to write even a fragment of his auto-biography for him. However, it is common knowledge that his formative period was passed first at Harvard, and then at the Sorbonne, the University of Marburg, and Merton, Oxford; and of those years the ones at Harvard and in Paris happen, in a sense, to bisect my own experience. Four years his junior, I grew up in the Paris of pre-1914. There can be no doubt, too, that the professor of French literature at Harvard in his time deeply influenced him, and before this professor died, in about 1935, I had the privilege of knowing him. To him may be attributed without protest the fostering of much of what is traditional in Eliot's understanding of both life and literature, and with equal impunity he can be said to have directed Eliot to proceed from Harvard to Paris as from the periphery to the centre.

There was, it is true, another signpost that pointed to Paris: the book by Arthur Symons entitled *The Symbolist Movement in Literature*. This book was published in 1899, and in all probability Eliot came upon it while still at Harvard. It acted upon him, he has written, 'as an introduction to wholly new feelings, as a revelation.' The reading of it may be taken to have put him on that road along which he was to hit upon the appropriate means of exercising his individual talent. The professor's teaching and Arthur Symons' literary survey combined to send the young Eliot across the Atlantic, and it is first in Paris that he can be considered to have struck that balance between the two elements, tradition and the individual talent, which is maintained in everything he was afterwards to write.

In Eliot's first book, *The Sacred Wood*, the professorial teaching and Arthur Symons' survey are alike dealt with critically, and of course nobody must imagine that at any time

51

was he inclined to take either for gospel. Indeed, the whole point of recalling some of the early influences which he underwent must be to bring out an instructive fact: how a young man destined to make his mark in literature may, without ever yielding a docile assent to his teachers, yet derive from them essential benefit. The man and the book I have referred to proved beneficial to Eliot precisely because he was content to obtain from each what each could give: the sense of tradition from the professor, the fostering of the individual talent from the Symons volume.

The Harvard professor of French literature could have given the individual talent no impetus. He was traditional to the point of being altogether anti-modern. I can still see the pain in his gentle face as he told me, one afternoon at the beginning of 1929 in his house at Cambridge, Massachusetts, that in London the previous summer he had visited Eliot at what he called his lodgings (actually, Eliot then lived in a flat) and had seen above the mantelpiece in the living-room a picture by Wyndham Lewis. How Eliot could live with such a piece of incoherence beggared his understanding, he said. A couple of years later, at an exhibition in Boston, he stood before a Cézanne in baffled silence, his tears too deep for words. This attitude to contemporary art he matched with his attitude to most modern writing. Apart from Emerson and Goethe, there was scarcely any author since Racine and Boileau for whom he had a kind word or even a pat on the back.

To listen to him, it seemed that upon the bulk of literature since the late eighteenth century there rested the blight of one man. Jean-Jacques Rousseau, the Citizen of Geneva, the Father of the French Revolution, was, in his eyes, at once the aboriginal and the archetypal criminal. Most of the great literary names from Wordsworth and Shelley to the present day stood, according to him, for subsidiary expressions of an evil the full enormity of which Rousseau alone had perpetrated. It is not for Rousseau to be defended here. I must say, nevertheless, that the accusation was excessive. The nineteenth-century French playwright and literary critic, Jules Lemaître, once delivered before a group of French monarch-

ists a series of lectures on Rousseau without having read his
works, and although he took advantage of the freedom of
abuse which his ignorance conferred on him, a lady in the
audience afterwards complained that he had not been sufficiently unjust. The ideal of being unjust enough to Rousseau,
which proved to be beyond Lemaître, it later fell to our professor to attain. If in that respect he was more credulous than
critical, this in no way vitiates, however, the cogency of his
demand for any new nostrum of human perfectibility, any eccentric literary experiment, any fantastic novelty in the practice of the plastic and graphic arts, to be contrasted, before it
was acclaimed, with the standards in honour in the past. It is
this demand that I fancy Eliot to have taken to heart as a result
of going to his lectures.

The name of the professor, by the way, was Irving Babbitt.
He went to his grave still relatively inglorious. America never
treated him to a fanfare of trumpets, and although his books
are published in England it is not to be expected that he should
be known over here. To most English people the word 'Babbitt' is solely the title of a novel by Sinclair Lewis. That an
American novel was given the title is proof enough that
Irving Babbitt's renown was esoteric. It must be presumed
that Mr Lewis – a Yale man – was unaware, when he chose
the name for his eponymous hero, that it was already that of
a giant of American literary criticism, or he would have picked
on another. As it turned out, the homonymity was to give rise
to a trifle of embarrassment.

In the time of Sinclair Lewis as in Eliot's time, on the
campus at Yale as in Harvard Yard, the name of names to
conjure with was that of H. G. Wells. Sinclair Lewis went forth
from his alma mater persuaded that the mercurial figure
whose name it is was little less than a god. Presently, on begetting a son, he could imagine no greater boon for him than
some of the Wellsian afflatus, and, in an attempt to attract this
by the approved means of verbal magic, he bestowed on the
boy the Christian name of Wells. Of how successful the magic
turned out to be I have no information, but that does not
matter. In the novels of Sinclair Lewis, the story and the

setting are of course always his own, but the inspiration is Wellsian. Needless to say, if Irving Babbitt had to speak of those novels, he could only animadvert on them. When the occasion chanced for him to do so in print in 1928, the problem arose of how to refer to the one bearing for its title his own surname. The ingenious but contorted circumlocutions thanks to which he avoided writing the particular word give his article more than a bibliophile interest.

Granted that minus the novel *Babbitt* the world would be the poorer, and still Babbitt the man is of notable importance. Afflicted with a bee in his bonnet about Rousseau he may have been. His learning was nevertheless encyclopædic, and he could communicate his passion for it. If, for instance, Eliot gave a couple of years to learning Sanskrit, very likely he is responsible. The Buddhism of *The Waste Land* may well derive from him also. By 1928 Eliot had not outgrown the conviction that his critical judgment was exceptionally sound. The raising of his monitory finger was timely, and there would be no harm if that finger were still held aloft to-day. As the raising of it was accompanied by a call for the recovery of the disciplined sanity of the French classical spirit, at this point let fair stand the wind for France.

Taking down Babbitt's book, *The Masters of Modern French Criticism*, in order to guide my memory of those now distant days, I see that the contemporary French books which are named in it with favour number precisely two. One, published in 1907, is *Le Romantisme français* by Pierre Lasserre, and the other, which had appeared in 1910, *L'Esprit de la nouvelle Sorbonne* by 'Agathon'. This second book I shall come to in its turn. In the first Babbitt thought that he detected signs of the rise of a new 'selective and humanistic criticism' in France. Yet he does not accept it without reservation. He regrets, he says, that the preoccupations which inspired it should be as much political as literary. But to see literature almost exclusively in a political aspect has long been characteristic of French controversy. While the book *Le Romantisme français* was still freshly topical there was a striking example of this. T. E. Hulme, in his *Speculations*, mentions that when, in about

54

1911, a lecturer at the Odéon Theatre in Paris let drop some disparaging references to Racine, fighting at once broke out among the audience. It was not over Racine's work itself that passions raged. Non-political writer though Racine was, his name had become a rallying-cry in French politics.

I myself remember the occasion, and in fairness I should say that there was something extreme, something we might now call 'fascist', in the violence displayed. The lecturer was pursued through the arcade that surrounds the theatre by a crowd of young men anxious to give him the boot. They were *Camelots du roi*. The French word *camelot* means 'hawker', and these young men were so called because, in their political enthusiasm, they hawked the monarchist daily paper, *Action française*, in the Paris streets. The paper took its name from a monarchist association of which it was the organ, and the brawls and scandals of which give movement and colour to the period. You might be quietly sipping your *bock* outside a café on the Boulevards and suddenly your neighbours scrambled away, tables were overturned, and the glass shivered and flew, as the *Camelots du roi* retreated up the broad thoroughfare before a truncheon charge by the police. To this monarchist group Pierre Lasserre of *Le Romantisme français* and 'Agathon' of *L'Esprit de la nouvelle Sorbonne* both belonged.

Its leader was Charles Maurras, one of the most extraordinary figures of the period. He divided his life between collecting money for his paper in the drawing-rooms of dowagers and supplying the paper every day with a leading article three or four columns long. His office was near the Boulevards and he never went to his bed on the Left Bank till the early hours. Under the moon, clutching his big stick, and surrounded by a bodyguard of *Camelots du roi*, he would tramp through the deserted streets and over the empty footbridge opposite the Institut, and from a distance the group would look for all the world like the watch of bygone days when France was still ruled by kings. Almost the only relaxation which Maurras allowed himself was the collection of newly published books which he never had time to read, and, as he lived in great simplicity, there came a day when the books overflowed from his overburdened shelves on to the floor, and then another day when the piles of books on the floor were so numerous that he could no longer walk, even sideways, from the front door of his flat to his bed. The only step he took to remedy the obstruction was to lock up the flat and go to sleep elsewhere.

To-day, at the age of eighty, Maurras is in prison. Throughout the German occupation of France, from 1940 to 1944, he was the stoutest supporter of Marshal Pétain, and it is for that that he is now paying the price. It has never been suggested that he favoured Germany; indeed, he was notoriously the most rabid anti-German west of the Rhine. He supported Marshal Pétain because he has always believed that government ought to be symbolized in a single individual. That is the whole secret of the attraction he felt for monarchism. In the halcyon days I now recall with a sigh, before August 1914, when the £ was worth only 25 francs, but a student could live in comfort in Paris on 150 francs a month, Maurras gave his allegiance to Philippe Duke of Orléans, then the French Pretender, who at Twickenham in England lived remote from the hurly-burly conducted in his cause.

The duke was a man born not to be king. His chances of gaining the French throne were ever nil. Likewise, Marshal Pétain's government was never what Maurras insisted on imagining it to be. Those are facts which go to show that Maurras is but an idealist. Moreover, it is not the confusion of his thought but the charm of his literary style that matters. If he was elected to the French Academy more than ten years ago, and if the manuals of literature in the French schools before 1939 assign a prominent place to him among contemporary writers, the reason is that nobody else in his time has made arid political topics so warmly entertaining to read about, or has made muddled ideas seem so lucid through the limpidity and humour of straightforward prose.

Not the least of the paradoxes of Maurras was that, himself an agnostic, he looked on the Roman Church as an indispensable social institution. Yet that was a main source of the attraction which the monarchist *Action française* movement possessed for French youth. This brings me to the second of the two books of which Babbitt speaks favourably, *L'Esprit de la nouvelle Sorbonne*. It was, I have said, by 'Agathon', and at about the same time there was another book bearing the same signature, *Les Jeunes Gens d'aujourd'hui*, which showed even more clearly that in the French universities and at the great specialist schools a substantial portion of the new generation was for both throne and altar. The years of which I am speaking were indeed years of a Roman Catholic revival in France, and with that revival as it concerns the new generation two names are especially associated.

'Agathon' was the pseudonym of a dual authorship. Together *L'Esprit de la nouvelle Sorbonne* and *Les Jeunes Gens d'aujourd'hui* made the instantaneous reputation of the two young men whose disguise success quickly penetrated. One was Henri Massis, the other A. de Tarde. Massis combined indefectible fealty to Maurras with the crusading zeal of a fresh convert to the Church. But in the apologetic activities into which he launched himself, it was not with A. de Tarde that his name became linked, but with that of another recent convert, a teacher of philosophy in the Catholic Institute in Paris, Jacques Maritain. Much later on, after 1925, the ways of Massis and Maritain were to diverge. Massis remained on the political Right; Maritain's sympathies with the Left became more pronounced. Massis concentrated on trying to expose the ideological deficiencies of such non-Catholic writers as André Gide and Marcel Proust; Maritain, on the contrary, being at heart a romantic, was ready to flirt with the godless if they showed the least sign of being touched by grace, and of his relations with Jean Cocteau, when Cocteau came into the Church for a short while, the less said the better. Massis is still a political and literary journalist; Maritain has been both professor at the College of Pontifical Studies in Toronto and French ambassador to the Holy See. Yet, whereas with Maurras, as I gather, Eliot had little more than a nodding acquaintance, with both Massis and Maritain he became friends, and his friendship with them is still close to-day.

In Paris then, and especially on the Left Bank, there was

much else to engage and stimulate a young man from America, in addition to the anti-romantic and royalist movement and the Roman Catholic revival of which I have been speaking. At the College de France, Bergson, in his stick-up collar and frock coat, was fascinating fashionable women with his lectures in which time and real duration were opposed. Just down the street from the main entrance to the Sorbonne was the tiny and crowded bookshop in which of an afternoon Charles Péguy rhapsodized to an attentive knot of admirers on the beauties of Chartres Cathedral and on their significance for faith. Georges Sorel, the philosopher of violence, whose book T. E. Hulme translated, had by then been excluded from Péguy's circle. But a self-effacing little man named Julien Benda was sometimes present. Sixteen or seventeen years later he was to sound his note of alarm at *La Trahison des Clercs*. Furtively up the Rue de Seine or the Rue de Médecis would steal the hooded silhouette of Remy de Gourmont, whose diseased face led him to shrink from social contacts. His book, *Le Problème du Style*, was of seminal value to Eliot. In a set of low-ceilinged rooms in the Rue de Grenelle were the offices of the most individual and advanced of French monthlies, the *Nouvelle Revue française*. It was founded in 1909 by André Gide and four others. Through the friendship which Eliot now formed with the editor, he became a contributor. The editor was Jacques Rivière, a vibrant young man destined to hover all his comparatively short life on the brink of conversion. His brother-in-law, Alain-Fournier, was often with him and spoke of being engaged in the writing of a novel. When the novel was published, it at once attracted attention and it has gone on being regarded as the most evocative piece of imaginative French prose of the new century. It is called *Le Grand Meaulnes*. It had no successor, for Alain-Fournier was killed in action soon after the outbreak of the 1914 war.

But it is time to say a word of the sequel to Eliot's reading Arthur Symons' book, *The Symbolist Movement in Literature*. When, thirty to thirty-five years earlier than this time, Stéphane Mallarmé translated a number of Edgar Allan Poe's poems into French prose, the undertaking was to have momentous consequences for himself. Already he was a poet. But hitherto the only kind of verse he had written was in the oratorical mode made inviting to new poets by Victor Hugo's virtuosity in it. The results had dissatisfied him. Now, in the course of translating Poe's poems, he grew intimate with their structure, and all at once he saw from them how he might follow his own bent. He hit on the kind of poetry which it would be congenial for him to write, and he went on to write it with success. He used words with revolutionary effect, and the result took the name of Symbolism. A whole group of his juniors, headed by Tristan Corbière, a native of Brittany, and Jules Laforgue, a Frenchman born at Montevideo, adopted Mallarmé as their master. They became known as the Symbolist school. When Eliot went from Symons's book to the French poetry with which the book deals, the poems of Corbière and Laforgue affected him as Poe's had Mallarmé. He understood all at once what kind of poetry it was that he had the temperament to write. His individual talent discovered its appropriate medium. A French debt to America was repaid. There could be no more instructive instances of how a poet may *see* how to write poetry by studying verse of another kind in another language.

However, when Eliot landed in Paris fresh from Harvard, there could be no question of his meeting the two French poets whose work was to be so illuminating for him. Both Corbière and Laforgue had died the year before he was born. Yet he was to form an affectionate association with another of Mallarmé's heirs. This was André Gide's long-standing friend, Paul Valéry, whose renown the *Nouvelle Revue française* was to establish after the peace of 1919. While Eliot was first in Paris, Valéry was earning his livelihood as a sub-editor with a news agency. He did not move in literary circles, and the day when Eliot would come to know him well had not yet arrived.

F. V. Morley

T. S. Eliot as a Publisher

'Let me say to that public, which has shown some interest in . . . the thoughts and actions of a very remarkable man, that they are not to blame me if I have not shared my knowledge with them, for I should have considered it my first duty to do so, had I not been barred by a positive prohibition from his own lips, which was only withdrawn upon the third of last month.'

Why, in writing of T. S. Eliot, should I at once refer to the Sherlock Holmes saga? I don't know, but it is natural for me to do so. There are a good many allusions which are pertinent. We met long ago at what might be called the Criterion Bar; and now at the occasion of this *festschrift* (the language of Goethe is always pithy), at a time when Europe is ringing with his name and when his room is literally ankle-deep with congratulatory telegrams, why shouldn't I choose a scheme of reference with which he himself is not unfamiliar? What I have to unfold is Eliot's career and long exertion as a publisher. I shall, however, tactfully restrict my description to a period which ended nearly ten years ago. My account of Eliot as a man of business will begin in the 'twenties, and will go forward only until the spring of '39. And if there are Holmesian allusions, that is as much his fault as mine.

I cannot speak of Eliot's conduct in the foreign department of Lloyds Bank, for that was before my time. I am ready to believe, though, that the City lost a fine banker, even as science lost an acute reasoner, when he became a specialist in literature. It has been said that Eliot is one who has wasted his gifts; he might have aimed high, if he had stayed in the City. But the profession he desired was publishing. In a monograph which he was writing at the time, scholars will remember that he invited attention to one of his chemical experiments. He was always a great man for chemistry; his knowledge of the science was probably profound; his friends of the time still recall his evil-smelling retorts. I mention this to show it is not without significance that the publishing house to which he turned was one which had started as The Scientific Press. Shortly after that I came to know him. He still looked very much the City man. His strong-set aquiline features and his well set-up figure were observed to advantage in the traditional costume of bowler hat, black coat and striped trousers which marked him as one of the class who give us our crack volunteer regiments, and who turn out more athletes and sportsmen than any body of men in these islands. Was that a deliberate disguise? It might fool you to know which of his disguises was which. He carried a malacca-handled umbrella which was always neatly rolled, and with which, when he wished for a taxicab, he paved in the air. Such a display, however, was unusual; for the most part his behaviour was subject to an iron control.

Now let me switch abruptly to a description of the publishing field in the twenties, which at the time seemed to some people not so much a verdant field, as a great alkali plain, or arid and repulsive desert.

It is hard to recall dates with any accuracy. It was round about 1925, I think, that one became aware of the intention of The Scientific Press to launch out into general publishing under the imprint of Faber & Gwyer. I had the pleasure of introducing to them Richard de la Mare, as a promising young production-manager. It was Hugh Walpole, I believe, who advised Faber to add Eliot to the team. It is curious, I repeat, how little one remembers about details. One thing I may point out which the public (the great unobservant public which can hardly tell a weaver by his tooth or a compositor by his left thumb) may not fully understand. I suppose most people think of Eliot's publishing career as that of a literary adviser, and as Editor, while it was going, of *The Criterion*. That needs a good deal of qualification. Even by 1925 Eliot's reputation as a literary man had not spread very far. His literary judgments were commanding only to a few. Some of the few were in high places, but for the most part those who followed Eliot were a ragged battalion. Now, in the publishing houses of that period the function of a literary adviser was fairly well defined. Edward Garnett was an example. To set up as a literary adviser it was not necessary that one's own writings should be popular, but it was essential that one should be known to have a flair for discovering and encouraging potential popularity in others. At the time when Eliot joined Faber & Gwyer, what is the evidence as to his position with the firm?

I suggest that there is very little evidence that he was taken on as a literary adviser. What was there in Eliot that could have appealed to his employers? There were his own writings, notably *The Waste Land* and *The Sacred Wood*, of which I suppose a popular impression, if any, was that he would pretty soon have to get off his high horse if he was going to get anywhere. There were Eliot's interminable debates with Middleton Murry, all very enjoyable no doubt, but not precisely popular. And to demonstrate Eliot's flair for discovery, there was *The Criterion* – 'Golly, what a paper.' No, if you look for circumstantial evidence as circumstantial evidence must have looked at that time, there is little to show for Eliot being taken into a firm as a literary adviser. It isn't even as if his colleagues at Faber & Gwyer were acknowledged or ardent admirers of Eliot's literary judgement. In 1925 I doubt if any of them saw any particular reason to defer to him in literary matters. What then were his assets? He was a gentleman; he was literate; he was patient; he got on well with difficult people; he had charm; and, he had been in the City. He had good qualifications for a man of business, and it was as a man of business, I suggest, that he was taken on.

Without there being anything in the least sinister in the thought, I am not sure that Eliot's best qualification to become a publisher wasn't the fact that he had worked in a Bank. He didn't put up any money to get into Faber & Gwyer; no money was needed; I'm sure no such question was born or thought of. But at the same time, at the start of a publishing house solvency is the greatest aim, and there was possibly something solid and comforting, something magical, in having a banker in the crew.

I hope I am not guilty of an indiscretion if I recall looking in
at Jonathan Cape's office one late evening about the time that
I am talking of. Jonathan's desk was piled high with manuscripts and untidy papers; his hair was ruffled and his de-
meanour was far from that of the pontifex that he is to-day.
He pushed back his chair, looked up at me, pulled at his jaw
(a characteristic gesture), and said, with a burst of feeling:
'Don't let anybody tell you publishing is easy. I've got to get
some more money, and I don't know where it's to come from –
and Garnett has discovered another bloody genius.'

Edward Garnett in those days used to lunch regularly on
Fridays at the Mont Blanc in Gerrard Street, and a group of
youngsters would surround him, of whom I was often and
happily one. I wish there were an adequate portrait of Edward
Garnett. He was an elderly man when I knew him, with a
large and shambling figure, with dun-coloured clothes rather
loose and untidy, and there was an impression that somehow
his skin was rather loose too, wrinkled and baggy, like an old
rhinoceros. His temper could be a bit uncertain, like that of a
rhinoceros, too. When he was at ease, Garnett took a liberal
view of geniuses. He was persistent at the occupation of swan-
upping, even when they were geese. (My brother Christopher
remarked of him, he was a great writer to the cygnet.) But he
certainly discovered a great number for Cape, and that was
his function as literary adviser.

Eliot's function with Faber & Gwyer did not appear to be
defined that way. Eliot wasn't an outside expert. He was in
the firm as a man of business, as one of the inner council,
making business decisions. And to the business he displayed
a complete loyalty. What do I mean by that? Well, anybody
who looks beneath the surface can see that Eliot has always
been an enthusiast, but I have never known him *use* his firm
or his colleagues for his own enthusiasms.

An illustration which occurs to me is an episode in the life
of *The Criterion.* That periodical, of its very nature, ran at a
loss. In the early days it was published through Cobden
Sanderson, and the loss was absorbed by an outside patron.
When Eliot joined with Faber & Gwyer I suspect that both he

63

and the firm were glad to let *The Criterion* continue with
Cobden Sanderson. I don't know; I wasn't intimate in those
days; I was only beginning to be aware of what was going on.
I didn't meet Herbert Read till 1925, and it was Read who
introduced me to Eliot. Read and Flint lunched fairly regularly, and Wheen and I and others took to joining them. This
lunch was fixed for Thursdays, and it had to take place near
the South KensingtonMuseums, and eventually a back room
was found in a pub called The Grove in Beauchamp Place.
After a while Eliot began to come regularly, and the lunch
took on a *Criterion* flavour. When *The Criterion's* patron invited Eliot to Switzerland to discuss the periodical, it was from
The Grove, in a costume much more sportif than the black
coat and striped trousers (he never could resist a touch of the
dramatic) that he set forth. It was also to The Grove that the
news was broken, that the patron's subsidy had been abruptly
discontinued.

This minor crisis must have presented Eliot with a conflict
of loyalties. Without financial support, *The Criterion*, and
whatever it represented to all concerned, would have to
dissolve. Eliot certainly valued it, and cared for its contributors,
as a group and as individuals. Not a great deal of money was
involved. Faber & Gwyer were prepared to lose larger sums
on experiments of less importance; for though the business
value of *The Criterion* was indirect, an indirect return was
assuredly there. So, looking on from the outside, I wondered
why Eliot didn't persuade his own firm to stand the loss, and
take it over. It would have been plausible for him to do so.
But, out of the costume sportif and back in the black coat, he
made no attempt (so far as I am aware) to involve Faber &
Gwyer. There must have been temptation, for the *Criterion*
crowd were all looking to him for a lead; but neither then, or
ever, would he put up to his firm a matter of special pleading,
or of self-interest. It turned out all right, for there were more
people interested in the continuation of *The Criterion* than
anybody had supposed, and the crisis was easily overcome, and
the periodical went on. My guess is, this was evidence which
startled Faber & Gwyer, and which, later, encouraged the

firm, on its own motion, to take over the publication. So there
was *The Criterion* at last conveniently housed with Faber &
Gwyer, yet not as a charge that Eliot himself had dragged in.
In the long history of things the episode is scarcely important,
but it is illustrative of Eliot's character as publisher. Because
he would not trade upon his influence, his influence grew.
Because he would not claim attention, more attention was
paid to him. Because he refused to over-estimate his own
enthusiasms, his judgements, within the firm, were more and
more respected.

On 1st April 1929, Faber & Gwyer was reorganized into a
new firm, Faber & Faber. Under that new imprint a good
many serious and useful books began increasingly to make
their way. They also began to exhibit a recognizable character.
This was observable in their physical appearance. Richard de
la Mare's superb gift for book-production had developed greatly
since his first days with Selwyn & Blount, and his later, but
still rather tentative, production for Faber & Gwyer. Now he
really hit his stride. He achieved full confidence in his own
distinctive style, which was beautifully adapted to the kind of
book for which the new firm became eminent. For though,
from the beginning, Faber & Faber published a wide range of
books, there developed a distinctive 'Faber' character. I think
there's no question who did most to shape this character. It
was not the character of any one individual; it was the ethos
of a group; and the group was shaped by its Chairman,
Geoffrey Faber. It is quite accurate to say that many diverse
books, not all of which gave Faber equal satisfaction, exhibited
a 'Faber' character. His was, and is, a very complicated, pene-
trative, sensitive, excitable and tolerant genius. The beauty of
the situation in 1929 was that by then Faber too had found his
style, and had found full confidence in it. His love for music
is really the clue. Faber's style was his team, and he made his
team organic. Then he gave it his full trust, and it worked.
The Faber policy demanded faith. What I have spoken of as
the Faber character in books, when you looked inside them
was seen to reside not so much in having been published for a
commercial reason, as for some other intrinsic quality: it

65

might be only some aspect of truthfulness or beauty. I don't believe any other publishing house gave more consideration to the intrinsic merits of a manuscript, or displayed more interest if it made any effective contribution to cultural conversation. The Faber faith was that the state of the world was not so bad, but that this policy could pay. It did. I can remember with amusement certain shrewd and solemn prophecies of failure; but the years proved that a bunch of Oxford amateurs could achieve some exciting publishing.

Eliot was a member of the team. I too was lucky enough to become a member when Faber & Faber started, and for a while I shared a room, and what was worse, a telephone, with Eliot. In the formal organization of Faber & Faber provision was made to exempt Eliot from the full duties of ordinary Directors, for by this time everyone was anxious to protect him, on the theory that poets should have just enough but not too much work to do. As soon as the business got to work, such anxiety was forgotten. Eliot might be no end of a *lumen et decus*, all the rest of us might be proud of the way his reputation was growing, but that did not prevent him from becoming rapidly submerged with just as many menial tasks as anybody else; with this difference, that on Eliot was dumped anything or anybody peculiarly difficult or peculiarly time-wasting. Each Director had his own bevy of authors, but Eliot's was a bevy and a half. (The word *bevy*, I believe is properly used of a company of ladies, roes, quails and larks; at least, that's the way I am using it.) I've never had such a time as when Eliot's Russell Square Irregulars were pattering in and out of our shared room. I don't mean to be disrespectful. In a *festschrift* it is permissible, I trust, to have the freedom of talking among friends. It is certainly necessary, in order to give a true picture of Eliot, to mention that he had to suffer an immense amount of author-trouble. Himself he cured of haste and vanity and fractiousness; others he could not cure. Of course anybody who did not speak English went to Eliot automatically, as did all correspondence and manuscripts in any foreign language. He had more manuscripts to read than anybody else, and the odd thing was, he really read them. He

was sought after not merely as a publisher, but as an employ-
ment agent; but in that capacity there was this consolation –
when you find a job for somebody, you don't always hear
from him again.

Conscientious, scrupulous, careful, attentive: one or other
of those uncommon epithets is needed to describe Eliot as
publisher, along with several other qualities which I'll suggest
in a moment. Of course he supported the Faber policy; he
could translate it into action. As to the geniuses who came into
his net he was conservative, preservative, painstaking, and
rarely in a hurry. On Wednesdays at Faber & Faber we had
what we called Book Committees, which lasted from lunch
till exhaustion. We would all surround an enormous octagonal
table, and each report on his special tasks and manuscripts.
At these meetings Eliot was the most self-controlled. He no
longer wore the black coat. His face, rather pale from over-
work, was now to be seen above an ordinary dark lounge suit;
but he had not given up the caution of the banker. He had a
theory you were not likely to lose money on the books you
didn't publish. It was difficult to bully him; he had the
courage to say No. But he could also say Yes. He was extremely perceptive in detecting the right character in manuscripts which might have been thought beyond his range. He
made mistakes, of course, but his mistakes as a rule were not
costly, and some of his far shots paid well. He was sometimes
a little mischievous in the way he would present things. He
might put something forward very diffidently, as if he didn't
care about it. If it was picked up, so much the better; if it
wasn't, it would come up again, some other time. We had
private zoological names for each other, supposedly expressive
of personal characteristics, which cropped up in the occasional
intramural verses which flew around. One of the nicknames
for Eliot was Possum (the reference here is to Uncle Remus),
and another was Elephant (because he didn't forget). I've
suggested that Eliot didn't often fight for his candidates.
Sometimes he did, though. He wasn't apt to fight for anybody
that any other publisher would publish; but he could fight for
people at whom no other publisher would look. It would be

indiscreet to give examples, but I can think of several.

Poetry was something we had in sheaves and droves and cartloads. The quantity overflowed even Eliot and afflicted all of us. He was never regarded as the sole arbiter, but he was made the chief interviewer of poets, and the chief correspondent, even for those who were not of his own choice. Within the Book Committee no marked deference was paid to Eliot's own views. If on occasion he would raise one of his questions which sounded to the Committee, let's say like this: ἀπόκριναί μοι, τίνος οὕνεκα χρὴ θαυμάζειν ἄνδρα ποιητήν; would everybody else be paralysed? Not a bit of it. We were no more to be bullied than he was. Each of us was prepared to correct Eliot in something. At that octagonal Board Room table there was no respect for persons. As to poetry or as to other things, Eliot had about as much preference as any scholar has among scholars. The one accomplishment for which he was highly regarded, was writing blurbs. Everyone admitted that he was our best blurb-writer. Blurbs! They are the curse of publishing. They may be dear to the heart of booksellers, but for all that, blurbs are in every aspect evil. They are torture to write. Eliot wrote thousands of them. I can testify, from personal knowledge both of Eliot and of blurb-writing, that during his publishing career he has turned out so many blurbs as to make it quite impossible that he should have had time or energy left over to write anything else.

A willing workhorse, is the picture that I draw of Eliot as publisher; a workhorse as to every kind of unpleasant detail. Author-trouble, threats of libel, griefs and woes of all kinds (there are agonies as well as pleasures in publishing) – he has had his share. He has never been above the battle. There may be less of that now? I speak of Faber & Faber in its first decade. That is the only period for which I can speak of Eliot as publisher, from my own daily observation. But I am conscious that my picture is not complete. I haven't made enough of his sensitive perception. I have also left out at least one other important aspect. On all levels of conduct and conversation we had fun.

I have read somewhere, possibly in some manuscript that

68

we turned down (for six-sevenths of a publisher's reading, like
six-sevenths of an iceberg, is forever lost to view), that in the
most respected business houses in China it was not uncommon
for partners to salute each other with firecrackers and to write
to each other in complimentary verses, and on commemora-
tive feast-days to celebrate with sought-for delicacies. Similar
courtesies spontaneously developed at Russell Square. The
delicate reminders which would appear at lunch – the Tio
Pepe, or the Brie! The cakes (from Fullers) on birthday
occasions – not by any means restricted to Directors, for among
so many Grecians there was always present a tachygrapher,
ready to ply her swift style on a stack of wax-coated wooden
tablets, and there were others behind the scenes. And sometimes things were not as they would seem: the OK Sauce (for
Faber) which was very far from OK, the coffee which foamed
over, the cigarettes which somehow produced snow-storms.
Such simple things went on sporadically, and you never
could tell when the solemn business of the afternoon might
not be punctuated with low comedy. Towards those offensive
jokes Faber was the most patient of men. The jokes were often
aimed at him, not in any personal way, but because he was
Chairman. As a mild example, I might give you the Fourth of
July. Eliot and Kennerley and I always attempted to teach the
Committee, and the Committee never could remember, about
the Glorious Fourth, on which the three of us harked back to
our boyhood customs in America. Bombs aren't funny now,
and it is tactless to refer to them; but at that time they were
merely comic. On the Wednesday nearest the Fourth of July
something noisy was sure to be rigged up. Eliot was fertile in
suggestions, and bland in the accomplishment. It was usually
his part to distract Faber's attention at the crucial moment.
The best of those occasions, though with many to choose from
it's a hard choice, was perhaps the time when we completely
filled a large brass coal-scuttle with what in America we used
to call 'giant' firecrackers. (They are prohibited now in
America as being too dangerous.) Eliot and Kennerley and I
spent most of the morning rigging up pulleys under the big
table, and rehearsing how the coal-scuttle could be pulled,

unseen, across the floor to appear between the Chairman's legs. It was a rather sultry afternoon. I can't remember what important matter we were discussing. I know that when the interruption came, it was terrific. The cauldron got going in a big way during its concealed approach beneath the table, and when the Chairman, startled, as was everyone else, by the noise and stench, looked down – there it was between his knees, banging and spitting like the mouth of Hell. One or two of the little giants popped out and got under the Sales Manager. That put him, also, on his toes. Now that I come to think about it, it was rather disruptive. Quite a lot of time had to be spent putting out fires and getting back to business. But I am glad to recognize that it was all very Chinese, canonical and civilized.

If I have now been compelled to make a clear statement of Eliot's career as a publisher, it is due to those injudicious champions who have praised him only as a man of letters. It is true, that is all he claims to be. His remarks about himself, however, need not always be taken at face-value; as when, in a favourite vein of irony, he says that his mind has no capacity for the abstruse. Secretly – who knows? – he may have an aspiration to be praised for something a cut above the ordinary level. That is what I am glad to do – to praise him for something at which he has worked more laboriously than at anything else, and at which he has done well – to praise him as a publisher. And I know why, at the beginning of my sketch, I fell into so many Holmesian references. In my own subsequent professional career, which took me elsewhere, I have often missed my Sherlock Holmes.

P.S. As the cognoscenti will have noticed, I borrowed the line of Greek from Aristophanes: *The Frogs*, 943:
Tell me, for what ought we to admire a poet?

Ronald Bottrall

Dead Ends

(Homage to T. S. Eliot)

Down the blind alleys where life is brutish and ablaze
    Among dead men, among rotted stumps,
We breathe the stale cigar smoke left by blunted fingers
    And play the wiseacre in a maze.
As we walk, the festering walls persecute the light
    Light too timid to risk a whisper
And our tamed bodies languidly resign their sinews
    To the city's mildew and soft blight.

When music rises like a fluttering pyramid
    Among the Gothic arches and smoke
Wreathes blue against the moss-green gables of cottages
    Are we not swathed in sweet dreams that rid
The rattling bones of sound and the lithe muscular words
    Of meaning? Are we not loitering
In a temple caught by brambles and the darkening
    Lianas in merciless dumb hordes?

If our mind's ear is touched with fire-coal that accustoms
    The whorls to a counterpointed chant
And the weave of divine pattern, the telephone rings
    Or the front door opens and in comes
A person from Porlock bringing with him the discords
    Of humanity and blotting out
Our vision of the bones leaping into place, alive;
    And we fall back among clashing swords.

What is the poet to say of the cyclic drama
    Where time resists sempiternity?
Is he to wait chilled in lethargy for the return
    Of the unbelievable summer?
Or can time grant a foretoken of the eternal

71

If on the brink of the monstrous gulch
The prophet speaks above the whirlwind, reaching the heart
   Of the sun and the atom's kernel?

Yet though the voice be heard it will become small and still
   In a lunar landscape where heaven
Is waxing old like a garment and man is bravely
   Stitching the holes in the living will.
The tongues of flame may dart lambent, fold and re-infold
   At the high moment our tired hearts;
But like the endless noiseless snow of Arctic forests
   Spreads the chaos of the level cold.

Emilio Cecchi

A Meeting with Eliot

In front of the old bombed church, St Anne's, in Wardour Street, there is a little cemetery now turned into a playground, with a few thin black trees and the tomb of that gifted and irascible man, Hazlitt. Here I noticed a flock of pigeons huddled together on a patch of grass fringed with icicles. They were steely-grey with greenish tinges and the sameness of their colour seemed to multiply their number. They were pecking at crumbs scattered by some kind hand, and the soft curve, dip and spring of their arched necks seemed curiously rhythmical and remote from the traffic and confused roar of the centre of the city.

Beside an area railing there prowled a restless and devilish dog with a long reddish dragging tail – a real witch's dog unearthed from the sewers. Against the dismantled tower of St Anne's and the bright bookshops of Shaftesbury Avenue, this seemed a kind of esoteric vignette not altogether out of keeping with the visit I was about to make to T. S. Eliot, perhaps the most authoritative present-day poet since Valéry's death.

Compared with his portraits, Eliot seemed taller than I had imagined and also perhaps a little more worn; not delicate, however, though he soon told me that he was passing through a period of ill-health. And of all the poets I have met – and some of them have been true poets – Eliot seemed to have the least manner of a poet or artist. He might have been a chemist or a philologist with the kind of intellectual aristocracy and aloneness that goes with that kind of discipline (the 'parfait chemiste' of Baudelaire): I might almost say there was about him a hint of the cleric.

We talked about mutual literary acquaintances, with tastes and tendencies very different from his, and I marvelled at the precision as well as the affectionate understanding of his judgments on them. In this he certainly differed from the dozens of revolutionary aesthetes who massacre and pull to pieces their contemporaries. In fact his very first words and the indefinable precision even of his physical appearance, fully confirmed the impression one gets from his prose work no less than his poetry – the impression that his temperament is strongly rooted in his reasons for living and therefore able to defend these with openness and objectivity.

When we spoke of that distinguished veteran, Hilaire Belloc, now stricken with illness and withdrawn from the struggles of the literary forum, Eliot commemorated (it is the proper word to use) the classical beauty of his essays and of *Esto Perpetua* and *The Path to Rome*. And when referring to the changes that have taken place in the relationship between Labour and the State, he praised the vitality of that old book, *The Servile State*. Belloc's name inevitably recalled that of Chesterton and I was surprised to learn that, in spite of collaboration in *The Criterion* and other reviews, Eliot and Chesterton had never met personally. Indeed I think that, compared with the Continent, English literary life seems to delight in maintaining specific divisions into schools, castes and trends – sometimes even topographical divisions as when Bloomsbury gathered round Strachey and Virginia Woolf.

I heard from Eliot an almost exact repetition of what the economist, R. H. Tawney, had told me a few evenings before. Perhaps it is the result of recent biographies and memoirs, but certainly what seems to stand out about Chesterton to-day is his moral stature. With one or two 'almost's' and one or two hesitations, Tawney, who is a man of pure learning, uttered the last word I should have expected from him: he said that for humility of mind, generosity and so on, Chesterton had made an impression on him which could broadly be called that of a saint. While Eliot, neither a man of learning nor an economist, but a Christian poet, did not go quite so far, I felt that the direction of his thought was not so very different.

Eliot's critical intelligence almost equals his creative ability – his faculty for re-presenting poets and writers who have been forgotten and whose stature has not yet been fully assessed –

74

and this intelligence has been brought to bear on Joyce and on Kipling, causing them to enjoy an unforeseen revival of attention and curiosity. But what interested me most was when he spoke of a literature nearer ours – of that kind of *koine* or poetic 'international' formed first under the influence of symbolism and successive French schools and fashions, then indirectly consolidated by Rilke, Yeats and Eliot himself, a school which welcomed an extraordinary number of adepts during and after the last war.

Now this seems all the more singular in Great Britain and America as up till now, and for various reasons, these countries have been unwilling to accept an aesthetic conformism even of a revolutionary trend. As Eliot was an indirect promoter, I was interested to know what he thought of the 'cult of poetry' now apparent in almost stereotyped forms in all the literatures of the world. Will artistic productiveness be substantially and lastingly benefited as a result of it? Has a more precise a swell as a more vital taste been matured among readers, one similar to that in every really creative period?

Eliot's opinions seemed calmly but sadly sceptical. If we make all the obvious and proper exceptions, poets are less equipped technically and culturally than they once were. Facile and indiscriminate acceptance cannot fail to weaken them; and they have to undertake wearisome collaboration with the age. Often they are working on a vague and easily alterable foundation of moral ideas and emotions. And further-more the modern cult or *furore* for poetry may not last. The public sets a poet's ideas of morality apart, possibly it is not even aware of them. And to conscientious and systematic study of a poet the public prefers chance encounters: in anthologies and reviews which have their merits but really provide less concentrated reading.

Now add to such unstable predispositions in both artists and the public the dissipation of war and post-war propaganda, concerning which we might go so far as to ponder whether the horror and undreamed-of cruelty of the days we have lived through have not sometimes been dwarfed by their idiocy. Thus (to remain in the field of poetry) Valéry's majestic

75

address: *Soleil, soleil, faute éclatante* has been charged with
gratuitous and decadent nihilism, as if something similar had
not been written by the poet of the *Book of Job* and by
Sophocles in his choruses – and these authors can hardly be
thought of as decadent. And we find a subtle humanist like
F. L. Lucas, in *Critical Thoughts in Critical Days*, rejecting
Virgil except for 'a few cadences of his music.' Whereas if
there is a poet who, for his sense of universal *pietas*, should
precisely be re-read to-day, it is Virgil.

Talk on this and that touched also on an extraordinary little
book which had appeared about that time: *L'Univers concentrationnaire* by David Rousset – so far, probably, the profoundest testimony regarding Buchenwald, Neuengamme,
Helmstadt and so on; a book not written as a story of frightful
descriptions, like so many others written with pens dipped in
colours of decay. Certainly physical and moral destruction has
never before taken on aspects of such calculated mathematical
perversion as those analysed by Rousset.

And Eliot wondered whether the gates of such hells, in the
spiritual and material order, can really be considered to be
closed for ever. Or whether mankind, now capable of reaching
such extremes of frightfulness, has a weaker resistance to new
and infernal suggestions; whether the wheel of bloodshed can
stop at last or will follow its murderous course. These things
were said lightly so as in some way to mitigate their frightfulness. But I felt that with the man I was speaking to, as with
myself, the dread was almost stronger than the hope.

Translated by Bernard Wall

Tambimuttu

O What a Beautiful Morning
(from *Natarajah:* a poem for Mr T. S. Eliot)

Life is the address between awning and yawning;
Have known them all, the blond and the black.
Reserve my ardour till the morning.

The editing, the ironing, the ozoning,
EVERYTIME – EVERYWHERE – THE CADILLAC;
Life is the address between awning and yawning.

Images resemble O but the warning
Is the day's paper and the newest tack;
Reserve my ardour till the morning.

At sixty, belief is still the horning
Of faith in Mac and Joe and the bric-a-brac.
Life is the address between awning and yawning.

May you prosper, sir, between the dawning and adorning,
Sweeney give you the things I lack;
Reserve my ardour till the morning.

Poetry is the inverse of the heart's pawning
(You told us) on the fading sound track;
Life is the address between awning and yawning;
Reserve my ardour till the morning.

Kathleen Raine

The Poet of Our Time

It is, I find, with difficulty that I can bring myself to think of T. S. Eliot in terms of years and anniversaries. His work forms, for my generation, so much a part of what for us is the permanent reality of our world that it is strange to realize that the man who has created so much that time cannot destroy, has lived for so short a time; for sixty years of life can so easily slip away without our ever finding the way between two moments into that eternity to which great poetry belongs. Mr Eliot's poetry we have experienced with a part of the mind that seems to have no concern with the passage of time.

The relation of time to human experience has, to be sure, been one of the major themes of Eliot's poetry, especially of the later poems. What is it, and how is it captured, the moment of eternity that exists between every two moments of time? Whatever that secret gate may be, we know that Eliot's poems have passed through it. With the world – or our own civilization, at all events – so near its end, it would be a small thing to say of any poems written to-day that they seem likely to last for all time. If Eliot's poems are for eternity, it is for quite another reason – because they belong to it already, because we experience them as part of the imaginative world which in each of us is timeless.

For my generation T. S. Eliot's early poetry, more than the work of any other poet, has enabled us to know our world imaginatively. All those who have lived in the Waste Land of London, can, I suppose, remember the particular occasion on which, reading T. S. Eliot's poems for the first time, an experience of the contemporary world that had been nameless and formless, suddenly received its apotheosis.

In the 'etherized' sky, the humming street-lamp watching through the night hours, the pathos of the London crowds expressed once and for all in the allusive line, 'I had not

thought death had undone so many'; the river carrying its
memories past modern gas-works; in the very name, 'the
Waste Land,' we recognized, as he created the images, the
world of our own experience. Eliot, we realized, was the poet
who had taken upon himself the burden of experiencing the
world for his generation, as kings were formerly supposed to
act and suffer for their tribes. It is in the nature of the poet's
vocation that he should thus take upon himself the imaginative
burden of his tribe. But it is not every poet who has taken it
upon himself to experience and transmute such a great weight
of human life and suffering; or who has found himself compelled to be the prophet of truths so terrible.

But Eliot has shown us what the world is very apt to forget,
that the statement of a terrible truth has a kind of healing
power. In his stern vision of the hell that lies about us in
modern London, there is a quality of grave consolation. In his
statement of the worst, Eliot has always implied the whole
extent of the reality of which that worst is only one part.
This is true no less of *The Waste Land* than of the *Four
Quartets*, whose philosophic hope is more immediately apparent. Belsen itself is only terrible because of the potential
greatness of man, in terms of a conception, in the truest sense
religious, of what man is capable of being. But for such a sense
of the greatness of the issues of human life there is a triviality
about the worst horrors of modern warfare and modern peace;
That Mr Eliot gave hell back to us, and with it the dimensions
of the universe to which hell belongs, is not the least of his
benefactions. If I seem to imply that, for myself, the early
poems have meant more than the *Four Quartets*, the reason
will, I hope, be clear. The shallow progressive philosophies
both religious and secular of our parents' generation sought
to eliminate evil from the world. Mr Eliot's vision of hell
restored a necessary dimension to our universe.

The imaginative work counts for most. But in the intellectual life of my generation T. S. Eliot has, besides, been the
guide and master. Again and again his criticism has pointed
the way to the books relevant to our problems. The rocks he
has struck have seldom failed to yield water for our wandering

79

tribes. In his critical writings he has pointed, always quietly and without any excessive enthusiasm, or desire to convert or to persuade, to those writers of the past who have some special significance for us; the Jacobean dramatists; Donne and the metaphysicals; Dante, Baudelaire. Hints dropped in a line of verse have set us off to try to discover what Krishna meant, or what St John of the Cross envisaged by the Dark Night, or why an allusion from Mallarmé stirred overtones so nostalgic. Never have these clues failed to lead us into some rich world of philosophic or imaginative experience.

Every young poet whose apprenticeship has fallen during the last twenty years must feel that T. S. Eliot's eminence cannot wholly be accounted for by the excellence of his verse and criticism. The achievement of Yeats and Joyce we have admired no less than Eliot's. But the veneration in which these two names are held is of a different kind. Their achievement is inimitable, self-contained, isolated. To writers who come after, their great work makes the task harder rather than easier, by its very completeness. Eliot, conscious always of the whole tradition of which any single poet's work forms a part has, in a sense dedicated his personal talent to the English poetic tradition. He has inherited the English language, and he has bequeathed it, both purified and enriched, to his successors. Not a poet among those who have written their first poems during the last twenty years but must have felt the influence of Eliot on the language as a force both of discipline and of liberation.

What perhaps is more than all the rest is that Mr Eliot has been a personal presence in our world. There are few young poets who have not at some time, between hope and fear, registered a parcel of poems to Faber & Faber, hoping not so much for publication (a hope more easily realized elsewhere) as in order to measure their work by Mr Eliot's exacting standards. Those who seriously desire to submit themselves to the severe vocation of poetry have always found in Mr Eliot's sternness a stronger incentive to creation than in the praise of others. It is hard to imagine writing poems in a world in which Mr Eliot's presence is not the measure of our work.

80

But his presence in the world has counted and still counts
for more than that. Human beings have a strange faculty for
knowing, unerringly, what a man is, without words; we can
often discern the stature even of those whom we have never
seen. T. S. Eliot is one of those whose living presence in the
world can be felt. Not because he is the intimate friend of
everybody – on the contrary, his life is private and retired, and
there is a ceremonious formality in his relationships with the
world; but we are none the less conscious of the quality, of
the mode of being that is his and no one else's; of the judgment on events that is implicit in his merely being there; of
the fact that he represents, in the contemporary world, what
Blake has called an 'Eternal State.' Most lives are too tenuous,
too incoherent for it to be said that they occupy, more than
momentarily, any place in eternity, or represent any state,
whether good or evil. Perhaps one of the things that we mean
by greatness is the assumption and upholding of one of the
spiritual modes of being that are possible to mankind. When
we think of T. S. Eliot we think of such a man.

Nevill Coghill

Sweeney Agonistes

(An anecdote or two)

One morning Mr Wystan Auden, then an undergraduate at
Christ Church, blew in to Exeter College for his tutorial hour
with me, saying:

'I have torn up all my poems.'

'Indeed! Why?'

'Because they were no good. Based on Wordsworth. No
good nowadays.'

'Oh . . . ?'

'You ought to read Eliot. I've been reading Eliot. I now see
the way I want to write. I've written two new poems this
week. Listen!'

He recited them.

I was brought up to demand a logical as well as a sensual
meaning in poetry, so his recitation was completely incomprehensible to me, though I was struck by some of the images
that had a sudden but seemingly irrelevant force. I can still
remember one of a man by a gate looking into a field, though
its 'meaning,' in a context unintelligible to me, escaped. I
complained of this, and Auden explained with clarity and pity
that to 'understand' a poem was not a logical process, but a
receiving, as a unity, a pattern of co-ordinated images that
had sprung from a free association of sub-conscious ideas,
private to himself. He again recommended the works of Mr
Eliot.

All this was towards 1926-7. I had of course already made
some tentative soundings in Mr Eliot's poetry and decided it
was too deep for me, or else one of us was off the track of
poetry. Perhaps he was a fad or fashion; if only my more
advanced pupils would stop talking about him, there was a
chance he might blow over . . . Or must I swot him up? It was
that morning's tutorial hour that convinced me I must.
'Auden,' I thought, 'is in the imperative.'

82

It was at first very hard for me to adjust myself to Mr
Eliot's apparently formless verses and (as I thought) Bloomsbury idiom. This of course will now seem derisory. I perse-
vered and understanding began to dawn with pleasure, and
pleasure to intensify into delight.

I was still for a long while perplexed as to the tone of voice
required for certain phrases; in *Prufrock*, for instance. Was
it right for ladies to come and go, talking of Michelangelo?
If not, why not? What were the dangers of eating a peach?
Was the 'music from a farther room' a room in Bloomsbury
or in some more heavenly mansion? When I asked these
questions, the adherents of Eliot looked at me (how rightly)
with compassion and turned kindly to subjects within my
capacity.

But slowly, over about two years, I think, the poems, at my
invitation, invaded me. The first to make a full conquest was
Sweeney Agonistes. I was at once moved by the quick, pert,
rhymes and rhythms, and the sense of how extremely effective
they would be on the stage. And there was that palmary jazz-
lyric *Under the Bamboo*. Although, as yet, I had absolutely
no notion what the 'fragments' of *Sweeney Agonistes* as a
whole portended, I could feel that they were portentous.

In the end, however, my eye fell on the title-page, and
there lay the two little latch-keys left by Mr Eliot for those
who wish to enter his intention: a quotation from Aeschylus,
countered by one from St John of the Cross. I fitted the keys
to the poem. In a moment it seemed to be unlocked.

I now entered the vision; it appeared to be about a normal
man of violence, the natural Orestes, the man who cuts his
way out of a problem. His natural motives of horror and
disgust have their natural expression in murder. But in an
obliquity no less natural, instead of plucking out his own eye
to enter the Kingdom of Heaven, he tries to pluck out what
his eye has seen; and this is murder, the wrong kind of
surgery, wrong and useless for (as in the case of Orestes) it
brings retribution. KNOCK, KNOCK, KNOCK.

The true solution of Sweeney's predicament, which he
neither knew nor took, was not natural but supernatural,

namely to divest himself of the love of created beings. (St John of the Cross.)

I had got this far in fathoming the governing idea of these fragments – how impressive they now seemed! – when a production of them in London was announced by Mr Rupert Doone. I rushed up to see it. About thirty of us were gathered round an almost empty room without a stage, but the almost fabulous figures of Lady Ottoline Morrell, Mr Aldous Huxley and Mr Eliot himself were pointed out to me in a whisper that deserved one. The play began.

It was performed with an exquisite blend of violence and restraint. The cool, rich, level voice of Mr Doone as Snow saying, 'Let Mr Sweeney continue his story,' sent a shudder down my back. He offered an almost entirely different interpretation of the play to that I had worked out. As he presented it, it was a study in the psychology of a Crippen; he made it seem that we were all Crippens at heart and that nothing was so true as that:

Any man might do a girl in
Any man has to, needs to, wants to
Once in a lifetime, do a girl in.

And this necessity led to nightmare and to the police. KNOCK, KNOCK, KNOCK. But it remained a necessity.

I went away overwhelmed and bewildered, yet reassured of the greatness of the play in this admirable production.

It must have been a little later that I came upon *Marina*, which of all Mr Eliot's poems I find the most revealing. It created for me a unification of all his work into which the later *Four Quartets* have easily fitted. Whether this unity I seem to perceive is the same sort of unity as Mr Eliot sees in and beyond them I do not know. I hope so. The governing idea (for me) is that of rebirth into super-natural life through a cycle of which a descent into the dark night of the soul is a recurring preliminary. This appears as a process for the common man as much as for the professed mystic, whether he recognizes it or not, and Sweeney is the common man, the average, decent, lout.

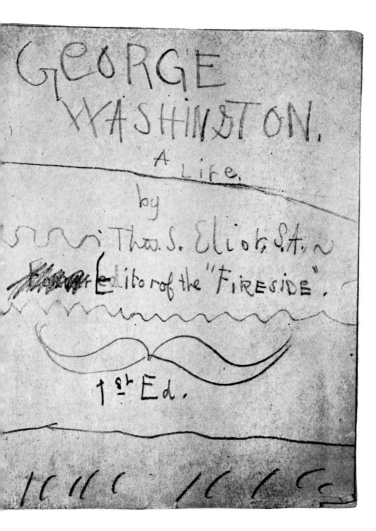

George Washington. A Life

The original Holograph Manuscript and the only extant copy of the Author's first and only Essay in Historical Biography.
Written in pencil on two loose leaves, folded into four (5" x 4"), consisting of: Title-page, *verso* blank; Text, one leaf written on both

George Washington.

BY

T.S. Eliot.

—

George Washington was born in plantation. He wanted to go to la bur his mamma didn't want im to, so he took to the army urst he killed French and Indians nd then British. freed his country and was president. hen J. Adams' was president he was

sides; pencil-portrait of 'G. Wash-ing-ton', *verso* blank; one leaf, *recto* blank, *verso* pencil-squiggle. The date of composition is not known, but was *c.* 1895. The only other surviving manuscript of the period, antedating the present one and therefore the author's earliest recorded work, is *The Fireside*.

an admiral of someting like.
And then he died, of corse. He was
never said to say a _lie_. He died at
Mr. Vernon.

G. Wash-ing-ton.

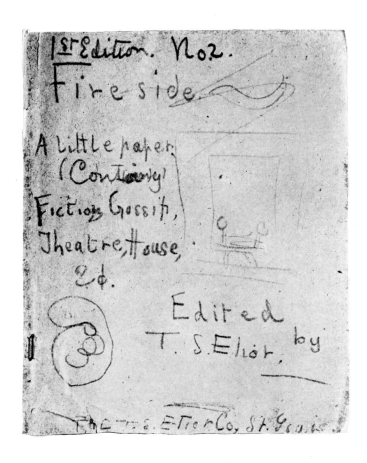

Each issue of this domestic periodical consisted of a single copy, written entirely by the 'Editor' in his autograph, and circulated amongst his family in St Louis, Mo. A few numbers are preserved in the collection at Harvard formed by his brother Henry Ware Eliot.

The title-page of No. 2 is reproduced here.

Such a man is put to torture by his soul, of whose existence he is at first but dimly aware, as a maturing man becomes aware of the upthrust of a wisdom-tooth. It hurts, and it drives him, naturally, to violence. So Sweeney, *l'homme moyen sensuel*, awakens to disgust and pain in his beloved *saeculum*, his frowzy world, and tries to cut his way out of it; the wrong surgery. But the Orestes-Crippen impulse masters him.

Mr Doone's interpretation (as I received it) was nevertheless a shock. It seemed to justify the ways of Crippen to woman, and thus to destroy my more metaphysical speculations, in that there appeared to be no alternative for Sweeney than to murder Doris. But his production was so convincing. Could it, after all, have been what Mr Eliot had really meant?

I do not remember the date on which I first met Mr Eliot. It was at lunch with Father D'Arcy. Conversation was about the Lambeth Conference, then recently terminated. As I did not know what the Bishops had been talking about I kept a tactful but ashamed silence and studied with admiration the zest of my companions in their theological discussion. Poetry was not mentioned and I had no chance to put the questions I had been nursing.

Not long after – a year maybe – I found myself once again seated at lunch next to Mr Eliot. It was at All Souls' College on Encænia Day and there were enough Bishops about to re-introduce Lambeth topics. Cantuar himself was there. I resolved to start straight into poetry rather than expose myself in theology; but what would Mr Eliot want to talk about? Would he rather not talk at all? Would he remember me?

To my great pleasure he seemed to know me at once. And in a rush I began to talk to him about the production of *Sweeney Agonistes*. So far as I can remember this is what was said:

Myself:

I think I saw you at Rupert Doone's production of *Sweeney Agonistes?*

Mr Eliot:

Very likely indeed. I was there.

85

Myself:

I had no idea the play meant what he made of it . . . that everyone is a Crippen. I was astonished.

Mr Eliot:

So was I.

Myself:

Then you had meant something very different when you wrote it?

Mr Eliot:

Very different indeed.

Myself:

Yet you accept Mr Doone's production?

Mr Eliot:

Certainly.

Myself:

But . . . but . . . can the play mean something you didn't intend it to mean, you didn't know it meant?

Mr Eliot:

Obviously it does.

Myself:

But can it then also mean what you *did* intend?

Mr Eliot:

I hope so . . . yes, I think so.

Myself:

But if the two meanings are contradictory, is not one right and the other wrong? Must not the author be right?

Mr Eliot:

Not necessarily, do you think? Why is either wrong?

This was to me so staggering a point of view that I could only put it down to modesty. I therefore abandoned this attack for one more frontal.

Myself:

Tell me, Mr Eliot, who *is* Sweeney? How do you see him? What sort of man is he?

Mr Eliot:

I think of him as a man who in younger days was perhaps a professional pugilist, mildly successful; who then grew older and retired to keep a pub.

86

I do not remember any more of this conversation, but what I have written is true so far as it goes, subject to correction from Mr Eliot, should he remember it at all. I was disturbed and excited by what he said and have often since then reflected on these occasions, and on the critical implications of his remarks. They repay thought. At least they have the merit of being authentic anecdotes.

Lawrence Durrell

Anniversary

Poetry, science of intimacies,
In you his early roots drove through
The barbarian compost of our English
To sound new veins and marbled all his verses
Through and through like old black ledgers,
Hedging in pain by form, and giving
Quotations from the daily treaty poets make
With men, possessions or a private demon:
Became at last this famous solitary
Sitting at one bleak uncurtained window
Over wintry London patiently repeating
That art is determined by its ends
In conscience and in morals. This was startling.
Yet marriages might be arranged between
Old fashions and contemporary disorders.
Sole student of balance in a falling world
He helped us mend the little greenstick fractures
Of our verse, taught polish in austerity.

Others who know him will add private humours,
And photographs to albums; taken near Paris,
Say, drinking among some foreign dons all night
From leather bubbles in a tavern: a remark
That silenced a fussy duke: yet these
Alluding and delimiting can only mystify
The singer and his mystery more, they do not chain.
Neither may we ever explain but pointing
To a new star one needs new vision for
Like some late hornbeam risen over England,
Relate it to a single sitting man,
In a high window there, beside a lamp,
Some crumpled paper, a disordered bed.

John Betjeman

The Usher of Highgate Junior School

In 1914-15 I spent two unsuccessful terms at Highgate Junior School. Mr Eliot was a tall, quiet usher there whom we called 'The American Master.' Some of the cleverer boys from Muswell Hill (I was from Highgate) knew he was a poet. How? I have often wondered, for I cannot imagine him telling them or anyone that he was a poet, and I did not know that he had published any poems in England as early as that. Anyhow, they persuaded me to lend (or did I present it to him?) a manuscript called *The Best Poems of Betjeman*. I had forgotten the incident until he reminded me of it, in as kind a way as possible, in the early 'thirties. I record this now purely out of self-advertisement, because I think I must be the only contributor to this book of my age who knew him so long ago. I wish my memory served me better that I might tell you of how he taught in what was then a rough place. All I can remember is that he looked exactly as he does now and that I have no unhappy memories of him.

I hesitate to write of his soul's journey though it travels in the same carriage as mine, the dear old rumbling Church of England which is high, low and broad at once. I know that we are both 'high' and object to certain weaknesses of the system and that we both regard the Church of England, despite these weaknesses, as *the* Catholic Church of this country. For this reason we remain in it, though it sometimes leads us where we would not. Other Anglicans better versed in theology than I am, who have discussed it with him at greater length will be able to enlighten readers more fully on his theological position. This great poet's Anglicanism does, however, draw my attention to an aspect of his poetry which is not theological and which is often missed. I refer to its delight in local-ness. The Church of England is the Church of this country. That is one of its attractions to someone who likes what is indigenous.

Eliot is certainly a visual poet, sensitive to the atmosphere of a street and a district, a country and a village. There have probably never been more graphic descriptions of the City of London than those to be found in *The Waste Land*. We all remember the Bloomsbury of Prufrock. Pimlico and South Kensington blossom from his pen. Indeed, I would say that he is a poet of London, and though three of the superb *Four Quartets* take their names from English villages, the villages they describe might be everywhere, while most of his poetry, particularly the earlier, is the product of someone who must have walked all over London and travelled in its trains and trams observing his fellow beings, the city men and the suburbanites, the cinema-fans and the newspaper-addicts.

Men and bits of paper, whirled by the cold wind
That blows before and after time,
Wind in and out of unwholesome lungs
Time before and time after.
Eructation of unhealthy souls
Into the faded air, the torpid
Driven on the wind that sweeps the gloomy hills of London
Hampstead and Clerkenwell Campden and Putney
Highgate, Primrose and Ludgate. Not here
Not here the darkness, in this twittering world.

He has the delight in place-names of the topographer and the further delight in the local atmosphere and industries. His fondness for Sherlock Holmes may *in part* be due to amusement derived from the plots and from Conan Doyle's inconsistencies about Dr Watson's possible bigamy and Holmes' education and family background. That sort of ingenuity is an intellectual pleasure which delights other theologically minded writers such as Monsignor Ronald Knox and Miss Dorothy Sayers. But I am sure he also delights in Sherlock Holmes for the vivid atmosphere which the stories convey of dark laurelled gardens in Norwood, of hansom cabs and gaslight and the Charing Cross Hotel. Conan Doyle and Eliot share the same poetry of the outer London of the steam suburbs. It is his pleasure in local association which makes him take an interest in varieties of English cheese (not forgetting the intrinsic excellence of the cheeses themselves) and which causes him to preserve a brass plate on his office door with the surname STEARNS engraved upon it, the relic of a Boston lawyer-forbear.

If it is a weakness in me to stress my own particular passion for topography which I find in Eliot's poetry, it is part of the strength of his poetry that it can appeal to so many different types of people. Topography may be a minor aspect of his work. It is one which strongly appeals to me. Others will admire in his poetry some of the other qualities which distinguish it.

In case it may be overlooked, I must stress his exquisite ear for rhythm. I remember an old poet of the 'nineties complaining to me that Eliot's poetry did not scan (this was before the publication of *Old Possum's Book of Practical Cats* whose metrical ingenuity is a combination of Gilbert and A. A. Milne). I can see what that old poet means – no sonnets, few quotations, no odes, no heroic couplets, no Spenserian stanzas. Eliot has rhythms of his own. Each line he writes is in itself a scanning line that could not possibly be mistaken for prose (except here and there where isolated from its context). And each line sets off the rhythm of the line that follows it.

O City city, I can sometimes hear
Beside a public bar in Lower Thames Street,
The pleasant whining of a mandoline
And a clatter and chatter from within
Where fishermen lounge at noon: where the walls
Of Magnus Martyr hold
Inexplicable splendour of Ionian white and gold.

The sudden contrast of the public bar all dactyls and short *a* sounds with the cæsuræ and spondees of those rolling lines which describe the cool still City church across the road need no conventional forms. They are a pattern in themselves. They are not free verse. But they are so difficult to write that they are disastrous to imitate which is why Eliot suffers more than most from imitators. He looks so easy and he is so hard.

I must conclude this note with an irrelevancy. The solemnity of his poetry and criticism, and that serious face, might lead strangers – and they will presumably be readers of this book – to imagine that he is an unhumorous person. Allow one doomed for ever to be thought a 'funny man' to say that Eliot is extremely funny. He has a slow deep, humour, subtle and allusive, the sort of humour that appreciates that immortal book *The Diary of a Nobody*.

Pierre Jean Jouve

Gravitation

I

Justement car tant d'or s'éloigne
Et tant de sang
S'écaille et justement
Tant de faim de mensonge est comme sur la mer

La lune atroce du vieux ancien Commandement;

Justement car tel doux bras traverse l'aube
Enchantant le mouvement saint
Tant de larme s'élance alors et tant de sang
Signifie résurrection calme des corps.

II

Tu m'as dit que j'étais le dernier de mon age
Tu m'as frappé de mélancolie au fort de tes guerres
Tu ne m'as plus donné de comprendre l'agneau
Sur un ciel ébloui de foudres embrouillées
Sur un sol bousculé de larmes (mon terreau
De ville blême rassemblant ses vils palais
Et ses hommes bouchés par entraille et matière
Qui n'ont plus d'homme que leur nom
Tel qu'au jour d'une matrice il est tombé)
Tu m'as donné ce mal d'apocalypse: aussi
Traçant ma croix au front comme un chevalier mort
De ruisselant espoir soudain je bénirai.

III

Quand tout est si coupable dans l'impur
Quand l'amour se procure à travers l'excrément
Quand le vouloir dépend d'une ligne sanguine
Quand les fantômes de l'horreur tiennent le ciel
Quand Dieu se fait poussière et absent;
Quand le vivant travaille pour le mort
Quand le mort fait la grève à travers le vivant
Quand rien ne sait
Ou nul, précipitant son orage, ne sent.

IV

D'après saint Bernard

Demande au Christ comment aimer
Le Christ et laisse au poids du Christ
En mystère, d'être le Christ
Et de rassembler l'adorable
Dans le pur mystère de force

Apprends du Christ comment tu dois
Aimer le Christ. Une tendresse
D'épouse. Et prudence de lion.
Et force flamme de la mort:
Zèle inflexible comme enfer.

94

Au sein de la guerre je te parle
Au soir de la guerre je te cherche
Du désert de la guerre je hache
Un cri vers ta stature céleste:

Du démon sur terre que je sache
Du fléau atroce de brulûre
Du sommeil atroce de sueur
De la honte de pays atroce

Regarder encor vers ta Sagesse
Et voler autour de ton Supplice
Avec un peuple fou de larrons

Autour de ta Consommation
Comme font les anges de la force
Oui graviter autour de ton supplice.

Bishnu Dey

Mr Eliot Among the Arjunas

It is a strange transposition: Mr Eliot in India. As Alun
Lewis wrote:* 'Don't you think India has reached the stage,
where the lotus becomes as much a 'lie' as the rose in Europe
(Mallarmé's theory) and there is need for a screeching, sweated
realism also, as much in the village as in the city? And why is
this realism so hard to attain? The sun teaches it every day.'

Further, 'And India is a hard country to mature in. There
is so much to anger you in the human scene, so much to dismay you in the social scene, so much to humble you in the
universal scene.' And again, 'But what untouched wealth the
Indian writer has – if only the climate of the soul was more
conducive to a free and deep development of his material!
Something seems to have gone wrong out here, and everything is tainted.'

And Mr Eliot reached this very British India about twenty-
five years ago. He came to be a fruitful influence perhaps in
the late 'twenties. Most of us came to know Mr Eliot through
the 1925 *Poems* and *The Sacred Wood*. One may be allowed
to be personal, because it was such an important event. I
remember the day when my secondhand bookseller showed
me copies of the *Poems* and *The Sacred Wood*, and how it was
only vague curiosity that prompted me to buy the two books.

And then came the impact of his poetry and his criticism.
It came at the right time of the happy though hollow 'twenties, before the fruit had turned bitter. It came at the right
time, even in India. And it came at the peak of a nervous crisis.
It is strange to recall the sense of the negative precision and
the intense frustration, Mr Eliot brought us accompanied by
his lyrical exultation. Idealist youth passed sleeplessly into
Gerontion and Europe was revealed to a young man in the

*Grateful acknowledgements to W. G. Archer for permission to
quote from these letters.

96

remote ruins of an empire as but another waste land. The
Ariel Poems grew out of that, as did *Ash Wednesday*, like
Mahatma Gandhi's Civil Disobedience with some 90,000
political prisoners, with their faith in torture, and their hope
with its hundred qualifications.

The Eliotites were a minority even among that minority
which could understand Gandhiji's pendulous ethics or
Tagore's open-air beliefs nurtured in strong seclusion. We
were among the few, and so we were self-conscious, but in
isolation, somewhat like Prufrock, or like that man who did
not commit the fornication.

Our self-consciousness was a burden to us, like that of the
lover away from his beloved. But it was creative, it was a progress in maturity, though it had not yet passed into the state
of the self-conscious lovers in embrace, as the old Vaishnava
lyric had sung: In each other's arms, both weep at the thought
of division. No, perhaps, our self-consciousness had not yet
arrived at Donne's *Extasie*. Our abstractions fed on themselves, as did the circular serpent of Valéry. Our solitude was
yet reminiscent of the Teutonic self-sufficiency of Rilke's nostalgia. We had more to learn, to know, to burn the mind out.

Indeed, Mr Eliot's great influence was that he sharp-pointed
us in our self-consciousness. Perhaps, his most important gift
was that; he made us poetically aware of self-consciousness
as a reality. The rest was subsidiary; he made us aware that a
poem has to be a good poem in order to be good poetry, he
helped us to be aware of literary history as a living source. He
widened and at the same time deepened our vision of literature, which is creative work. In an odd way he did in literature
what Marx had done in the broader sphere of social and
political life. And just as anti-Marxists point out the rather
negative and inconclusive nature of Marx's communist society,
so the anti-Eliotites have told us of the ultimately tentative
nature of Eliot's somewhat negative ideas and ideals.

It is that undogmatic nature of Mr Eliot's mind which has
influenced writers and readers in India; as far as the obviously
dogmatic persona of Mr Eliot are concerned, we in India are
debarred from contemplating and accepting them for im-

mediate political reasons, for reasons of climatic difference, and for the reason that we cannot ponder over the dogma of the Christian Church. Our life has worn away Mr Eliot's dogma – for us.

I do not know how I shall convey to an English reader this picture of Mr Eliot in India, convey the nature of our homage to him – Mr Eliot teaching Indian writers how to write and how to read – not merely the literature of Europe, but that of India, of Bengal. Our fathers and grandfathers had been full of Shakespeare as a solitary Elizabethan, of Milton, the Romantics and the sturdy Victorians. One can see however, how Shakespeare must have helped, as did Burke and, most of all, Matthew Arnold, through the backdoor. Mr Eliot was not altogether a stranger in his tastes. Michael Dutt, our great poet of the nineteenth century, was keener on Milton than on Shakespeare, on Dante, Virgil, Tasso rather than on Wordsworth, Blake or Keats, on Byron rather than on Shelley. And there was the great European, who was also a Brahmin Pandit – Vidyasagar – who translated from Sanskrit as well as from Shakespeare.

However, to cut short this unimportant topic of the local history of taste, it is true that Europe in India was largely the Europe of the French Revolution down to Queen Victoria, and to find Pater's *Renaissance* among the ancestral books was like a discovery.

No doubt, there is the towering figure of Rabindranath Tagore. He gave us professional competence without which technical advances remain but fortuitous triumphs. Tagore has been admired by a number of Europeans, but insufficiently understood. It is primarily as a great and versatile writer that he should have been appreciated. But that requires an approach which only writers themselves could have supplied: and very few writers in England or elsewhere – E. M. Forster is but a noble exception – had either the interest or the knowledge of the background. I would not compare Tagore with Homer as a German did, but English readers may arrive at an approximation if one thinks of Goethe in Germany, or Chaucer in England. Just as one can call the latter 'Father of Modern

English' etc, and at the same time miss in him the melancholy, the nostalgia, the romantic discontent and fervour so characteristic of English poetry from Beowulf to Eliot, similarly one finds that Tagore, after all that he has done for us, is a magnificent interlude; and with his heritage enriching our minds we have to search for roots elsewhere, in the popular as well as highly esoteric literature of the past, and in the actual life of the present.

It is not a paradox to say, and such is the measure of Mr Eliot's influence, that Mr Eliot has been of great help in realizing this active, creative, dialectic of our tradition. The difference between Mr Eliot's background and ours is quite obvious. But experience has parallels – more or less approximate, as the conditions differ. Parallels imply no similar excellence, but one thing should be borne in mind, that in India, though one finds great backwardness, definite retrogression and misery for the last 200 years, the life of the Indian people has a wide tradition of centuries of sophistication, Sanskrit and vernacular – at least as far as the basic human life is concerned: birth, copulation and death, as Mr Eliot has sung. An English reader has only to turn to Elwin's *Folk Songs of Chhatisgarh* to find this out.

This sophistication, in its cultural aspects, acquired certain popular patterns. In Bengal, at any rate, due to geographical and ethnic reasons, the patterns had been various, both in their width of prevalence and frequent renewals of tension. As far as actual writing was concerned there was naturally the shelter of habits which conventions tend to become. Tagore brought us, by his almost elemental genius, out of the walls of this sometimes dull and sometimes deadening conventionality. Eliot taught us how to recognize their necessity and thus utilize the resulting freedom.

Mr Eliot's influence as a poet and critic has thus been, on the one hand, a releasing force: it has widened the experience and the attitude of our very limited English educated minority, and at the same time, it has intensified our sense of isolation and thereby made us acutely aware of ourselves and the world. This is, indeed, a pathetic or a heroic situation, as one looks at it. It is the heroic aspect, the aspect of exploration, of activity, of readjustment which is of genuine interest to us.

It is quite likely that this exploration would be more punctuated by failure, by confusion, placed in the Indian scene, the empire, than in the English, the metropolis. Even in England with its comparative prosperity and cultural opportunities, the contradictions have been baffling enough. Therefore it is no wonder that there has been less understanding, and by less people, of this modern poetry business in India than in liberal England. Unable to share this apprehension of an active tradition and the individual conscious talent, critics have been misled into crying against peculiarities of individual writers. Efforts, however, were made towards understanding. For example, *Parichaya* (the old series) came out eighteen years ago, (inspired as Sudhindra Datta and his friends were) by Mr Eliot's *Criterion*. Datta wrote the first essay, I suppose, in an Indian language, where he stated that poetry had come to the dead-end of its development in the work of writers like Eliot. We came to realize that poetry must have a certain purity in its process of being, and in its immediate, one might say, manual purpose – though pure poetry might be quite impurely applied just as impure application might go with great formal purity and genuineness.

But the opposition was there. Tagore wrote quite a long essay on this modern poetry, mainly on Eliot, Pound and Amy Lowell. His main theme was what he thought were these poets' claims of impersonality. In one passage he said: If this modernity has any ideology, if it can be called impersonality, then one must declare that this rude suspicion of the world, this derogatory attitude is, after all, but a personal maladjustment, due no doubt, to some revolutionary change. This also is a kind of delusion: there is not that depth here which can accept the reality easily, with detachment. Some people think that this excess, this Goliathic challenge is modernity. I do not agree with that. Influenza to-day affects thousands of people, but it does not mean that influenza is the nature of the living body in its modern aspect.

Towards the end of his essay, Tagore said that this attitude

100

did not suit poetry at all, though it might have suited those ascetics of Europe who hated the body and the concrete reality. And he concluded that this antithetic outlook was sentimental, as was the excessive acceptance of the Victorians.

This highly interesting essay appeared in *Parichaya*, and Tagore referred in it to some of Mr Eliot's early poems. In those days Tagore was experimenting with *vers libre* in Bengali, and in that field I was for Eliot rather than for the garrulous prose-poems of Lawrence. So in my youthful impertinence I argued with him, and then sent him a poem with prose rhythms moving into verse rhythms as the need arose, and asked him to re-write it according to his canons. He turned it into prose altogether, and then it was triumphantly revealed that it was really a translation and the author was T. S. Eliot. *The Journey of the Magi* moved him profoundly, whereas the little early poems had failed to do so.

Translation went on. *A Song for Simeon*, *The Hollow Men*, *Marina*, *The Wind Sprang Up*. Two other writers joined: Kabir tried *La Figlia che Piange*, Hem Bagchi *The Preludes*.

It might be of some interest to consider how these translations happened. They really happened after months, and even years of preoccupation with them. *Ash Wednesday* and *Burnt Norton* came off in a rush, but *Gerontion* had taken years before it burst, and so had *Coriolan*. *Gerontion* rushed into a faithful translation when Gandhiji went on a fast unto death, in Calcutta, last year, against the communal riots over the Mountbatten award, and when young men and women went out in peace processions and kept guard at street corners, and when some of them gave their lives. It really throws light on my consideration of the pure greatness of Mr Eliot's verse technique. Impelled as one was by awful thoughts of Gandhiji's death and our terrible shame, and hopes centred in our youth, one found that the Bengali equivalents of Hakagawa, de Tornquist, Von Kulp, Mrs Cammel, all these – whirled beyond the circuit of the shuddering Bear in fractured atoms – very naturally led – in the fabric of the faithful Bengali translation and in the context of the translator's immediate life – to

101

a different *dénouement*. Of course, the translator's intruding six lines had to be cut to keep the translation exactly like Mr Eliot's *Gerontion*. But it was with a shock of pleasure that the translator learned how the fasting and the tears of a great man of nearly eighty years, and the boys marching through mad streets of secret death had poetically and formally nothing alien to:

Thoughts of a dry brain in a dry season.

The *Landscapes* ripened after a trip to the Santhal country. Similarly *Coriolan* came to be translated all on a sudden, when Pandit Nehru had formed the Interim Government and there used to be frequent talk of his resignation.

All this does not mean that the growth of the technical maturity of the translator was not the main factor, whatever the worth of the translations may be. But it throws light on the nature of Mr Eliot's poetry, as it worked as an influence in the remote mess of a colonial country with a long tradition. The influence has been deep and subtle, it has opened up awareness of depths and subtleties which we had lost sight of, in our poetry, in our active apprehension of our past tradition, and in our critical judgments. It is as if Hoelderlin had read Marx. The influence has worked through decades, at various levels, at various degrees of intensity and at the end – which is no end – of one such progress, it has released itself into the kind of freedom which Hopkins must have had in his mind when he spoke of Milton, and of how he wanted to write differently. That is one level, and there is the other, when we find some of our orthodox romantics at last thinking in terms of their frightful efforts at self-consciousness. Such is Mr Eliot's influence in this Waste Land where Krishna admonished Arjuna and where 'a poet's poet consistently and persistently has to try to be a people's poet'. In one's end is one's beginning.

One wonders what Mr Eliot would have thought of Tagore's last phase, the poems he wrote after his illness, after hours of unconsciousness; stark poems which cannot be translated, poems of Death, the lady of lifelong illusions, but defeated, at the last, before his naked self, as he awoke, alone, on the banks of Rupnaran, and none answered its primal query.

102

E. F. C. Ludowyk

T. S. Eliot in Ceylon

Time past in Europe after the lapse of several years becomes time present in Ceylon. This is particularly true of change in established traditions in the arts. This time lag has its disadvantages, but where, as in the case of the work of T. S. Eliot, the modifications for which he was responsible have become the established tradition, and the taste by which he is enjoyed has been the creation of the artist himself, there is a slight advantage to be gained from the delay in knowing the work – that of being able to appreciate, as it were simultaneously, early and late, the beginnings as well as the development.

Eliot's poetry came to be known in Ceylon in the early 'thirties. Naturally only the English educated minority would know either his work or his reputation. To the general reader literate in either Sinhalese or Tamil only, the name of T. S. Eliot would convey nothing. In India one hears of poetry in Bengali which has been influenced technically by poets as different as Eliot and Hopkins. In Ceylon a few writers of poetry in English wrote as they did because certain things had become clearer to them through Eliot's example. It could, I think, be said that though the influence was not considerable, it was important. The painter George Keyt caught some of Eliot's paradoxical tones in *Poems* (1936) and *The Darkness Disrobed* (1937). His material was as far as anything could be from Eliot. There were many things in Tambimuttu's work *Och* (1936) which were released by the exhiliration of reading Eliot. Jayanta Padmanabha – he is by the way an excellent reader of Eliot's poetry – produced for *The University of Ceylon Review* a useful discussion of the background of allusion in *The Waste Land*. All this seems slight, but in numerous undergraduate journals and reviews occasional verse which had previously been Shelleyan and Swinburnian took on a new accent and developed a new subject matter. In the higher forms of secondary schools and in the University where English is the medium of instruction, the poetry and the criticism are studied – a development which Eliot himself would probably regard as being of dubious value.

If it were asked, on the occasion of his sixtieth birthday, what readers of Eliot's poetry and criticism could derive from it, there could be only one answer. They could only derive that which a limited control of language and a different range of experience, from that of the poet, could reveal to them. What is true of almost every single English poet would be true of Eliot too in Ceylon. Perhaps Shakespeare would be an exception, because of a tradition in schools which probably makes Shakespeare seem less difficult to apprehend.

What has come through, and what has been gratefully received, has been that notable quality of Eliot's poetry early and late – the sharpness of his perception of the external world, recording through the sensory image a world changing in roughly the same ways in both West and East. This is as meaningful here as in Europe. The sensitiveness of the discriminating mind, the surprise of the images in the early poetry like *Portrait of a Lady* and *Preludes* might tempt one into hazarding the remark that here lie the distinction and the strength of all Eliot's poetry. To the reader in Ceylon to whom *Four Quartets* and *The Love Song of J. Alfred Prufrock* seem scarcely separated by an interval of time, and to whom the former must necessarily be more difficult to approach than the latter, the power of the sensory image would offer itself as the easiest aspect of the poetry to grasp. As the eye travels over the unsightly rash of 'oil-tanks', modern cosmopolitanism and war have left upon what is no longer 'India's utmost isle' but a strategic base in an Empire's network of bases, then the reader here can appreciate at least the force of lines like:

The worlds revolve like ancient women

Gathering fuel in vacant lots.

One feels that one's experience has been enlarged in ways that did not previously seem possible.

Not only has the sensory image compelled admiration because it has registered change in an environment to which ours

104

approximates daily, but there also seems to be an attitude of
mind in Eliot's poetry which is so frequently met with as to
seem almost typical of him, and which might even be called
his characteristic aptitude. There is a tendency in the poet,
much in excess of any other poet's revelation of the unfamiliar
(as it lies hidden under the covering of the familiar) to see
through and beyond the world of the senses. We could say of
this poet that his characteristic mode seems to have been, and
still is, the descent into Hades, whether, as in *The Love Song
of J. Alfred Prufrock*, it is only the might-have-been:

I am Lazarus, come from the dead,

Come back to tell you all, I shall tell you all

or, as in *Little Gidding*, it is the meeting with the 'familiar
compound ghost'. This readiness, to see the object not as it is,
but in its symbolic setting, would appeal to readers to whom
the idea of Maya is familiar, if not through knowledge of its
philosophic import, then because of the assumptions one tends
unconsciously to make in the East when judging the validity
of experience. Furthermore, it would not be too rash to say
that this attitude of mind in the East has been strengthened as
a result of several centuries of increasing misery, the consequence of alien rule and the breakdown of indigenous social
systems. What Krishna meant no longer matters much to the
East, and the glow of the original Fire Sermon has paled considerably. But Eliot's way of communicating his reaction to
what he has called 'the boredom and the horror' is fresh and
vital. This may be only the least part of his genius; that little
more has come through to us is our deficiency and our fault,
not his. To attempt to say more about his genius would be
presumptuous.

Stephen Spender

Speaking to the Dead
in the Language of the Dead

I

So this young man reeled out
Of gambling den or brothel –

                       his face white
His hair ebony –
             his waistcoat was
Embroidered with small roses among stains
Of wine.

He drove into the night –
Hooves cannoned snow to moonlit smoke –
Black buttocks tossed under the sprinkled bells –

And remote childhood bells mourned for his life.

Pursuit of happiness had exploded
A mine within his mind.

The lamentable word AGAIN
Exploded in his brain –

Kaleidascope of turning mistresses
– Black and red upstarting images –
Heart club diamond spade.

II

He ran past stone dogs of the palace gate
Up arching stairways aching like his head
Into his room – flung himself down
His world revolving – on his bed.

Then in the lifted darkness images
Fixed into angels and devils for his pages.

Speaking to the
Dead in the
Language of the
Dead

'Again, again,' he sighed –

Rose, filled a tumbler, lit the candles
On each side of the rosewood table with brass handles.

III

Within that darkness where I see his room
    – Pavemented floor, star-pointed ceiling –
Within this midnight and beyond his tomb,
    He incised with a quill his vein of feeling
And wound the thin red blood out through the gloom
    To set down here for us: revealing
That dancer – his despair – at which we look –
His blood behind the white mask of his book.

Passion of women, flushed from his embracing,
    He dipped his pen in: his great night-limbed lovers
In operative moments of enlacing
    Were experiments for sensuous manoeuvres
From which he formed those tears and blushes gracing
    To-day's libraries. And that sigh, which hovers
Through spaces between letters, white and far,
Is, on his page, the print of what we are.

His moon, *his* nightingale torn from *his* time,
    Her tear, falling down centuries, hour by hour,
Her letter weeping *her* wish through *his* rhyme,
    Her footstep, immanent; from such, his tower
Whose base of violent deaths stands in quicklime,
    But whose high gleam reintegrates the flower,
Petal by petal, of time-outworn fashion,
In omnipresent coexistent passion.

It was enough for him that what is, is,
  To cut his jewels on time like jewels in clocks.
The tears, the diamonds, duels, the moons, the kisses,
  He shut within his stanzas' iron locks
For us to look at. What was, what lived, still is his
  Ecstasy. Marriage, ennui, pox,
And the long disenchantment, were unreal.
His life was the bright cutting edge we feel.

Enough to praise it all! To burn! To live!
  Dip women, cards, remorse, avenging fires
In the poetical preservative!
  Brush all the nightingales to wires
Strung on the trees, behind a sigh! Oh give
  The absolute affirmation when the choirs
Mass onto silence. Beyond ultimate harm
Trumpet that opening O! Call death life's balm.

IV

Pock-marked face of stinking breath,
Bones heaped over tavern tables,
Sweet-tooth for ill-wit, pen dipped in fumes
Of a scribbling age without sewers –

An age of pox, hard-drinking, and no cures
To look down-time onto whose huddled lanes
Is to encourage
The pail of garbage falling on one's head –
Stench of urine and rotting cabbage.

Stiletto glance, hog-bristling arm, treacherous, lecherous
Companion, poet –
                how is it
Your songs have sails which glide through death
With tackle clean as print,
                        and your transfigured head
Curves back all futures to obeisant waves,

And the upsurgent deck as fresh as paint
Bridges its crowded hold
Loaded with ore of still-impassioned days
Still burning through our senses?
                                    And you
Are multiplied by all you did create,
Male captain, female hostage, neuter crew,
Your world become our world, and you still you,
Blotches deleted from your brow,
Where now the laurel scarcely dares
Stain with praise the skin,
And future ages trembling near
Have thoughts like footprints across snow!

How can you, despised of mistresses,
Have made posthumous time your bride,
And laid posterity down by your side,
With all the world a lover to atone
For love your world denied?

Speaking to the
Dead in the
Language of the
Dead

V

Perhaps we live on time as on a plain
Where the present is the blurred and cutting edge
Of past humanity:
                    and we, the living,
Hack out the blind obsessions of our wills
Upon each others lives, Our violence
Enslaves our knowledge to our ignorance.

But yet within our minds there gleams that plain,
One total coexistent history,
Where within our edge of living, the dead are near:
As though to live were to be doomfully blind
In wilful acts of all we are,
While the dead show within our living mind
An art of chiaroscuro,
Using their shadows to become more clear.

109

And thus within this harsh and cutting edge
Where we lay waste our world-inventing powers
Like children who make, to throw down, towers,
Deeper than our blood upon our hands
The dead move through us into ordered lands.

You who were once this blurred and cutting edge
We suffer now in being, become you
Within our omnipresent coexistence:
In us you are of you what was most true,
Purged of time's derelict irrelevance,
In us you live your death's significance.

Through us you enter into your ideal,
Through us the heart of all becomes the real,
And you become the world, and we are you.
We bring to birth your poem's perfected statue,
Out of our lacerated flesh of violence,
Within this edge of life you also knew.

Ashley Dukes

T. S. Eliot in the Theatre

Our new dramatic poetry in the English theatre did not begin (as is often supposed) with the production of *Murder in the Cathedral* at Canterbury and the Mercury. It began with the occasional work of the Group Theatre around 1930 under Rupert Doone, and with the writers Auden and Isherwood, Stephen Spender and Louis MacNeice. Eliot's only contribution to this particular movement was a permission to perform *Sweeney Agonistes*, which had been written some time earlier.

The Group Theatre was at first a Sunday Society, and it may be said to have taken the pioneering place of the Incorporated Stage Society which flourished before and after the first World War and was responsible for bringing the work of Shaw and Granville-Barker as well as many Continental dramatists on to the English stage. There was the difference that the main quest of the younger play-producing unit was for original verse drama in the English language. Its discoveries were varied and significant.

The owner of the Westminster Theatre, Anmer Hall, made it possible for the Group to give its Sunday performances, and later a public season, on his stage. Here Auden and Isherwood (at one time the chief hopes of the movement) proved themselves as dramatists with *The Dog Beneath the Skin* some years before their Everest drama *The Ascent of F.6*, directed like the former play by Rupert Doone, was produced at the Mercury under my management. A light-hearted willingness to collaborate with original musicians and scenic artists was shown by most of the authors, indeed this was a mark of the whole Group. The older dramatic critics, who had been long trained to think of any poet's theatre as solely a dramatist's creation, were perhaps unduly repelled by the atmosphere of youthful experimentation that surrounded its work. A political bias to the Left was another inevitable character. England as the home of middle-class complacency is also the home of violent reactions against this complacency on the part of the youthful middle class.

But independently of all this, Eliot's pageant play *The Rock* was created from a scenario by E. Martin Browne, its producer, and performed at Sadler's Wells on behalf of the Forty-five Churches Fund of the Diocese of London. (The Church of England began to assert itself as a powerful element in the dramatic audience.) The production was overlooked by some observers within the theatre, but it was of great significance to Eliot himself. He learned from it something of the collaborative process of the stage; he became interested in the possibilities of the dramatic form; and in fact he was prepared for the writing of plays as perhaps no dramatist of our present century had been prepared before him. An Elizabethan spirit of respect for the poet combined with theatrical inventiveness began to be abroad. The new poet's theatre, clearly, was not going to accept any of the conventions of the author of *Saint Joan;* it was even in full rebellion against them. In asking everything in the way of inspiration from the dramatist, it asked merely for a text with entrances and exits – no more material than is handed down to us in a seventeenth-century text as we read it to-day.

Both the secular and the religious tendencies in our new dramatic poetry had declared themselves already before 1935, the year when the tragedy of Becket was first performed in Canterbury and London. Other tendencies had manifested themselves as clearly; for example it was plain that the poets meant to restore tragedy to our English stage, and with it the tragic chorus as a personage of drama. Even earlier, in the 1920's, there had been hints of such a development in the plays of Sean O'Casey. But now all the writers of a varied school not only accepted the Chorus but broke away from the convention of iambic or 'blank' verse which had dominated English dramatic poetry for centuries, and chose for themselves trochaic and yet freer forms interwoven with a great deal of dramatic prose. Had it not been for the second war and the departure of some of the writers for diverse reasons to dis-

tant spheres, dramatic poetry might well have advanced rapidly along this wide front. For *The Ascent of F.6* was very nearly
a great play, and *The Family Reunion* in the succeeding year
was as exciting a stimulus as a young dramatist could receive.
This outline of history is significant because to-day dramatic
poetry is recognized as the one notable contribution of our
country to the newer drama of the world. Without it, we
should have little to set beside the drama of Odets and Wilder
in America, or of Sartre and Anouilh in France. Our prose
writers are not of comparable importance.

I met Eliot in the early months of 1935, when we conferred
several times at the Mercury with W. B. Yeats and Martin
Browne on the possibility of establishing a poets' stage for
regular performance in London. This was long before the days
of CEMA or the Arts Council, and the risks of such an undertaking in a small theatre were bound to be my own. But the
prospect of new plays by Yeats and Eliot was decisive, and a
season was provisionally arranged. It was then also that I read
the first draft of the Becket tragedy, which was called, if I
remember rightly, *Fear in the Way*. It was suggested that this
work (which had already been commissioned for the Canterbury Festival) would be available for the Mercury, together
with a double or triple bill of plays by Yeats, as the foundation
of a repertory. Martin Browne as director of productions was
to be closely associated with the project. Then however came
the proposal that he should first produce *Murder in the Cathedral* (under this title inspired by Mrs Martin Browne and wil-
lingly accepted by the author) at Canterbury the following
June; and the notion of a Mercury production was accordingly
deferred, together with the Yeats bill which would in any
event have to wait upon the producer's freedom to undertake
it. The postponement until the autumn of 1935 suited us well
enough, and there was the further prospect that the Canterbury production might be taken over, as indeed it eventually
was.

Festivals, even of a dramatic nature, were nothing new to
Canterbury. In yearly cricket weeks or on similar occasions,
Old Stagers of much eminence in other professions than that

113

of acting had adorned the stage of the local theatre before county gatherings for a great many years. What was newer was the gathering, in the Chapter House opening from the Cloister, of an audience much less social and clad in homespuns and flannels if not in sandals, paying their modest price of admission in aid of the restoration of the cathedral fabric. Newer still was the appearance before them in these august surroundings of a small band of actors bringing, like artists of the Middle Ages, their own gifts to the service of such a cause. And hitherto unknown was their performance of a play by our foremost poet, author of *The Waste Land*, within a few yards of the spot where Becket, protagonist of the tragedy, had been murdered seven and a half centuries ago. But these were only the outward circumstances that made the occasion memorable.

It is hard perhaps to recapture the mood of that summer of 1935, which seems nevertheless oddly near to us instead of far-removed by the sequence of violent events. An acceptance of the religious theme of the play united the poet, the actors and the Canterbury audience as surely as the Greeks were united in acceptance of any tragic myth on their hillside in the theatre of Dionysos. The listeners knew enough of modern poetry to follow the rhythms of the speakers and the chorus of the Women of Canterbury, and even to be reconciled to the author's more surprising images. It was for such initiates, that the 'catherine-wheel' and the 'prize given for the English Essay' figured among life's disillusions as they were recited by the tempters. The presentation was accepted as natural and at the same time theatrical. Such innovations as the absence of a curtain or of conventional stage lighting linked the conditions of performance with those of the Elizabethan stage, even in this elongated hall with its inconvenient platform fitted only for the assembly of the Chapter.

Other things conspired to remind us of the play's actuality; indeed it was never allowed to become historical drama for a moment. Hitler had been long enough in power to ensure that the four knightly murderers of Becket would be recognized as figures of the day, four perfect Nazis defending their act on the most orthodox totalitarian grounds. Echoes of one war and

114

forebodings of another resounded through the sultry after- noon. All of this spirit Martin Browne had contrived to impress upon his team of players headed by Robert Speaight, an actor of spiritual force having behind him a notable stage history, including a Hamlet played for the Old Vic. It may not have been a very great Hamlet, but it was beyond doubt sensitive and lively-minded. Speaight proved himself in the part of Becket, as every one now knows. And if the Women of Canterbury were no peasants or poor townsfolk, as they might have been in some subsequent productions of the play, they were young women of individual perception who had passed through the best school of verse-speaking, that of Elsie Fogerty, available to our stage. This Chorus, too, was a gift brought to the service of the play and the Festival.

London dramatic critics came down to Canterbury and wrote handsomely about *Murder in the Cathedral*, though without a full understanding that a masterpiece had been born. On the other hand, one heard of few if any theatre managers who had the curiosity to visit the city in search of a new drama- tist. They recognized him afterwards but not at the time. The brief run of afternoon performances was soon over and the holiday season came; then toward the end of it Martin Browne and I drove down to Canterbury one Sunday morning and brought to London the costumes and properties which we had acquired from the Festival authorities and had packed in a couple of hampers. Some of these, I believe, are still in stage use after the thousand-odd performances that we have given since. The general design of the presentation remains in its full integrity.

Perhaps no one was more astonished than Eliot by the suc- cess of his play, which ran nearly a year from the date of its first performance at the Mercury (1 November 1935) before it was transferred to the Duchess Theatre for a further run of several months. In the West End it even survived the crisis of the Abdication, which lent unforeseen point to some of its lines ('King is forgotten when another shall come' or 'If the Archbishop cannot trust the Throne') and embarrassed actors and audiences alike. In the University cities, to which we sent

115

the play at an early stage of its history, the scene of the Knights' Meeting was always the highlight of the performance. In the big theatres of the industrial cities, which were visited in the course of the first tour, the Knights were heard with respectful attention mingled certainly with decorous surprise. In Boston and New York, on the other hand, we found this scene to be apprehended as a dramatic masterstroke and accepted (as it should be) both light-heartedly and seriously. Nothing is gained by allowing actors to make it comic in the obvious sense; it is a scene of self-revelation in the classic spirit.

In these much later days, thanks to a roving commission in the cultural world of Western Europe, I see a number of productions of *Murder in the Cathedral* in translated form. The most interesting so far was that of the Vieux-Colombier in Paris, in 1945–46, in the version of Fluchère. What it may have lacked in humour it made up in subtlety, especially in the treatment of the Chorus by a well-trained group retained semi-permanently by this little theatre. The first run lasted many months and there will be revivals from time to time. In Germany the play began its career almost simultaneously in the autumn of 1947 in Cologne, Göttingen and Munich. The text of Rudolf Alexander Schröder (*Mord im Dom*) should hold the stage fifty years hence as firmly as it does to-day; but the Germans are inclined to give an operatic importance to the production by their use of incidental music, and to indulge in choreographics both in the scenes of the Tempters and the Chorus. The play can fill a large theatre as has often been proved; but its appeal is always strongest in a simple setting and by the direct impact of words. There are certain difficulties for the German Knights in addressing their own countrymen with the lines 'You are Englishmen and therefore you believe in fair play.'

The Family Reunion presents difficulties in any country, and perhaps most of all in England. John Gielgud wanted originally to play Harry, Lord Monchensey, as Orestes is named; and perhaps he will yet do so, or actors of his intellectual sensibility will do so in other generations. The play was dubiously

116

The Earliest Poetical Manuscript

The original Holograph Fair-copy of the first poem by T. S. Eliot 'To be Shown to Others' Eyes'.

Written in ink on one side of a single sheet of ruled exercise-paper (11″ x 8½), signed on the reverse: 'Eliot January 24 1905'. The question-marks and underscoring in the text, and the credit mark 'A' on the reverse – all in red ink – were added by the English Master at Smith Academy, St Louis, Mo., Mr Roger Conant Hatch who according to the poet 'conceived great hopes of a literary career for me'. Eliot was a pupil at Smith Academy, a day-school founded by his grandfather, before he went as a boarder to Milton Academy. Although this is his earliest surviving poetical manuscript and the first poem he is *known* to have written, it was actually the second to be printed. It was originally published as a lyric, in the April 1905 issue of the Smith Academy Record, two months after the publication, in the February issue of the same magazine, of the Byronic 'A Fable For Feasters'. It was reprinted, as 'Song', with the first stanza re-written, in the *Harvard Advocate* 3 June 1907 while the poet was a freshman.

'Difficulties of a Statesman'

The first and last pages of the original Holograph draft of 'Difficulties of a Statesman'.

Written in pencil on one side only of six loose ruled leaves (6¼″ x 4½″), from a block of scribbling-paper. First printed with a

in the silence of the Croaking
night
                    in the dew
Come (with the sweep) of the
small Cat's wing, with the
small flare of the fire fly (or
the lightning bug)
"Rising and falling, Crowned
with dust", the Small creatures
The small creatures chirp in
the dust, within the night.
On o the
What shall I say?
We demand a committee,
a thoroughly representative
Committee of investigation.

Resign resign resign.

French translation by Georges Limbour, in *Commerce* XXIX (Winter
1932), and in *Hound and Horn* Vl. 2 (Oct.–Dec. 1932); first published
in book-form in *Collected Poems* 1909–1935, 1936. Few of these preliminary autograph drafts of poems have survived, the poet's usual
method being to work from his own typescript draft and subsequent
typescript revisions.

T. S. Eliot 1932; at Randolph.

T. S. Eliot 1926.

cast and imperfectly understood when it was first seen in
London, and perhaps the Mercury revival of 1947 brought
out for the first time its qualities with some defects. Martin
Browne, as producer, well as he responds to the depth and
humour of the work, does not give final clarity or reconcile us
to the basic realism on which Eliot lays stress. Perhaps no one
could do these things fully, in the theatre and in the round,
even though Eliot sees them completely on a stage of his own.
One should be able to accept these members of a country-
house family in the North of England as being what they claim
to be. They and their background of the family doctor, the
police sergeant, the parlourmaid and the nobleman's chauffeur
should be fully convincing before the Eumenides begin (rightly and inevitably) to appear in the picture. And they are not
entirely convincing in this habitat, under these names of
honourables, with these superbly imagined womenfolk. They
seem somehow to belong to the old-colonial city of Boston, to
Beacon Hill and Back Bay where maidservants more Kensingtonian than Kensington peep from behind lace-curtained windows before answering the bell at front doors, themselves
flanked with wooden pillars painted to look like the stucco
porticos of the Cromwell Road. They are surely readers of the
Boston Evening Transcript, with whom Eliot's readers will
be already familiar by proxy. The Hon. Gerald and the Hon.
Charles are real in everything they say – real that is to say as
clubmen and cultivated gentry – but not in everything they
are. It is even characteristic that the Hon. Arthur, who backs
his car into that shop-window in Ebury Street and incapaci-
tates himself from appearance on the stage among these others
of his kin, proves himself in a realist sense the most rounded
of any of them. But then the Hon. Arthur is a newspaper report, he is a sardonic observation in which Eliot excels. Were
we really to see him, we might not believe in him very
heartily.

The test of *The Family Reunion* will be not only its enduring hold on the stage, but its capacity to inspire other dramatists. A work so profoundly original must lead somewhere.
Agatha and Mary and Amy must prove memorable by a fruit-

fulness of their own; for who can be satisfied to write of ordinary women after knowing them? And Eliot's theatre of the mind is now the most notable possession of the actual theatre; so far we have come since those early days of the 1930's with their fugitive efforts to erect the standard of a new verse-drama.

Meantime we should acknowledge thankfully the value to the cause of a single and indubitable success. The theatre, of whatever kind, needs one of these in every three or four productions in order to live at all; and it needs one in every three or four hundred for the maintenance of its prestige and the renewal of its art. Eliot has already given it this latter and rare impulse, which in the experience of stage history is oftener given, for some reason, by a first play than by a second. Others are yet to come, and we should therefore look hopefully and confidently forward.

Ernst Robert Curtius

T. S. Eliot and Germany

In the summer of 1922, when I was a professor at Marburg
University, the Rhineland was occupied by English, Canadian,
French and American troops. Marburg itself was outside the
occupation zone, and one could breathe more freely there.
One morning a letter from T. S. Eliot turned up out of the blue.
I knew nothing whatever about him. He proposed that I should
contribute to *The Criterion*; for Hermann Hesse, apparently,
had mentioned my name to him, very likely because I had
recently published something about certain contemporary
French writers. At that time France seemed to me – as it did
before 1914 – the most important country beyond the frontiers
of Germany. I thought of France and Germany as the two vital
centres of the West. In those days we believed in a new Europe.
I myself believed in a new European France. For me the most
important representative of France was André Gide, whose
books I had known since 1910. I became acquainted with Gide
himself in 1921 in Colpach. This is a hamlet consisting of a
few houses which is situated in a small country between Germany and France. There was a beautiful country house in
Colpach standing in a large park. Under the ancient trees of
the park there were bronze figures by Bourdel, Maillol, Des-
piaux and Kolbe. It was a friendly and hospitable house. One
could meet Walter Rathenau there, and Jacques Rivière,
Annette Kolb or Jean Schlumberger. The park adjoined the
lonely forests of the Ardennes. It was a fabulous oasis in our
disintegrated Europe, a Prospero island in the middle of the
Ardennes mountains. From Colpach I had to go to Pontigny.
This town in the nineteen-twenties was one of the spiritual
centres of Europe. One ran into Oxford students there who
imported Donne and Eliot. Back in Paris I met Jane Harrison,
Roger Fry, and James Joyce. In the bookshop of Shakespeare
and Co., in the Rue de l'Odéon, it was possible to find a copy

of T. S. Eliot's *Poems* (New York 1920), as well as *The Waste Land*, published by the Hogarth Press. This poem made a more powerful impression on me than anything I had read since Paul Valéry's *Le Serpent*. Even to-day I consider those first four lines as the most superb musical opening of any poem of Eliot's. 'To please me,' said Coleridge once, 'a poem must have either sense or music.' I did not always find it very easy to follow the meaning of *The Waste Land*, but its music carried me over its obscurities. I studied this work just as I had formerly studied Dante. In the process of translating it and trying to reproduce as nearly as possible the metre of the original, I succeeded in assimilating it. This translation appeared in the *Neue Schweizer Rundschau* in 1927 together with an essay on the poet. Not more than five or six readers took any interest in either of these efforts. My attempt to make a place for T. S. Eliot in German literature was so quickly and completely forgotten that he had to be entirely rediscovered twenty years later. Some time after this I made one more attempt to focus attention on Eliot (in *Die Literatur*, October 1929), but this had the same result.

In the notes appended to *The Waste Land* there occur some phrases from Hermann Hesse's *Blick ins Chaos*. This medley of languages in the poem is one of the stylistic devices that can often be found in the literature of late antiquity. It exactly resembles the manner of Ausonius:

Nobiscum invenies ἐπέων πολυμορφέα πληδύν

In Dante this technique is given a true poetic value. He decorates his cantos with Latin and Provençal verses and also with resounding Hebraic rhymes. Eliot's poetry is made up of such polyglot elements; French, Italian, Provençal. Also German. The opening lines of *The Waste Land* contain fragments of a *poème conversation* in the manner of Apollinaire.

Bin gar keine Russin, stamm' aus Litauen, echt deutsch

The speaker continues: *In the mountains, there you feel free*
This reminds one of earlier verses:

En Allemagne, philosophe
Surexcité par Emporheben
Au grand air de Bergsteigleben.

120

Eliot is a poet who had studied philology. One aspect of his poetry has an Alexandrian flavour. For this reason it is possible to interpret it in a philological sense. There is a parallel passage in *The Sacred Wood* to 'En Allemagne, philosophe':

No one who had not witnessed the event could imagine the conviction in the tone of Professor Eucken as he pounded the table and exclaimed 'Was ist Geist? Geist ist . . .'

It seemed therefore that Eliot was once upon a time in Jena and also in Munich ('Went on in sunlight into the Hofgarten'). When I made his acquaintance and we had breakfast together in Soho, our conversation was of other matters. But in 1945 I came once more upon 'Emporheben', in *East Coker:*

Erhebung without motion.

Writing poetry is a kind of alchemy of transmutations. Eliot appears in his youth to have had some fleeting contacts with Germany. Among the Aristophanic protagonists of his earlier poems there are certain German sounding names such as Prufrock and Bleistein. But these are 'Chicago Semite Viennese,' just as the hero of Joyce's *Ulysses.*

For a young American coming to Europe in 1910, England and France were the natural avenues of approach. Bloomsbury, Soho, and the Latin Quarter formed a resort for intellectuals, a modern Arcady touched by the charm of decadence. Its inhabitants, *'florentes aetatibus,'* were

Et cantare pares et respondere parati.

The Luxembourg Gardens formed a pastoral setting which was haunted nightly by the ghost of Rémy de Gourmont. In Paris, Eliot absorbed the Gallic spirit in all its variety from Petronius to Baudelaire and his successors. Ezra Pound discovered these on the banks of the Arno – '*Arcades ambo.*' Seen from Anglo-America the Latin Spirit was in fact Europe. To Europeanise England meant injecting into it the Latin spirit. And Eliot proclaimed that England was a Latin country.

In this kind of Europe there was no place for Germany. I shall always remember with amusement a sixteen year old French girl, who told me many years ago: 'En Allemagne, vous avez la musique: pour le reste, c'est creux.' It strikes me as important that after 1944 Eliot excludes Goethe from the classical literature of Europe. He demanded a universal quality of classic writers, and continues: 'We may for instance speak justly enough of the poetry of Goethe as constituting a classic, because of the place which it occupies in its own language and literature. Yet, because of its partiality, of the impermanence of some of its content, and the Germanism of the sensitivity; because Goethe appears, to a foreign eye, limited by his age, by his language and by his culture, so that he is unrepresentative of the whole European tradition and, like our own nineteenth century authors, a little provincial, we cannot call him a universal classic.' This was said on the sixteenth of October 1944 in the course of a lecture given to the London Virgil society. The date of *The Sacred Wood* is 1920. After a quarter of a century Eliot's opinion of Goethe undergoes a transformation. It involves the formal exclusion of Goethe from Europe; but also the exclusion of Germany, her language and her culture. In 1920 as in 1944 Eliot speaks like a legislator of Parnassus. His judgment shows that criticism can also be an expression of politics. It is possible that Eliot would have modified it, if he had found time to read more of Goethe. In 1944, it is true, there was still war. But when, during the first world war, French propaganda tried to discredit the German spirit, Gide wrote: 'Comment ne comprenez-vous pas, vous qui voulez rejeter tout de l'Allemagne, qu'en rejetant tout de l'Allemagne vous travaillez à son unité? Quoi! nous avions un Goethe en otage, et vous le leur rendez! . . . Goethe et Nietzsche sont nos otages. Je tiens que la dépréciation des otages est une des plus grandes maladresses à quoi excelle notre pays.'

When a critic of standing speaks about the European tradition, it involves taking up an attitude towards Goethe. Thus, in speaking about the literary tradition Saint-Beuve in 1855 characterized Goethe in a few words: 'Il est toutes les traditions réunies.' The European spirit acquires definition in Goethe's work. Perhaps that is more obvious in 1948 than it was in 1944.

When Eliot gave a talk in 1946 over the British radio network in Germany, he somewhat modified his judgment of

122

Goethe. He spoke of the unity of European culture. A part of Germany had become a British occupation zone, and therefore the perspectives had shifted somewhat. As a contrast to Goethe, Eliot now chooses Wordsworth. This leads to an ambiguous comparison, a synkresis, as the Greeks would have put it: 'I do not know of any standard by which one could gauge the relative greatness of Goethe and Wordsworth as poets, but the complete work of Goethe has a scope which makes him a greater man.' Is it really impossible to compare Goethe and Wordsworth as poets? I consider that an open question. But even if we do not attempt to answer it, it strikes me that the coupling of these two names is questionable. Its sole motification is the fact of their contemporaneousness. One can no more judge the greatness of Goethe by measuring him against one of his contemporaries than one can Shakespeare. His greatness is of a kind which excludes comparisons, that is to say, it has the representative character of the unity of its epoch. This is not in any way an irresponsible view. It can be proved by an historical factor, namely, his influence. Wordsworth is a poet whose influence has never reached beyond the English-speaking world, just as little as Pope, Dryden, Tennyson and many others. And this suggests a very interesting question to a European critic: how far can the influence of an English author in any case be of world-wide importance, in the sense that Dante, Montaigne, Cervantes, and Racine are important? Such questions are nothing more than intellectual experiments, but a concrete situation can thereby be illuminated. The actual situation to-day is that England's frontiers are on the Rhine and she is therefore compelled to play a European role. She has the military means to do so, but what of the spiritual means? These are imponderables, but still they have a great importance.

Ever since 1945 many Germans have been busy trying to master the difficulties of Eliot's work. The *Four Quartets* are the focus of these studies, but as yet it is impossible to give much information as to their results. The *Four Quartets* present great difficulties. After Hölderlin's later hymns and Rilke's *Duinese Elegies* our present-day youth is ready for anything. But the obscurity of this poet is rooted in mythical and philosophical materials. This is precisely what recommends itself to our young critics. They feel themselves at home in this atmosphere. But there are entirely different grounds for the difficulties of the *Quartets*. Their obscurity is related to their very great precision. We are not accustomed to that. And there is something else. Eliot's poetry is full of all sorts of allusions. It is necessary to have read a great deal in order to understand and enjoy this subtle web of allusion. The method of alluding to previous literary works is one of the most important artistic devices of Greek and Roman literature. Dante too employs it when he introduces echoes of Virgil into his verse. The German reader, however, is not prepared for this. He searches for what is truly modern, and doesn't understand that Virgil and Dante have always been modern. Stefan George has borrowed the *levique malva* of an Horatian Ode for a poem on Leo XIII. He also introduced an old French line which he had found in the *Chanson de Roland* into a German poem. This practice therefore occurs also in our literature, but only occasionally. With Eliot it is fundamental.

To purify the dialect of the tribe
– this is an echo from Mallarmé, therefore a comparatively simple case. But very few are as simple as this.

The German reader likes to find a philosophy in the works of a poet. But unfortunately one always finds only that for which one has been looking. It is somewhat astounding all the same when suddenly one comes upon something entirely unsuspected, namely Christian theology. That, too, is something to which we are unused except in the work of professional theologians. And we now discover Lancelot Andrewes and St. John of the Cross. Should one not attempt to interpret all this metaphysically? For all I know such attempts have been made. The ontological antinomies, which in Eliot have the formal character of rhetorical antitheses, would seem to demand such an interpretation. All the same such attempts at interpretation must necessarily fail, and for many a German reader of Eliot this failure would become a *via purgationis*.

The Waste Land and the *Quartets* are poems, the material

124

for which has to a great extent been derived from myths and various philosophies and religions. Perhaps there is no other material more capable of giving meaning, weight and structure to a poem. But the value and, I might also add, the interest, of a poem are not dependent on this. These depend on the handling of the language.

The greatness of the *Divine Comedy* depends on the *terza rima*, on the controlled tension between rhyme and meaning, on new and daring images, on a skilful interplay of sound and allusiveness.

One can read Eliot's poetry in many different ways. A philosophical, historical and theological commentary might be of use for those who feel need for such a manner of interpretation. It seems to me, however, that this could only be a preliminary to full understanding. In order to value Eliot's art properly, one would have to make a philological study of it. One would have to trace certain images of actual things in their kaleidoscopic transformation throughout the whole work.

Let us suppose that to-morrow one could buy all Eliot's works in every German bookshop. This certainly would be a miracle, not in the precise theological sense, for there would not be anything supernatural about such a situation, but simply in the sense of its being a fairy tale. What would be the consequences? Thousands of students would buy the book, that is to say, the complete works in one volume. Dozens of critics would immediately get to work on it. It would become a subject for lectures and study groups. All young people interested in poetry would be reading it, discussing it and learning it by heart. Eliot would lead them back to the European tradition and reveal to them the meaning of literature and culture. How wonderful and how productive that would be! I recommend these aims to all whom it may concern.

Translated by Richard March

George Seferis

T. S. Eliot in Greece

My dear friend,

Circumstances have forced me to answer your letter about Eliot in an autobiographical manner. I'm sorry about this, but I happen to be here without my books and manuscripts. I am a traveller here – and that must be my excuse.

From 1932 until recent years I have often lived in the company of Eliot's poetry. Among the many debts I owe him by no means the least outstanding is the better knowledge I acquired, through the study of his work, of the English language and literature: an important gift for one who is self-taught in these matters, as I am.

I remember the time – it now seems so long ago – when I was making my first faltering discovery of London, which I thought of as a gigantic sea-port, and of the English language, whose music sounded so much more fluid than that of our own tongue. Also, the shock I experienced at the sour taste of death in the fog, and the intensified circulation of fear in the arteries of the great city. Death, I kept thinking, is for us a sudden wound; here it is a slow poison. I carried with me a great nostalgia, which was awakened on many occasions by the kind of formless sensitivity and patient, really rather cold politeness with which I was surrounded. I had no friends in England then. My only acquaintances were the crowds in the streets and the museums. The pre-Raphaelite paintings in the Tate Gallery bored me. I often had to rush out of my house to see again a fragment of the Greek marbles, especially – for reasons I won't dwell on – the one of the Ilissus, or a small portrait by El Greco at the National Gallery. An unconfirmed idea had taken root in my mind, that the model for this picture must have been a Cretan boatman. Some days before Christmas 1931 I visited a bookshop in Oxford Street to look for some Christmas cards, and for the first time, among the colourful engravings, I took a poem by Eliot in my hands. It was *Marina* from the series of Ariel Poems.

What seas what shores what grey rocks and what islands
What water lapping the bow
And scent of pine . . .

From that time onwards up till the time when I first read *The Dry Salvages*, one afternoon in 1941, in Cape Town, to this very day as I write to you from a high plateau surrounded by the naked steppe, this lovely bow which forges slowly ahead has impressed itself on my mind as one of the most striking features of Eliot's poetry. In case this may seem strange to you, you must bear in mind that for many of us the bows of ships have a special place in the psychological background of our childhood, as perhaps do the shapes of footballs or the photos of deceased relatives for other people.

Anyhow, I went back home with *Marina* and a small volume of poems, bound in mauve material, the one that ends with *The Hollow Men*, if I am not mistaken. The proverb from Petronius σίβυλλα τί θέλεις made me glance at *The Waste Land*. I don't think I understood much of the pattern of that poem. The inner regions of English literature, of which it assumes some knowledge, were mostly unknown to me; but the dramatic manner of expression had aroused my interest. After the outburst of Dadaism and the experiments of surrealism which I had witnessed in France, after these tremendous excavations and explosions of the ego which had brought into the atmosphere of that time the sort of electrical tension one finds in tropical climates just before the advent of the rains, the renewal of the dramatic tradition which I found in Eliot brought me back to a more temperate zone. I feel it may be surprising that I talk in this way of a poem like *The Waste Land*, which, more than any other, gives the sensation of thirst among the dry cactuses, a sensation with which we were so familiar in those happy-go-lucky days. The difference is that this thirsting despair found its expression in France in the search for a technique of Despair, whereas in the England of Eliot it was treated less abstractly in terms of actual human character.

You who were with me in the ships at Mylae!
That corpse you planted last year in your garden,
Has it begun to sprout? Will it bloom this year
Or has the sudden frost disturbed its bed?
Oh keep the Dog far hence, that's friend to men,
Or with his nails he'll dig it up again!
You! Hypocrite lecteur! – mon semblable, – mon frère!

It was a long time since I had heard such a note, and the 'Hieronymo's mad againe, moved me long before I had read even a line from Kyd. To put it in simpler words, apart from the image of the Mediterranean *Marina* the poetry of Eliot offered me something much deeper, something which was inevitably moving to a Greek; the elements of tragedy.

I am still grateful to that unknown shop-girl who offered me these poems instead of *Ash Wednesday*. If my acquaintance with Eliot had started with that poem, I fear that this first spark of emotion, this gift of God which counts for so much in such circumstances, would have been lost forever. You see, we are a people who have had great Churchmen, but no mystics; we are devoted to emotions and ideas, but we like to have even the most abstract notions presented in a familiar form, something which a Christian of the West would call 'idolatry'. Also, we are – in the original sense of the word – very conservative. None of our traditions, Christian or pre-Christian, have really died out. Often, when I attend the ritual procession on Good Friday, it is difficult for me to decide whether the god that is being buried is Christ or Adonis. Is it the climate? Is it the race? I can't tell. I believe it's really the light. There must surely be something about the light that makes us what we are. In Greece one is more friendly, more at one with the universe. I find this difficult to express. An idea becomes an object with surprising ease. It seems to become all but physically incarnated in the web of the sun. On the other hand, at times you cannot discern whether the mountain opposite is a stone or a gesture. The *logos* in its disembodied form is something which transcends our powers. And horror when it falls in our country falls with mechanical exactitude. Perhaps this explains some aspects of our character

128

which shock the foreigner; and perhaps this too may have
some relation to the structure of the ancient drama. You must
excuse me if I have departed from my subject. I only wanted
to find a way of expressing the fact that, though I have often
in the past had discussions with English friends who admired
Ash Wednesday without reservations or even thought more
highly of it than of any other of Eliot's poems, my feeling
remains that in these lines,

> *Who walked between the violet and the violet*
> *Who walked between*
> *The various ranks of varied green*

the effect is rather that of an heraldic decoration than of a
sensitive image. I also feel rather guilty that I cannot respond
to the following lines:

> *If the lost word is lost, if the spent word is spent*
> *If the unheard, unspoken*
> *Word is unspoken, unheard;*

The *Quartets* are far more difficult poems – though the word
seldom means anything in poetry – yet they function in a very
different way. That is why I sometimes think that in the case
of *Ash Wednesday* one finds the same thing as that to which
Eliot draws attention in Shakespeare, in Hamlet; a certain
difficulty in his use of 'the objective correlative'. Yet it is more
probable that the fault is mine. Poetry does not mean the
same thing to all people; it does not create the same impression
on everyone, and sometimes it brings the same result with
different means. Take, for example, *The Waste Land*. I
believe that in one way or another, in a positive or negative,
direct or indirect manner, the feeling 'Waste Land' (let us
call it this for short) runs through all the poetic expression of
our times. The person who might be said to have expressed
this feeling in Greece is an old man – I nearly said Gerontion –
who carried, inherently, a tradition enormous both in depth
and quantity. But he has no inclination to reform. On the
contrary, he has an obvious dislike for any reformer. He writes
as though he were telling us: 'If men are such as they are, let
them go where they deserve to be. It is not my business to
correct them.' He is a mythologist with an astonishing feeling

129

for history, history, I mean, in Eliot's sense. One is never quite
sure when one reads him whether a youth who works in a
poor blacksmith's shop in contemporary Alexandria will not
turn up in the evening at one of the dives where the subjects
of Ptolemy Lathyrus are holding their revels, or if the
favourite of Antioch Epiphanus has not in mind to discuss
with the King the outcome of Rommel's operations in Libya.
Surrounded with tombs and epitaphs – it is Kavafis I am
speaking of – he lives in a huge cemetery where with torment,
a mellow kind of torment, he invokes endlessly the resurrec-
tion of a young body; of an Adonis who, as the years pass,
seems to change and become vilified by a love which is continually more vulgar. It seems as though the mind of the poet
in his despair soaks in vitriol the dead body he cannot revive.
This old man has really no sense of the Purgatory in his veins
(anyhow, Purgatory does not exist in orthodox Christianity),
nor of Hell. He cherishes his sins. He is sorry that the decay of
his old age does not allow him to commit more. His only
aspiration is to remain Hellenic. 'Humanity has no capacity
more precious than this,' he used to say. They say that on the
last piece of paper he held in his hand before he died – he had
by then lost his voice – he marked a dot and round it a circle,
to underline it. That was all. He ended his life with a dot, in
the same way as his carefully written poems. This grammarian
sometimes gives that impression that he is a 'Mystic without a
God' – if this phrase of Mme. Emilie Teste's means anything
at all, it applies to him.

I mention the case of Kavafis, for it can show, approxi-
mately and with a great deal of simplification, the geographic
position in which one might place Greek poetry in relation to
that of Eliot. Yet, though Kavafis – in his own manner and
with his own traditions, and after all the necessary distinctions
have been taken into account – did write a 'Waste Land,' defined, that is to say. the region from which we feel so pressing
a need to escape, he could never have written the *Quartets*.
However, Greece, as my friend Rex Warner has remarked,
though a small country, is in reality many Greeces. Kavafis
represents only one of these. The poet who could, if he had

130

not been born 150 years ago, have come nearer to the *Quartets* is Dionysios Solomos. He, like Eliot, is an extremely sensitive reader of Dante, and, like Eliot, gifted with an extraordinary 'auditory imagination'. He was '*Il miglior fabbro del parlar materno*' for us all, I believe, not so much for what he achieved as for what he strove to achieve. It is a remarkable trick of fate that the new Greek poetry began with him, whom we could much more easily imagine a contemporary of Mallarmé than of Byron. The precious inheritance he left us consists only of fragments of work which were never completed, and terrible blank spaces. It is a heritage which underlines our limitations. However this may be, the contemporary reader must experience a strange feeling when he reads in the introduction to Solomos' poems (written by his best friend who, after his death, preserved all he could of his work) sentences such as these:

His art was a spontaneous and incessant effort to merge his personality in the absolute truth, applying the axiom of Heraclitus: 'There is a truth that is common to everybody, yet most people live as though they had a wisdom of their own.' This extract, written in October 1859, will remind you, I am sure, of the phrase Eliot wrote in *Tradition and the Individual Talent* ('The progress of an artist is a continual self-sacrifice, a continual extinction of personality'). The axiom of Heraclitus, on the other hand, serves as a motto to the *Four Quartets*.

This is my answer to your question on the relation of Eliot to Greek poetry, and I am afraid it is not very satisfactory. Apart from this, as far as contemporary matters are concerned, I am not much use as a witness. Incidentally, there are critics in my country who say that in the few poems I have written they discern the influence of Eliot. This does not surprise me, for I believe that there is no parthenogenesis in art. Each one of us is made up of a number of things, and the lion too, 'est fait de mouton assimilé,' wrote Paul Valéry. Precisely, for it is the assimilation that matters – but it is very difficult to discuss such an obscure process. The fact is I attempted to translate *The Waste Land* into Greek, as well as some other poems of

Eliot. I did this for two reasons. First, because I had no other means of expressing the emotion which Eliot had given me, secondly because I wanted to test the resistance of my own language. Now that I look back after twelve years, I think that it was rather a useless effort from which I profited more than did the reader. It obliged me at least to dig up a fairly large field of English literature. I worked like a student, seven hours a day, for five or six months. I remember how much it tired me trying to discover whether the word *burning*, with which the Fire Sermon ends, refers to Augustine or to Buddha. I am not sure whether I have ever discovered this. However, I recall the work I did with some nostalgia. It was the last time that I could give myself up to a literary work in a carefree way. Then came the disorders of the war. But, even among the disorders, Eliot remained for me, as I imagine he did for many – I am also thinking of the prematurely lost Sidney Keyes – one of the rare lights in a darkened world.

I said to my soul, be still, and wait without hope
For hope would be for the wrong thing; wait without love
For love would be love for the wrong thing; there is yet
faith . . .

These lines are related in my mind to the roar of the first Hurricanes in the Greek sky. The English friend who had lent them to me was killed on our soil. They show, I think, the power and the weakness of those who are still trying to look upon human life with independence.

You will hardly expect me to comment on Eliot's work in this letter, nor is it my intention. I find that there have been too many commentaries already; they merely disturb the reader's attention and end up in remarks such as the following, which I happened to overhear: 'Eliot is not a good poet, because he writes about the Tarot pack of cards without really knowing it.' Of course, Eliot's experiences are complex. But why should we imagine them to be more complex than they are. For example, it has been said about the lines,

The whole earth is our hospital
Endowed by the ruined millionaire,

that the 'ruined millionaire' is really Adam. Someone else

would have said that he is the *Zeus le Banquier* of Gide. I would beg them not to force me to explain. I prefer these lines as they are written. The poet comes towards us with his own experiences, and we go towards him, if we can, with our own. That is why I would tell the reader to enjoy the poetry of Eliot (I imitate the words he himself wrote about Shakespeare) with all the capacities he has for such enjoyment and with all the emotions he possesses, even though his feelings do not coincide entirely with those of Eliot. I would also advise him to try and follow the certain emergence of the poet in his search for life among all the perishable things which surround him: that sure road which begins from the garden of *La Figlia che Piange,* if you wish, and ends in the rose of *Little Gidding.* I am not trying to simplify things which can't be simplified, but I, too, have strayed a great deal when trying to verify the details of Eliot's poetry, a thing which cannot always be done without doing damage to the poetry itself, and I think that when one has wasted much thought in trying to understand the meaning of 'the redeeming from Time' by abstract analysis, it is worth asking oneself whether one could not have approached his meaning more directly by turning towards the experience of those moments when one has been struck by the emotion of love:

There are hours when there seems to be no past and future
Only a present moment of pointed light
When you want to burn. When you stretch out your hand
To the flowers.

I would advise the reader to try and hear one of Mr Eliot's *Quartets* in the same manner that he would go to hear the *Canzona di Ringraziamento* and to notice whether he does not feel, there also, the rise towards life of a wounded body. Here many distinctions would be needed. Let them be. But the dream of the old Mallarmé: 'Reprendre à la musique, le bien de la poésie' (I am not sure if I remember the phrase correctly), which provoked so many aberrations and delusions, has been brought by Eliot far nearer to its realization than it has been by anyone else.

Along with the great services he has offered to poetry, I

133

would like to add that we must not forget the integrity Eliot has, as an honest man, both in his attitude towards his art and towards himself and his fellow men. It is not a small thing when you remember that in these days there are poets who use the word 'truth' or the word 'freedom' with the same indifference with which they say to a stranger 'I am pleased to have met you,' and that we have entered for good a period of mechanized stupidity, mechanized falsity and mechanized self-destruction. We have experienced some of these things in Greece, the fruits of contemporary inventions and we pay dearly for them with our 'blood and tears' as you used to say in the years of the war: I stop here. I would say bitter things and it is not the moment for them; however:

What is woven in the Councils of Princes
Is woven also in our veins, our brains,
Is woven like a pattern of living worms . . .

Let us continue our conversation. In those days when I first read these lines a phrase of St John of the Cross kept coming back to my mind, a small phrase that to me seemed to throw more light than a score of essays on the intangible poetic function: 'He who learns the finest details of an art always goes forward in the dark and not with the initial knowledge, for, if he does not leave it behind him, he could never be liberated from it.'

This phrase describes in my opinion better than any other the image I have of Eliot's progress. Not only because Eliot progressed in this way, discovering the finer details of his art, but also because it corresponds to the air of quiet and humble agony which this phrase gives out. In an age of overbearing pride that such a significant poet should be the poet of humility – is it not strange indeed? – 'Humility is endless.'

I will make one final point. One morning in spring, roaming in the streets of Chelsea, I entered a deserted church – I cannot remember its name – to seek refuge from a sudden storm. From a stained glass window I watched a tree struggling dishevelled with the wind and the rain. Then, without any warning, suddenly, the organ started playing, accompanying a solitary female voice, and then, after a few moments it stopped. I looked round me, there was no one there. Only the ornate tomb of Lord Dacre with the bodies of a man and a woman in stone on it, and the coat-of-arms with its motto: 'pour bien désirer.' 'The empty chapel, the wind's home,' I imagine, or the lost song, brought Eliot to my mind and I thought that one loved him, 'parce qu'il a bien désiré.'

Yours,
George Seferis

Translated by Nanos Valaoritis

George Barker

Verses for the 60th Birthday
of Thomas Stearns Eliot

I

By that evening window where
His accurate eye keeps Russell Square
Under perpetual judgment so
That only the happy can come and go
About these gardens and not be
Tested in that dark neutrality
Which, in between love and disgust,
Hates most of all its own mistrust,
I see this gentle and gothic man
Tame Apollyon with a pen.

II

I never knew the juggernauts
Go bulldozing through my thoughts
So that everything I own
Is trod down and overthrown
Without remembering that worse
Than thunder in the hearse
Is the supernatural sigh
Of illusions as they die –
But in the room of Eliot
The visions whistle as they rot.

III

To him the dead twig in the gutter
Cries across all law to utter
Confidences that would bring
Tears to the eyes of anything.
But that set imperial face
Has looked down on our disgrace
And, without betraying so
Little as a twig of sorrow
Seen all grief begin again –
A gentle and long-suffering man.

IV

Outside the huge negations pass
Like whirlwinds writing on the grass
Inscriptions teaching us that all
The lessons are ephemeral;
But as these huge negations ride
And depredate all things outside
His window, he puts out his hand
And writes with whirlwinds on the ground
Asseverations that tame
The great negations with his name.

G. B. Angioletti

Encounters with Mr Eliot

Eliot to-day, if he has not become a 'popular' poet in the ordinary sense of the word, is nevertheless among all living poets the one who is best known and most highly thought of in Europe. People in general no longer say that he is a mad alchemist, the critics no longer cling to their subtle discriminations between being ingenious and having a heart, between being the master of an elaborate technique and being really inspired. To the great surprise of his not very numerous admirers of the old days, each edition of a work by Eliot is rapidly exhausted and cannot be reprinted in time to satisfy the growing demand. He has been translated into very many languages. His poems are imitated, they are used as texts for detailed study in universities. What does all this imply?

There may be those who believe that public taste has improved. But when I saw Eliot again last year, both in London and in Rome, public taste appeared to be even worse than it was fifteen years ago when he first told me, 'People no longer care for art, what they like is sensationalism.' The public cared even less for art, and it liked sensationalism even more. Why, then, was Eliot so highly esteemed by those who read him – why was he known even to those who had never looked at a single line of his?

In my opinion, the reason for the admiration felt by those who had actually read him was this: in Eliot's poems the imaginative and emotional elements have always been present, but so shyly hidden that a good deal of time was necessary before the ordinary reader could become fully apprised of their presence. In these poems there was a profound human suffering, which, to disguise itself, made use now of irony, now of parody, now of learned allusion, as well as of disgust and cynicism; and in the long run the ordinary reader has succeeded in discovering the human truth that was hidden

138

behind these painted and grimacing masks.

As for the crowd of people who have never read the poet, but who are now aware of his existence, we have to admit that the people, in the end, begin to feel a certain remorse for their own intellectual condition. People in general have an unconscious desire to redeem themselves from their low intellectual state; when, by a sort of instinct, they feel themselves in the presence of art, of poetry, they remain fascinated by it. Moreover, intelligence in itself (and intelligence is sovereign in Eliot) has an irresistible power of attraction . . . so, it may be said, has stupidity an irresistible power of attraction; but the power of attraction of stupidity, since its roots are in matter, not in spirit, is of brief duration. People in general, therefore, have *felt* the fascination of a great personality. And they have thronged to applaud that personality.

We Italians, if I may be permitted to say so, were among the first to recognize the poet in Eliot. He has entered into our taste, into our imagination; and even those of us who, not understanding his language, have to be content with translations, remain under the wand of the enchanter. Another reason why we have taken to him so strongly is that he has been able to infuse a new breath of life into that classicism which, in Italy, is the tradition from which we all derive; and because the cast of his mind is lucid, penetrating, and calm, as in Italy we like the cast of a mind to be; and because, studying Dante with love and care, he has given back to us the significance of a kind of poetry which was ours to start with; a kind of poetry of which the notes are at once intellectuality and the loftiest inspiration, composed at once of harmonies and of profound conceits, of aspirations towards the divine and of a disillusioned knowledge of the things of the earth.

To us in Italy his reserve is also pleasing, his sense of an order freely accepted, and his aristocracy of spirit – at once so disinterested, so spontaneous, and so engaging. And we are also enchanted by the spirit, in his work, of dedication to his art; a spirit serious, active, and yet passionate.

139

That is why thousands of listeners, of whom the greater part did not understand English, thronged in Rome to applaud him. In him they saluted Poetry – which, a creature almost of the angelic order, exists as a presence to us even before its nature has been divulged; and in him they also saluted a Personage: a personal presence noble and full of dignity, in a world that to-day needs, and lacks, and thirsts for nobility and dignity more than ever before.

Translated by **G. S. Fraser**

Henri Fluchère

Défense de la Lucidité

It is now a little over twenty-five years since the name of
T. S. Eliot was mentioned to me for the first time. I was then
at Cambridge, a painstaking and not altogether confident
candidate for the '*agrégation d'anglais*', when F. R. Leavis, in
more ways than one my literary adviser, directed me to *The
Sacred Wood*. What a name for a collection of essays! I was
tired enough, as any one who has been in my position might
well have been, of learned criticism, and I suffered from a
surfeit of erudite disquisitions on sources, bibliographies and
all manner of academic foot-notes and glosses. I was craving
after original thinking (one may well be that at that age),
clear reasoning (the ever-present nostalgia of a Frenchman),
and, chiefly, the freedom to believe I could form my taste and
shape my own judgment without the props of *la science de
manuel*. What I wanted was a new approach to the problems
of a foreign literature, something which would give me the
impression I was not treading on forbidden land, but could
hope to find my way about without feeling too much of a
stranded alien.

The difficulties of a foreign literature, studied in the
foreign language, will naturally make the foreigner diffident
of what critical attitude he may safely assume with any quali
fication to honesty. But, after all, critical problems are bound
to be the same in the end, for any reflective mind – that is
after one has mastered the language well enough not to be lost
in its subtleties and original nuances of meaning. What one
really needs then, is the refreshing excitement of a discovery,
the illuminating comment which will throw an entirely new
light upon an old problem, but in such a way as to allow you
to think the discovery, the comment, might have been your
own finding. One is led to hold the simple view that the good
critic is the beneficent critic who, quite detached from the

teaching profession, offers you new tools of criticism, and, at the same time, without any show of didacticism, *la manière de s'en servir.*

That is what Eliot did for me at the time, and I cannot be grateful enough to Dr Leavis for having brought me to him. As it happened, Grierson's *Metaphysical Poets* were that year included in the *agrégation* book-list. This was a mere coincidence, but it led a long way. I need not blush to own my curious love for the metaphysicals from which, for me, there can be no recantation) and for Elizabethan and Jacobean literature, dates from those days. It matters little to me if some critics today ironically refer to the fashion then set by T. S. Eliot in the 'Cambridge school'. Fashions come and go, at Cambridge as elsewhere, and, maybe, 'incense no longer fumes upon local altars with quite the old intensity.' Nevertheless, what Eliot did for me is much more than make of me an adept of a literary fashion. For one thing, he taught me a lesson of modesty, and sincerity. Eliot's style of writing, clear as it was, yet was not one *écriture littéraire.* One felt he was carefully tracing his way, following his *raisonnement* with that kind of detached intensity which is so particular to him, and which gives to his statements their unmistakable ring. Valéry, compared to him (and one must, sooner or later, come to the comparison), is too much of a conscious artist, he is far more preoccupied with the way in which he puts a statement, than with the statement itself. *C'est trop bien écrit.* Eliot's prose is never more than the best possible way of communicating his thought (exactly what Middleton Murry describes as 'style') – and does not want to be more. It proceeds slowly, often repetitive, and not seldom far from easy-going, as an instrument of investigation should, which would not leave any stone unturned, any hypothesis untried, and yet reaches the conclusion with unerring firmness. It always gives an impression of sincerity, in the sense that one follows the efforts leading to the discovery, and one feels the satisfaction of the attained end. I would not say either it is the prose of a purely intellectual writer, as a subtle interplay of irony and emotion is felt throughout the pattern of the style, colouring the state-

142

ment and giving to some of his pronouncements the ir-
refutability of a profoundly personal truth.

But then, there was, I believe, something still more important. As in the case of Paul Valéry, here we had a critic who was also a poet, and who was investigating the art of poetry, at the same time as he was writing it. It was difficult to say which should be put foremost: the critic, or the poet. Each was helping the other, and the 'awareness' of the critic served the 'lucidity' of the poet. The case, indeed, is not rare in the history of English letters. Coleridge was a great poet, and a great critic. And many others have applied their thought to their own art, were it only to name Matthew Arnold and Edgar Poe. But, in France, poets had rarely been good critics at the same time (and with the same effects) and very few had, apart from school manifestoes (which are anything but criticism) investigated their art with the intent of improving it, and still less with an actual profit for their production. Now, the two famous essays: *The Function of Criticism* and *Tradition and the Individual Talent*, brought about a well-defined and very clear view of what the relation between critic and poet should be, not only in the co-existence of the two functions in the same man, but in the perspective of the past as well. The most arduous problem, for a student of literature, and particularly so when it comes to an appreciation of contemporary production, is to take one's bearings, to situate and evaluate a work of art in the perspective of the centuries, as it rightly should be to be rightly appreciated. Witness the countless blunders which critics of some renown, and even capacity, have made, when committing themselves to a judgment of value on their own contemporaries. The elucidation of a work of art, though apparently easier than an appreciation of it, is something to be praised. How does the mechanism work, and to what purpose? And, as it should, it helps us towards a just estimate of the quality. But far more interesting is the critical activity of the mind when applied to the very problems the creative writer is trying to solve for himself. It seems as if T. S. Eliot never wrote a poem without having an eye cast towards his own critical experience, nor ever set pen to paper to write an essay without having his own poems at the back of his mind. This, of course, may be nothing more than a formula, for who will ever decide whether Eliot's taste for the intellectual forms of poetry of the past is the outcome of his writing 'intellectual' poems himself, or, conversely, if his own inclination for the intellectual was induced from his love, say, for the metaphysicals.

I see no reason why one should, at this stage, reproach Eliot with having 'set a fashion.' Eliot, after all, readily acknowledges his debt to such anti-intellectual poets as Jules Laforgue and Tristan Corbière. Both of them were *'romantiques attardés,'* but they keenly felt the ridicule of their position. They scarcely indulged in some sentimental effusion without suffering the pangs of their own revolting consciousness, and this was, to all accounts, the way in which *'la conscience de l'homme moderne s'éveilla'*. Contrasted moods, from which an ironical, and not infrequently sarcastic attitude to one's self will spring. It may lead to a superior grasp of the contradictions in man, it may even lead to despair. It will, safely enough, if the power of expression is given to a man of refined sensibility and clearsightedness, lead to the writing of no indifferent poetry.

It has, anyhow, helped men of my generation to reach what should not be an object of mockery, and which goes by the name of 'awareness' in English, and *lucidité* in French. Awareness is the fundamental, and, as Valéry Larbaud would perhaps put it, unpunished, vice of the transitory epochs when one has ceased to believe in the current creeds of the age, and when the resulting uncertainties try to shape themselves into more hopeful tenets. This does not call in question the permanent value of the poetry, nor of the criticism produced. Though I believe Eliot to be a major poet, and one of the best critics that ever plied the trade, this is no place to discuss or develop the point. My contention is only this: living in an age of spiritual disintegration as we did, the only *planche de salut* was to take stock of the wreckage around us. And we needed the strength to take in what blows had been dealt us. We had to submit to humility, to accept the ordeal of misery and

144

anguish, in order to salvage what vital values could be saved. But we have sunk even lower down since then, and our discoveries, still more terrifying, have been, and are still being, expressed in the post number two world war literature, which is much more inclined towards metaphysics than the preceding one, and, indeed, than any literature in any age.* The reason being, clearly enough, that man's last twigs of hope have withered and been brutally blown off, and the conception of what is human has receded to still more remote perspectives. *The Waste Land* of T. S. Eliot, with its dried out stretches of sterile ground, its drumming threats of thunder, and its death by water or fire; his *Hollow Men*, whose empty heads and hearts one could hope to refill with human thoughts and emotions, come short of the horrors spread out over '*l'univers concentrationnaire*', and look like a mild purgatory as compared to the dehumanized hell into which we have been hurled. What else can we do, but affront such misery, and, courageously, try to establish new assets over the ruins of an absurd world.

By linking the past with the present, by assigning to the work of art a prominent place in the hierarchy of values, by trying himself to insert his own view of the modern man into a living tradition of poetical expression, Eliot has done much for the keeping up of human dignity. When he tries to define a classic, when he is concerned with the unity of European culture, or when he writes his *Four Quartets*, these are only different aspects of the same preoccupation. The problem is always how man will survive man, that is, how intellectual activities may be maintained at the highest level. It therefore matters little, after all, if we come to disagree with Eliot on his way of solving Hamlet's problem, or on his views on Milton. The fine curve of Eliot's spiritual and literary development since his achievement is far from being completed, will remain as a model for succeeding generations. His superb alertness of mind, his utter sincerity, and his unshaken faith in the future, still make of him the living force of the age.

*In France, at least, and, to some extent, in America.

Louis MacNeice

Eliot and the Adolescent

It is a truism that different generations react differently to the same body of poetry; so does any one reader at different points in his own life. Thus in our time T. S. Eliot has been many things to many and many things also to oneself. To summarize this Protean impact is impossible but a reader's memory by checking certain shifts of emphasis may throw light on the organic unity which persists through these permutations. It is useful, I think, to sidestep the broad disputes about 'classicism' and 'romanticism' or 'personal' and 'impersonal' poetry and turning back to the poems themselves to turn back also to one's earlier self who encountered them. I first read Eliot's poems in 1926 during my last term at school. What they meant to me then is something considerably different from what they mean to me now, yet certain constants remain. Undoubtedly my adolescent self (like most adolescents?) missed a great deal in Eliot. What interests me is to try to remember what I *got* from him.

How did we schoolboys come to read Eliot at all? The answer, I am afraid, is largely snobbery; we had seen reviews proclaiming him a modern of the moderns and we too wanted to be 'modern'. We had already seen, if we did not own, many reproductions of Picasso, Matisse, etc, and we had not yet found any English poet whose daring in form and content would rank him as a 'modern' beside them. So we got hold of Eliot and, though at a first reading he seemed unheard-of heavy going, we sensed straight away that he filled the bill. Having said this, I must add, as my solemn belief, that snobbery on the reader's part does not prevent what he reads from hitting him hard and truly. Otherwise there would be no point in adolescents reading books at all; we are all snobs in our later 'teens, if not afterwards.

The paradox of my generation, who were aged about

eighteen in 1926, is that while (again like most adolescents?)
we were at heart romantics, i.e. anarchic, over-emotional and set on trailing our coats, the date of our birth had deprived us of the stock, i.e. the Nineteenth Century, 'romantic' orientation. A year before I read Eliot my favourite long poem had been *Prometheus Unbound* but this had already cloyed; Shelley's enthusiasms were beginning to seem naive to a child of the Twentieth Century, even to a child who had only fleeting contacts with its over-industrialized, over-commercialized, over-urbanized, over-standardized, over-specialized nuclei. What we wanted was 'realism' but – so the paradox goes on – we wanted it for romantic reasons. We wanted to play Hamlet in the shadow of the gas-works. And this was the opening we found – or thought we found – in Eliot.

What we should have found in the *Four Quartets*, had it been published then, is a puzzler; youth finds it easier to face the end of the world than its beginning. The volume available to us began with *Prufrock* and ended with *The Hollow Men;* the last had a more immediate impact than the first. Your adolescent likes a dream atmosphere and among dreams prefers nightmares. The images, the rhythms and the hypnotic, incantatory repetitions of *The Hollow Men* were not too alien to anyone brought up on the Bible and on Shakespeare's tragedies and even on the autumnal Victorians. In the same way the pock-marked moon of *Rhapsody on a Windy Night* fell naturally into place beside Shelley's 'dying lady'. But *The Love Song of J. Alfred Prufrock?* At a first reading I saw no form in it and, with the exception of the mermaids at the end, got little kick from it. And the opening image shocked but did not illuminate – perhaps because I was used to dominantly sensuous imagery, having read at that time very little of the Seventeenth Century Metaphysicals. Realism, the mention of things topical or sordid, I was prepared for – but Wit (in the older sense of the word)? Especially (in spite of my acquaintance with the Cubists), especially Wit about a sunset? The image a few lines later, of the yellow fog rubbing its back and muzzle on the window-panes, was different. It was little more daring than some images in A. E. Housman – the beeches that

147

'*stain* the wind with leaves' or the evening that '*bleeds* upon the road to Wales' (italics mine) – but freed from Housman's ti-tum-ti-tum framework it seemed to pull much more weight. At the time this release from limitations seemed to me mere release; I probably thought of *Prufrock* as *vers libre* and it was only unconsciously and insidiously that Eliot's extraordinary rhythmical skill rang its bell in my nerves. After a few readings I knew this poem by heart.

But after a few readings what did this poem mean to me as a whole? Certainly not what it means now. All poems, even the most direct of lyrics, are in a sense dramatic but few adolescents – and not many book-reviewers – see this. *Prufrock* is a dramatic poem in a more precise sense, yet even here the adolescent tends to bypass its dialectic and resolve it all into a one-way outpouring of self. This is perhaps why we used to read this poem aloud in an over-emotional booming monotone. We identified ourselves with Prufrock, having first (in flat contradiction of the text) identified Prufrock with Hamlet. Prufrock was obviously up against the world and so – like all good adolescents – so were we and, all being ill with the world, it was a most exhilarating makebelieve to stand among the dooryards and the sprinkled streets proclaiming one's *Weltschmerz* and announcing at the top of one's voice with the cynical arrogance of virginal youth:

... *I have known the arms already, known them all –*
Arms that are braceleted and white and bare.

As a result of this egotistical (romantic, if you like) approach, Prufrock himself ceased to be a character and became a mere mask for the young reader's ego, a mask which like those on the Greek stage also served as a megaphone. Eliot's delicate balance of satire and sympathy was shattered. For us it was merely a case of Prufrock (meaning Us) versus Society; that Prufrock himself is a product of that society was something we chose to ignore. So when he says, 'Do I dare disturb the universe?' we assumed that he could if he wanted to. It will be seen how much we missed in concentrating on the self-pity and the masochism (two things as natural as breathing to an adolescent). The nostalgia of that startlingly 'modern'

I should have been a pair of ragged claws

Scuttling across the floors of silent seas.

seemed to suit our mood perfectly, even though what *we* had
to scuttle away from was not the soullessness of the City office,
of a banal sex-life, of a weary intelligentsia, but merely the
soullessness of the Sixth Form Room. Yet this travesty of ours
was not a complete travesty. Prufrock does embody self-pity
and masochism – his creator's as well as his own, I would say
(Eliot was under thirty when he wrote him). And anyhow
lacrimæ rerum are not a monopoly of the mature adult.

Of the other poems in the volume the *Portrait of a Lady*
meant little to me then because I did not know that kind of
lady; yet this too was rendered memorable, if not intelligible,
by its sheer technical brilliance. Eliot's supple line which could
so exactly and without fuss convey the slightest *nuance*, change
of mood or variation on his theme, seemed admirable even to
someone on whom that main theme was largely lost. In such
a poem as *Preludes* we felt more at home. Before ever hearing
of Eliot we schoolboys had tried introducing into our own
verses such modern properties as telephone wires and com-
bustion engines and this, whatever our elders thought, was
not on the whole an affectation. The adolescent is peculiarly
sensible of his physical surroundings. To take myself: I had
only occasionally visited great cities – London, Belfast, Liver-
pool, Birmingham – but the fact of these cities was mysterious,
compelling, frightening; it was one of the great inescapables
of my world which a poet, I thought, must recognize. But,
until I met these poems of Eliot, I had not seen it recognized
duly. In *Preludes* I found not only that 'smell' of a modern
city which your first visit establishes as part of your mentality
but also the human element below that surface, something
which even the young and innocent can guess at –

'The conscience of a blackened street

Impatient to assume the world.'

However sheltered our young lives, however rural our
normal surroundings, however pre-Industrial-Revolution our
education, we knew in our bones, if not explicitly, that this

which Eliot expressed so succinctly and vividly, this was what we were up against.

The Sweeney poems had too much salt in them for our liking and, while we relished what we thought was a smack at the Church of England in *Mr Eliot's Sunday Morning Service*, we resented its vocabulary – polyphiloprogenitive, superfetation, pistillate. In a year's time or so W. H. Auden would be deciding that all poetry to-day must be 'clinical' but my school-friends and myself, lacking any scientific training, still thought of poetry more as effulgence (Dr Johnson's word) than as analysis. Such an effulgence, though a sombre one, we found in those also analytical poems, *Gerontion* and *The Waste Land*. 'The tiger springs in the new year' or 'I will show you fear in a handful of dust' – these were in a language of emotion that we knew, the same language as 'Brightness falls from the air' or:

> The Son of Morn in weary Night's decline,
> The lost traveller's dream under the hill.

The Waste Land, needless to say, was the poem in this book which most altered our conception of poetry and, I think one can add, of life. We knew few of its literary allusions and it was not till years later that I even bothered to ascertain, for example, the meaning of '*Poi s'ascose nel foco che gli affina.*' The cosmopolitan world upon which *The Waste Land* is based was as unknown to us as its anthropological symbolism. Yet it had such an enormous impact on us that I am almost forced to explain it by some such hypothesis as Jung's archetypal myths (as has, I believe, been done by at least one critic). The cinema technique of quick cutting, of surprise juxtapositions, of spotting the everyday detail and making it significant, this would naturally intrigue the novelty-mad adolescent and should, like even the most experimental films, soon become easy to grasp; but that the total complex of mood-and-meaning remains for me now, for all its enrichment by experience and study, qualitatively the same as it was then, strikes me as astonishing. It is possible that at the age of eighteen we knew, however unconsciously, more about waste lands than most earlier generations did – or than any adolescent ought to know. Possible . . . but what is certain is this: to have painted the Waste Land so precisely that those who had never to their conscious knowledge been there could so fully recognize it at first sight and at every subsequent meeting could find it still as real or more so, was the feat of a great poet.

Edwin Muir

A Tribute

In paying tribute to the greatest poet and critic of our time, I should like to say something of the influence he has had on my generation and the following one, for it seems to me that the probity of his intelligence is shown there as clearly as in his writings. He is one of the few figures in the history of a literature who alter the direction of the writer's activity and the preferences of the reader's taste. If the best poetry that is written now is different from the best poetry that was being written when *The Love Song of J. Alfred Prufrock* appeared, Mr Eliot is mainly responsible. Not solely, of course; he could influence the poetry of his time only by himself coming to feel and understand the many influences which were agitating writers in the first two decades of the century. It was in understanding that he was pre-eminent among his contemporaries then; and it was understanding that led him to choose a policy for poetry which seemed to most observers rash, perverse, and without hope. It has since become the accepted policy of the younger poets. In the early poems and essays, probably Mr Eliot was merely working out his own problems, making his own choice, without knowing that he was making a choice for many of the poets who were to follow him. That choice at that time was, I think, important and decisive. It made one kind of poetry impossible, and another possible.

Mr Eliot's influence became so powerful so quickly because there was a vital connection between his theory and practice, between his criticism and his poetry – the mark of a writer of exceptional courage and integrity, capable of choosing a direction and of continuing in it even in the face of misunderstanding and unpopularity. The observations on the nature of poetic activity, of tradition, originality, and such things, in his early essays, appear to be made always with an eye on the current difficulties of poets, and on practice. He writes about the

152

Elizabethans and Dante and Baudelaire not so much to make
us enjoy them as to pick out those elements in them which are
peculiarly alive now, and capable of being incorporated in our
poetry. In doing this he has done more than any other contemporary writer to add to the potential resources of poetry;
and he has shown in his own work how these resources can be
used to embody a new and serious conception of life. These
two activities, which sprung from the same root, a root in
character, decided the direction of poetry in our time, and gave
it a new lease of life. And even those of us who, like myself,
are not Mr Eliot's disciples, remain his debtors.

Luciano Anceschi

T. S. Eliot and Philosophical Poetry

Vie più che indarno da riva si parte

. . . .

chi pesca per lo vera *e non ha l'*arte

E di ciò sono al mondo aperte prove
Parmenide, Melisso . . .

Dante: *Paradiso, XIII*

It seems to me that when we are studying an author, any precipitancy or short-cut to understanding the free movement of his living personality, while being a forcible restraint on our own desire to read him exhaustively and comprehensively, is also a deplorable want of respect to the man himself, and his hard, devoted and laborious work, the conscious effort with which he builds his own truest humanity. So let us pursue that humane method of critical investigation which prefers to trace the curve of all the internal developments of the æsthetic categories, in their own slow reflective tempo, thus extracting from them the successive mutations of their organic life. We shall then choose to dwell on the early Eliot in his lively æsthetic prime, when his intellectual love of art, with a subtle rare and felicitous achievement, redeemed his desolate consciousness of the human condition. And we see that Eliot is supported by a mature conception of the impersonality of art particularly in the irritation, the almost moral indignation, which he feels towards the romantic frenzy, whose sentimental and unrestrained utterance dissolves 'personality', while it is burdened with an altogether too eloquent and pervasive conception of Man, like a physical presence; and towards the impressionistic and symbolic lyricism of the *fin de siècle*, in which romanticism expresses itself, with an allusive and atmospheric musicality, the final effort of the inexpressible individual to put himself into words.

154

Eliot's conception of the *impersonality of art* does not and cannot deny the individuality of the artist – how could it indeed? Rather it redeems that individuality in a special pointed sense. But if we are to get near to the inner meaning of such a conception, we must dwell on a fundamental consideration: on the fact that this poet is a man whose whole cultural background has made him believe in the fundamental epistemological truth of the senses, and whose point of departure is therefore a theory of perception; and in fact he has re-echoed the famous Aristotelian proposition, interpreted in the philosophical light which is predominant in the English tradition, and said that 'Not only every kind of cognition but every feeling has its location in perception.'

Within the ambit of this general conception he has essayed a modern revival of the old idea of the poet as a *medium*, and interpreted the poet's mind as a *means of combining* sensations and thoughts into a new unity according to a law by which neither the special personality, nor the private history and particular emotions of the poet-as-man, nor even his individual outlook, are finally determinant in favouring the rare act of poetic generation.

This definition is liable to astonish a reader whose background is strictly modern and Continental, but he will soon feel less inclined to wonder if he thinks of the æsthetic tradition of the English poets and of their different and romantic tradition of enlightenment – for example, of Burke's idea of the imagination as the faculty which combines 'sensible ideas', freely varying their relationships, and then of the romantic and post-romantic developments which this doctrine has had in Coleridge, as well as Shelley and Keats.

Of course, this is a statement typical of the most genuine civilization of the century, particularly as it developed between the two wars (I am speaking of a poetic civilization which came into being in the dry intellectual light of a *disconsolate awareness of art*), and therefore there is no question here of conceiving the writing of poetry as an unconscious act, analogous to an æolian harp, or as the inspiration of a pagan frenzy, and even less as a sort of surrealist automatic writing: all ideas

155

which must appear strange and irritating to such a man as Eliot, a man, I mean, who has doubled the part of poet with that of acute and expert critic, and who, finally, has never been disposed to renounce the separate function of the 'intelligence' proper.

On the contrary, for him this idea of the poet as *medium* and not as a personality, is the very pivot of an organic system of poetic creation capable of guaranteeing that broad clear consciousness, which alone can give a poet strength and certainty and an acute sense of responsibility towards words, extending into the subtlest literary associations and to the profoundest originality of poetic language. Therefore, in examining the nature of imaginative activity as he conceives it, Eliot is naturally disposed to see all the questions set out on the plane of the 'eternal present', in which all the typical aspects – characteristic, historical, in one word, individual – of the art, tend to vanish and dissolve: indeed towards everything which is characteristically individual Eliot nourishes an invincible distrust which is sometimes expressed in a way more fitting to a mediæval mystic, and which once again witnesses to his irritated opposition to all forms and theories of romantic subjectivism.

In this sense, Eliot rejects every kind of *nominalistic* solution: rather his doctrine of sensibility is a kind of *Eros* – in a spiritual sense – a metaphysical impulse towards a pure ideal order. It was by such a path that he came quite early to a method of founding his own thought on the universal guarantees of Averroism. I am referring to a revivified form of Averroism, whose historical curve can be traced, via our own Renaissance and via the Cambridge School till at last, the most refined and precious flower of empiricism, it finishes as a new and extremely subtle version of the recent American realism. Only such a doctrine – later contradicted – which admits the *substantial metaphysical unity* of the soul, can account for the otherwise incomprehensible hints of a future poetic, made in youthful audacity, whose meaning might be summed up by the Spanish motto 'Intensity is eternity', as their motto and key.

This is the only explanation of the significance of the 'passive role', exactly like that of platinum in the production of sulphuric acid, which he ascribes to the working of the individual poetic mind. This mind is nothing but the medium – the more finely developed, the more efficient – which selects and encourages infinite ever new and unpredictable combinations among its special very varied feelings, in an intense and rapid fusion. Here Eliot seems to be trying to purify a conception already favoured by Keats, according to which the natural state of the poetic mind was a sort of imaginative and receptive passivity – to purify it, I mean, from all elements and relics of romanticism ('The romantics did not know enough' he states): and indeed Eliot immediately warns us that the poetical fusion will produce an intensity of its own kind, which has nothing to do with the intensity of the particular and personal emotions, but is an artistic intensity obtained only by the violence of the internal relations, which are defined in their expression. Even in this sense, intensity again implies impersonality: the result will be more intense the more it approximates to the eternal form of the art, the more it renounces typically individual characteristics, to 'conform' to a perpetual archetype of expression, in which everything which is æsthetically true and genuine in human poetry finds a higher harmony. The poetic operation is made actual only in the endlessly rich internal articulation of a relation between the emotive and the sensuous which, according to Eliot, who has studied it in various aspects, resides in the words themselves, when they are purified from all purposes of ordinary intercourse.

Thus, referring to the Elizabethans, he speaks of a form of 'sensible thought' and of 'thinking through the senses' or of 'thinking senses', or again, apropos of *Hamlet*, of the adequate correlation of external facts and emotion: and thus, finally, artistic expression takes a concrete valid form only when it appears as the *correlative object*, as it finds, that is, for every thought and emotion which it is required to express, a series of objects, a situation, a chain of events, which will be its formula.

So we can clearly understand what Eliot means when he points out that, by impersonality in art must be understood that the important thing, after all, is not the poet, but the poetry – or when he insists that the feeling and emotion, as they are felt in the mind of the poet, are always something different from the feeling, emotion and vision which result in *poetry;* and when, finally, he points out that in reading poets, it is not correct to look chiefly for the ways in which they are essentially different from one another, but rather to look for the causes which unite them in the single tradition of poetry. Is this not perhaps the conception which makes clear what Dante signifies for him?

Indeed, here a consideration reveals itself which is central to our discussion because it is central to Eliot's preference for Dante. I refer to that profound poetic reason, because of which *thought* (for example philosophical thought) can be released into a new poetic intensification, only if it succeeds in transforming itself into a relation of sensible and visible objects. That is to say, if 'knowledge is made flesh' in the analogical and symbolical functioning of the living word, in Allegory, in the action of figures or representations, rather than that of images, and on the other hand, of *Ideas*, that is, etymologically, *Visions*, rather than of intellectual abstractions.

He has a somewhat singular mind, but a truly organic one and one which, in an age of poetry when critical consciousness is a general obligation, can be held second to that of no other poet of the century. In Eliot everything can be said to *cohere:* and indeed his method of poetic dissertation harmonizes with other themes: taste and preferences, unusual, even far-fetched, but always justified according to a definite scheme of judgment: and finally, his critical method, which is so exact and subtle. And does not his feeling which analyses the world into a dense interplay of symbols, of the freest poetic syntax, in which moments of concentrated, almost clotted, lyrical passion, alternate with long, discursive and even directly dialectical passages, contribute to determine his conception of poetry and to maintain certain principles derived from Dante? And too, his love, in moments of the greatest intensity, of certain syntactical forms – forms in which a precise and concrete image sums up and brings to life a whole rich, swift concen-

158

trated field of thought, resulting in a condensed and powerful figurative truth which is immensely active and stimulating: and the manifest desire, which he has actually admitted, to attempt the poetical expression of our contemporary *Summa* – does this not all contribute?

And so, with Praz, we can see in perspective, the cultural and environmental causes and the objective reasons, in general, which have favoured Eliot's choice of Dante as an example. But here we also imply some particular and subjective causes: which we find, for instance, in the open desire, henceforward attested in various ways, to resolve the traditional opposition between poetry and philosophy, with proper respect to the natural rights of their declared autonomies: in the reasonable aspiration to harmonize an idea of the integrity of the poetry with that of the poet as a kind of 'control'; in the impersonal conception of poetry as a movement of straightforward regeneration after romanticism and symbolism; finally in the poetics which follow like a corollary on this desire for a new order in art which will be, in a certain sense, classical – I refer to the *objective correlative:* in all these causes a vivid and varied comprehension of the figure of Dante is rooted. If we have read it correctly, the brief essay written in 1920, with one or two other signs scattered through *The Sacred Wood* opens up a highly concentrated movement which develops into numberless acute, particular investigations and which reveals itself as a lively, indeed an exciting anticipation, though only in germ, of a kind of thought which he will later elaborate very differently. And what has Dante to do with *The Sacred Wood?* He certainly isn't the useless straw puppet of a certain scholasticism which is still operative, the 'real Dante'. The ancient poet is here living or rather, is brought to life again, at the heart of a present problem and one which troubles our consciousness of art. This *Dante according to Eliot* involves a participation on our part and is a pattern and example of 'contemporary literature' of the most engaging and sympathetic kind, the product of a lively and intelligent 'creative eye'.

With the exalted support of Dante, Eliot calls in question a famous assertation of Valéry's (quoted moreover as the expres-

159

sion of a whole critical and poetical civilization) – which would exclude philosophy of every kind from the subject matter of poetry. On the contrary, he sees in Dante precisely the most certain guarantee of the possibility, indeed of the indisputable justification of philosophical poetry, the most solid and impressive witness of this high and difficult truth. And here we have the delicate and decisive point of his argument. He definitely takes sides and distinguishes a lesser and impure form of philosophical poetry, that of Parmenides and Empedocles, a form that is, in which a partially impure philosophical inspiration mingles with a poetical inspiration which is not free, to give something which is neither poetry nor philosophy. Dante and Lucretius, on the other hand, within their different limits, are shown as the true protagonists of a poetry where the solution is acceptable and in which the relation between philosophy and poetry is guaranteed by a mutual respect for their distinct meanings and purposes. They are poets, and what counts in them is the poetry, but, precisely because of this, their poetry becomes capable of making visible and sensible the integrated movements of thought, of 'making them visions'. In them, in fact, we can see that a *concept*, an *objective truth*, becomes something which can be *perceived*.

It is not accidental that I have used the words, *concept*, *objective truth:* philosophically, the poets, according to Eliot, have nothing to add to the knowledge of their time, to the thought which happens to be the living expression of the form in which truth is offered to their time; they are competent only to work it out according to the possibilities granted to their natural disposition, to give to thought some sort of imaginative concreteness. In this way – and I should like to stress this point – the autonomy of philosophy and poetry, their respective 'territories' guaranteed by right, can always be safeguarded: and if we keep in mind that Dante appears to Eliot as one who reached the 'greatest intensity of emotion and feeling' in some essential directions of his poetic achievement, then from that point we shall begin to understand the developed and inner meaning of that definition of the poet's activity which, at the beginning of our discussion, seemed

160

specially difficult and obscure: 'the poet is one who offers the greatest intensity of emotion, of emotion based on that which constitutes the truth of his time, *whatever that may be.*' This means Dante – and, if Eliot arrives slowly at such an exact formulation, for us, after an attentive reading of *The Sacred Wood*, it is already justified. I should say that it is there almost implied in his meaning and already announced in terms proper to the imaginative logic of poetry, clearly, openly and comprehensively, as an ideal indication of poetic *Type*.

I said at the beginning that in his *Imitatio Dantis*, Eliot aspires, in the sense which we have seen, to be the poet of the *Summa* of truth for our century. But if Dante was the poet of that very fruitful crisis of mediæval civilization whose principles were of such remarkable power and such prolonged validity and were directly transformed into the forms of a victorious humanism, Eliot seems to be the poet of a twilight age, of one of those transitional ages to which Hegel somewhere refers, pointing out, very convincingly though somewhat over-confidently, how a deep inner anxiety characterizes them and a diffused sense of ennui and fatuity, revealed in the disintegration of their civilized forms and their obscure dread of the unknown. What I mean is, that, more so even than Valéry, Eliot has almost become a symbol and seems to be the poet of the condition of crisis which more and more involves and afflicts the civilization in which we live. A detailed investigation would be needed to collate all the successive passages which express this feeling from *Prufrock* to *The Waste Land* and up till the most recent times, through his conversion and 'return to his father's house'. But certainly, beneath the suggestion of an 'Elizabethan restored' which he often betrays, there is revealed a wan sense of a sham and dissolving society, of the grim silence of a world whose inner authenticity and self-integrity is already lost. Mirsky has spoken of the 'end of bourgeois society', and Praz of an 'intellectual élite in decline'. Eliot on the other hand is probably concerned with a world already empty of any meaning, physical or metaphysical: until in the end, even the rhythm 'birth-copulation-and-death' seems vain, and as it were irrevocably bound over to irony.

161

As Krutch says 'that animal acceptance of life by life, which really decides the continuation of life' suddenly weakens; it is a reflection of supreme ennui, a dissertation on disgusts, in which the notions of life and death are reversed with an effect of anguished humour and a delirium of logic: 'Life is death and death is life.'

At this point, only one path remains, the one indicated by St John of the Cross, a 'divestment of the love of the creature', a transference elsewhere of the ideal value, a Christian renascence and finally an orientation, as a student of English letters has put it, 'towards the haven referred to by the Mariner of *Marina*', to the 'logical conclusion' of this truth:

> *This form, this face, this life*
> *Living to live in a world of time beyond me; let me*
> *Resign my life for this life, my speech for that unspoken,*
> *The awakened, lips parted, the hope, the new ships.*

And the early Averroism is transformed into the 'eternal present' of Christianity.

But in the process of his development, in which this truth of the 'eternal present' tends to turn into a gnomic figure, I mean of 'white' metaphysical gnomics, Eliot has continued to meditate on Dante: and the essay on Dante and Donne of 1926, is certainly very acute and full of unexpected and revealing observations: and of course, the essay on Shakespeare and Senecan Stoicism of 1927, is also very much concerned with the relations between poetry and philosophy (also in Dante): while the definitive essay on Dante of 1929, can be taken as fundamental.

In the meantime, Eliot has been investigating the notion of a poetics of 'sensible thought' in all its ramifications, with a sensitive analysis based on experience of the imaginative and expressive forms of the Elizabethans and of the metaphysical poets, and at the same time, with an inward sense fortified by the principles of his religious conviction. This 'sensible thought' reveals itself, in his own case, as the truest and most subtle expression of a heart which has been sweetened and regenerated by the continually urgent sense of an extramundane presence, and the sense also of religious refreshment which a

162

man, who has passed all the crossroads and witnessed all the uncertainties of our civilization, might well come to feel. Of this civilization, in fact, with its many aspects and confused truths, we may say with Eliot himself:

A heap of broken images, where the sun beats.

Donne, Dryden: and apropos of Dryden, we have Eliot indicating very precisely and pointedly, the condition in which, for these cultural reasons, poetry finds itself to-day, in the intricate reality of time – 'The poets of our time must be difficult. Our civilization is very complex and varied, and this variety and complexity, operating on our refined sensations, must give rise to complex and varied results. The poet has to become always more *compressed*, more allusive, more indirect, even doing violence to language, in order to express himself.'

I will not yield to a very strong temptation to diverge into an examination of the nature and diction of modern poetry: what concerns me here is still the vigilant attention bestowed on Dante, but the reference to the poets of our own day may be taken as an illuminating revelation of a difficult and reserved disposition of taste. Meanwhile, in the essay of 1926, we find something which bears on our exercise in the understanding of the relations (to be found in Eliot, through his own interpretation of Dante), between 'sensibility and intelligence'. 'To sum up' says the poet, 'I have tried to show the connections between the mysticism of St. Vittore and the poetry of Dante, on the one hand, and on the other, between sixteenth century mysticism and the poetry of Donne; and to indicate that between Dante and Donne there is a difference in the conception of soul and body which corresponds to a difference in the philosophies of the two epochs.'

If we had examined such a critical proposition before having understood the meaning of Eliot's poetical theory in its rich inward significance, it is very probable that after reading the essay and the words with which it concludes, we should have found ourselves admiring certain particular observations, which would seem valid in their concrete meaning and expression, but also perhaps we should have been unprepared to accept the general sentiment which stimulated the inquiry, the comprehensive moral impulse which justifies it. It would have been easy to allude to a sort of 'romantic confusion', or else to suggest an intellectual examination of the poetry, or even an extra-æsthetic interpretation. Possibly the fruits would have been scanty and in the end we should have laid aside a writing so steeped in tradition that it often employs figures and personifications of a learned, an intellectual subtlety to which we have no parallel. After the prolonged analysis which we have made, we know, instead, that behind this proposition there is something which interests us directly as critics and readers, a theme which compels reflection: it is a question which concerns the very structure of our idea of *poetry as poetry*.

Even if we are obliged to adduce certain fundamental categories, we must always be able to refrain from stereotyping the thoughts of poets, even where they are being employed in a critical activity. But it certainly will not seem to be an arbitrary crystallization of Eliot's thought, to bring forward one of its revealing orientations, its determining principles. Referring to the relations between poetry and philosophy, during a careful examination of the differences and analogies in the poetic functioning of Shakespeare and Dante, he does in fact indicate some considerations which are very much connected with the clarification of this much disputed question. When Eliot remarks that from the point of view of poetry it is absolutely unimportant whether the poet has before him an organic system, as Dante, for instance, had that of Aquinas, or a free trend of unsystematized thought (as Shakespeare had Montaigne or Machiavelli or some reading in and feeling for Seneca), and that the great poet 'writing himself, writes his own time', while it doesn't matter whether he believes the philosophy or not – he shows a clear awareness of the specialized nature of poetic practice: what matters is that the poet should make use of these themes to the end of making poetry, and as it were releases theory through poetry. The poet writes poetry, the metaphysician writes metaphysics, the bee makes honey – it is very difficult to say what any of them believes, says Eliot. Finally, in the essay of 1929, Eliot collects and arranges all the themes of this meditation on poetics and on what seems to him his highest witness of the world, which we have been tracing, and does so in a fashion which is at once unassuming and decisive, with something of an old-world English dignity and courtesy: concluding his *Itinerarum Mentis* in Dante, a journey which has certainly been productive of brilliant and fertile hypotheses, of stimulating suggestions and mental nourishment. Among these we will single out a problem which particularly interests us at the present moment and is a result which can readily be appreciated – that profound analysis, from the angle of the poet's sensibility of the relations between *Time, Thought and Poetry*, by means of which, redeeming Allegory as the visualization of impersonal thought, he arrives at their living interpretation, and the poetry succeeds in embodying the philosophy. It is clear that such a solution is consciously opposed to another idea – more in accordance perhaps with the necessities of pure lyric – which would have poetry exclude, and even in some ways repudiate, every contact with philosophy. By such paths Dante has regained the position which he now holds in our everyday discussions of poetic theory and, through Eliot's loving concern, he has come down again among us from the kingly exile in which he had remained for so many years.

I have said that to speak of the connections between Eliot and Dante is the same thing as to speak of the crisis which involves the years in which we live: and I have already shown to what extent it is permissible to surmise an *Imitatio Dantis* in Eliot. Could we call Eliot the *Dante of the crisis of our time?* If according to his view, writing poetry is not a 'criticism of life' nor even a 'useless substitute for philosophy', it is clear that for him the ultimate truth concerning poetry consists in the absolute impersonality of the poetic form, which expresses the feeling of 'Time' and the 'Timeless'. (We can see what we call *objectivity* and *universality* converging in this notion.)

It is not possible here, as I would wish, to describe Eliot's poetry, the philosophy *within* Eliot's poetry, and his effort to open up a path from Laforgue to Dante, or his awareness of the necessity to accept a certain *prosaic state*. I shall confine

165

myself in conclusion to recalling a pathetic episode which has in some ways the intensity of a symbol: in a work dedicated to the memory of Valéry, Eliot tells us, that his last meeting with the French poet, just before he died, had an apocalyptic note: 'Europe is finished' said the old poet. And Eliot comments 'I must admit that in the main my own Europe is what is meant.'

Translated by Kathleen Nott

G. S. Fraser

A Language by Itself

I would like to express the gratitude which, like every poet
of my generation, I feel towards Eliot in language worthy of
himself. I feel, of course, that this is beyond me: as Lord
Herbert of Cherbury, struggling to express a similar gratitude
towards John Donne, said, I could do it

> *. . . did I not need*
> A language by itself, *which would exceed*
> *All those which are in use; for while I take*
> *These common words which men may even rake*
> *From dunghill-wits, I find them so defil'd,*
> *Slubber'd, and false, as if they had exiled*
> *Truth and propriety, such as do tell*
> *So little other things, they hardly spell*
> *Their proper meaning, and therefore unfit*
> *To blazon forth thy merits, or thy wit.*

That quotation, besides expressing one's sense of embarrassed
inadequacy on an occasion like this, suggests something else:
Eliot resembles Donne in having given the more sensitive
spirits of his time a new, a critical awareness of language. That
is what Lord Herbert intends to suggest, and that also is what
Thomas Carew suggests in his more famous, more brilliant
elegy, which is, indeed, perhaps the best piece of criticism in
verse in the English language:

> *The Muses' garden, with pedantic weeds*
> *O'erspread, was purged by thee; the lazy seeds*
> *Of servile imitation thrown away,*
> *And fresh invention planted . . .*

That is as true of Eliot in his time, as of Donne in his.
Donne, like Eliot, had refreshed the language, and in every
innovator and renovator there is a certain quality of harshness;
the classics of an age of experiment may be thrown somewhat
into the shade in a succeeding age of established convention.

167

They are likely, however, to reassert themselves as soon as convention has exhausted itself. Such, as Carew foresaw, was to be the fate of Donne; such perhaps may be the fate of Eliot.

> *Thou shalt yield no precedence, but of time,*
> *And the blind fate of language whose tun'd chime*
> *More charms the outward sense: yet thou mayst claim*
> *From so great disadvantage greater fame,*
> *Since to the awe of thy imperious wit*
> *Our stubborn language bends, made only fit*
> *With her tough thick-ribbed hoops to gird about*
> *Thy giant fancy, which had proved too stout*
> *For their soft melting phrases.*

Their soft melting phrases: there was a difficulty, as Carew saw, in keeping up along 'the line of masculine expression' opened up by Donne – there was a counter-attraction, against his harsh genius, of the mild, the gentle, the soothing cadence; against his precise and passionate thought, of a noble and vague eloquence. Therefore, Carew thought

> *. . . thy strict laws will be*
> *Too hard for libertines in poetry.*
> *They will repeal the goodly exil'd train*
> *Of gods and goddesses, which in thy just reign*
> *Were banished nobler poems; now, with these,*
> *The silenced tales o' th' Metamorphoses*
> *Shall stuff their lines, and swell the windy page,*
> *Till verse, refin'd by thee, in this last age*
> *Turn ballad-rhyme, or those old idols be*
> *Adored again with new apostacy.*

These passages have a certain relevance, also, to Mr Eliot's position to-day. They cannot, of course, be applied to him literally. Unlike Donne, he is not a writer who is ever likely, in any age, to seem metrically harsh to any educated ear. Unlike Donne, he cannot be said exactly to have banished 'the silenced tales o' th' *Metamorphoses*' from his verse; classical mythology, but understood with a historical breadth of view and a religious depth of feeling, is one of his main sources of allusion. But, like Donne, he came on his age with a peculiar shock of immediacy. Extremely learned, as Donne was extremely learned,

168

he nevertheless, like Donne, was to bring poetry almost uncomfortably close to the language and the feelings of common
life. For our age, like Donne for his, he has been a salutary
disturbing factor. He is also, like Donne, an eminently masculine writer and a writer who sets standards both of aim and
execution which are hard for weaklings to follow. We have
only to open, to-day, the latest anthology of work by young
Oxford or Cambridge poets, we have only to look, even, at the
accomplished but, in comparison to Eliot, quite academic diction of such a promising and regretted young poet as Sidney
Keyes, to realize that Eliot's laws are, indeed, 'too hard for
libertines in poetry': and we have only to read the critical attack by a contemporary of Eliot's, like Herbert Read, on the
'line of wit' in poetry – on the tradition, that is, which Eliot
has drawn onwards to fresh triumphs – to realize that wit, like
Eliot's or Donne's, is not at every man's fingertips, and that
for those who lack it, it is hard to admit that it is an essential
ingredient of the highest poetry. Why is it, for instance, that
in spite of the enormous talent, the enormous industry, of
Browning and Tennyson, a faintly musty odour still hangs
about their work? Dr Johnson's answer, in another connection,
will tell us. It had not enough vitality to preserve it from
putrefaction. It had not enough wit to keep it sweet.

I am talking, then, of Mr Eliot especially as a poet (not as
a critic, as a teacher, or as a representative of any particular
beliefs) and from the point of view, especially, of what other
poets of his time have got from him. He has, I am suggesting,
for all of us, refreshed the language of poetry. I first read him
myself when I was about fifteen or sixteen. Much of what he
was talking about was beyond my experience or above my
head. I found myself, nevertheless, reading him with tingling
excitement, and pausing, with absorbed delight, on, for instance, such lines as these:

In the mountains, there you feel free.
    I read, much of the night, and go south in winter
or these:
                . . . turning

169

Wearily, as one would turn to nod good-bye to Rochefoucauld
If the street were time and he at the end of the street
or these:
Would she not have the advantage, after all?
This music is successful with a 'dying fall'
Now that we talk of dying
lines which, for the ordinary reader, may well seem not among his most absorbing or most exciting. They are transitional not climactic passages. For the reader, on the other hand, who is beginning to write poems, such lines are absorbing and exciting; he thinks he knows how to manage climaxes, but transitions are what stump him.

A struggling young poet, coming for the first time on Mr Eliot's work, is struck by such transitional passages because they reveal to him the possibility of conveying in verse, with exactness, an equivalent of his passing moods and of the tone, and even of the shades of tone, of his individual speaking voice. Such lines reveal to such a young man a new possibility in verse as an instrument. Donne, of course, reveals the same possibility; but still, his voice, though still a living and individual one, is the voice of another age; and his metric meets the demands not only, one might say, of a special rhetoric but of a special physique. It is the metric of a preacher, who has learnt to cast his voice to the back of the hall; the metric is successful, but behind the success there is strain, and the voice, loud, slow, harsh, resonating – with what Saintsbury called its 'sad clangor' – is not a voice for most young poets to imitate. Eliot's voice in verse, in spite of a certain dryness, is much nearer to the common tone, the common cadence of poetry. It is an easy and graceful voice, and it could have revealed to us, if his interests had been other than they were, the possibility of combining that 'natural, easy' manner with a highly wrought artificial form. The poem which, as a boy, I knew by heart of Eliot's was *La Figlia che Piange*. It is one of his slightest poems; perhaps his only strictly conventional one; and certainly one of his most purely beautiful:
So I would have had him leave,
So I would have had her stand and grieve,

170

So he would have left
As the soul leaves the body torn and bruised,
As the mind deserts the body it has used.
I should find
Some way incomparably light and deft,
Some way we both should understand,
Simple and faithless as a smile and shake of the hand.

Such a passage is not typical of Mr Eliot, and yet I felt it to
be typical of something. In its simplicity, its transparency, its
lack of larger implications, it has its equivalent in a famous
passage in Donne, where he, too, for the moment lays aside
his usual apparatus of scorn and irony:

Sweetest love, I do not goe
For weariness of thee,
Nor in hope the world can show
A fitter love for mee

Yesternight the Sunne went hence,
And yet is here to-day,
He hath no desire nor sense
Nor halfe so short a way . . .

It is a mark of some very fine poets that, even in slight, occasional pieces, outside the main line of their development,
they can suggest new lines of development to others. In an
essay of Ezra Pound's, I was to discover what *La Figlia che
Piange* is typical of. Pound was comparing Provençal lyrics,
which had specially influenced his own lyrical writing, with
early Italian lyrics. Provençal is for singing; its metric is elaborate, but its sentences are short and abrupt, like Pound's sentences in many of his own poems. Early Italian verse, the verse
of the *dolce stil novo*, is to be read, and to be read on the page;
the sentences are longer, the words more weighted with
thought, the connections of thought more carefully worked
out. The type of poetry which I divined through *La Figlia che
Piange* was, I think, that of the *dolce stil nuovo*. Similarly, what
one feels about 'Sweetest love, I do not goe' is that Donne, if
had not had other work in hand, might have developed the
conventional Elizabethan lyric towards a new deep and sober

171

intimacy of tone. I am not a very original writer myself; I am lost, on the whole, without a convention of some sort, and so, I suppose, I may have been the only person to notice that, if Mr Eliot had not had more important things to do, he could have become a poet of restrained and sad lyric grace in a quite conventional tradition. That possibility would naturally not be of much interest to anybody else. What must, however, have interested every young poet who read him was that immediacy of language to which I have already drawn attention: what has been called, too vaguely, his conversational tone.

What do we mean, in fact, by his conversational tone? As his work progresses, that description becomes less apt: the language of *Ash Wednesday*, of some of the Ariel Poems, of the *Four Quartets* is, indeed, 'a language by itself.' It can hardly influence anybody, for it has exhausted its own possibilities. (In saying this, I suddenly remember Tambimuttu's extraordinary complimentary exercise in this very style for this volume. Only, however, this occasion could have produced that exercise; and only a person, like Tambimuttu, who felt some strange temperamental affinity with Mr Eliot could have carried it off.) For the ordinary reader, admiring Mr Eliot's later poetry, the first impulse must be, not to go and do likewise, but to go and do something else; and such contemporary writing as has modelled itself on that later manner (some of Mr Henry Reed's poems, for instance) strikes me as mere accomplished cold pastiche. *Prufrock*, on the other hand, the first poem of Mr Eliot's that we all read – for we all open the book at the beginning, and we all find it impossible to dip or skip – is another cup of tea. As the first thing of Eliot's that we read, and are absorbed by, it has a great practical influence on our own work. And *Prufrock* is very largely an exercise in Mr Eliot's peculiar conversational tone, and may help us to define that.

Eliot's conversational tone in *Prufrock* is not, for instance, that of Pope, even when Pope is most direct and least mannered:

Nothing so true as what you once let fall:

172

'*Most women have no characters at all.*'
It is not that of Byron in *Don Juan*, a garrulous, loquacious
tone. It is not the buttonholing, breathing-down-your-neck
tone that Browning has sometimes. It may, however, have
something in common with all these three writers; like Pope
Mr Eliot gives an effect of frequenting always the best company, who can quickly pick up a hint or an allusion; like Byron,
he can be apparently inconsequent and flippant; like Browning
he can conceive a poem most effectively as a sort of dramatic
soliloquy. Yet it is more illuminating to go back, once more,
to Donne. Compare these two passages of verse in a conversa-
tional tone, one by Donne, the other by Pope, rewriting him:
(Donne)
Sir, though (I thank God for it) I do hate
Perfectly all this town; yet there's one state
In all things so excellently best,
That hate towards them breeds pity towards the rest.
Though poetry, indeed, be such a sin,
As I think, that brings dearth and Spaniards in:
Though, like the pestilence and old-fashioned love,
Riddlingly it catch men, and doth remove
Never, till it be starved out; yet their state
Is poor, disarm'd, like Papists, not worth hate.
(Pope)
Yes, thank my stars! as early as I knew
This town, I had the sense to hate it too:
Yet here, as e'en in Hell, there must be still
One giant vice, so excellently ill,
That all beside, one pities, not abhors:
As who knows Sappho, smiles at other whores.
I grant that poetry's a crying sin:
It brought (no doubt) the Excise and Army in:
Catched like the plague, or love, the Lord knows how,
But that the cure is starving, all allow.
Yet like the Papist's is the poet's state,
Poor and disarm'd, and hardly worth your hate.
Pope, in correcting Donne's 'rugged and most unmusical versi-
fication', has missed his point. Donne's stretch and contortion

173

are deliberate, they have a rhetorical purpose, as in the blank verse of another of Mr Eliot's models, Cyril Tourneur. What Pope has lost, rhetorically, by a metrical regularity may be seen by comparing

Is poor, disarm'd, like Papists, not worth hate,

where the asyndeton accumulates the climax (and the phrase 'like Papists', where the climax piles up, looks both back and forward in the line) with the flat amenity of

Poor and disarm'd and hardly worth your hate.

Donne adapts his language and his metrical framework to his thought: Pope adapts his thought to a conventional language (how weak, for instance, is the polite, pert 'Thank my stars!' compared to the fierce, 'I thank God for it!') and to a strict metre. His passage seems smart and vapid, at the most mildly facetious: Donne's, on the other hand, has sinister force. That comes out in things that Pope just leaves out – the adverb 'riddlingly', and the phrase, 'old-fashioned love' – which might mean normal love, as opposed to homosexual love, in which one ran less risk of the pox; or even love itself, the romantic and chivalrous love of the Petrarchan tradition, as opposed to fashionable lust . . . Eliot has a perpetual elegance of language, a conscious refinement, which makes him in one sense more like Pope than Donne; but like Donne he dramatizes (and we should remember, in justice to Pope, that the background of Donne's passage is Elizabethan tragedy; the background of Pope's merely the Addisonian polite essay, gentlemanly chatter about literature); and like Donne he is always adapting his language to his thought, never his thought to a fixed convention of language.

What shall we say, then? The language of *'Prufrock' feels* like conversation, but it is rather a dramatic imitation of conversational language: heightened, condensed, contorted, with an uncanny precision which ordinary conversation could never have. *Prufrock*, for all its setting at a fashionable party, for all its air of being a Henry James short story, drastically boiled down (the 'story' left out, and the moral, the atmosphere left in) is essentially a tragic soliloquy. It makes remarks which one doesn't, in fact, make at parties, though one may think

174

afterwards that one has made them; but one is remembering
odd thoughts and perceptions that flashed, unbidden, to one's
mind,

And I have known the arms already, known them all –
Arms that are braceleted and white and bare
(But in the lamplight, downed with light brown hair!)

What it creates rather (and memories of a party create this
too, for if one arrives at a party late, sober, one finds that very
trite and disconnected things are being said) is the *illusion* of
conversation: the illusion that, in a quiet corner near a noisy
group, one is being talked to quietly, or is quietly talking to
oneself. That illusion creates a lull, a soothingness: against the
lull, the images flash out, like lightning against a dark sky,
with all the more startling effect, the famous evening

. . . spread out against the sky
Like a patient etherized upon a table;

the paragraph in which the fog is stated to be a great animal,
the crustacean velleity,

I should have been a pair of ragged claws
Scuttling across the floors of silent seas

and then at the end in a passage, after so much petulance, wit,
and triviality, after such a deliberate excess of the 'personal
touch', suddenly purely formal, utterly impersonal, drained of
all these polite hesitations of the voice, the mermaids:

I have seen them riding seaward on the waves
Combing the white hair of the waves blown back
When the wind blows the water white and black.

We have lingered in the chambers of the sea
By sea-girls wreathed with seaweed red and brown
Till human voices wake us, and we drown.

As the Russians all came out of Gogol's *Overcoat*, we might
say that we all came out of Prufrock's drawing-room. Nearly
every important innovation in the English verse of the last
thirty years is implicit in this poem. If some of the younger
poets, at least, know when to be easy and when to be formal;
if they know how to lead up quietly to a startling image; if
they know that the point of highest concentrated feeling in a

poem must be the most objectively, the most impersonally expressed – they could have learned these things, and to a large extent they *have* learned these things, from *Prufrock* and from Mr Eliot's other early poems. Our gratitude for the later poems is, as I have already suggested, of another sort; it is a gratitude which we share with the general reading public, for these later poems mark out a path which only Mr Eliot himself could have trodden – there is everything in them to admire, but, from the point of view of a young poet who is just beginning, there is nothing in them to imitate. It would be as fatal for him to imitate the language of *Samson Agonistes* or *The Tempest*. But *Prufrock* is a beginner's poem, and it has lessons for all of us in the art of how to begin. It refreshed, as I have already suggested, the whole language of poetry in our time. Thinking of Mr Eliot's work, poets must share the general admiration of the public for enormous talent, for enormous learning, and for a steady, sad, and noble vision of the world; but they have also, as I have been trying to suggest, this special gratitude to him, as a craftsman who has provided them with new, sharp tools, and as a teacher from whom they have learned how to use these tools and how to keep them clean. Our time has been a terrible one, and for poets that terror has expressed itself as a struggle to say anything at all, to find any resource in language. Yet, like the 'girl of Tereus' in the *Pervigilium Veneris*, Eliot, by his example, has helped us to transform the grief of the time to art:

iam loquaces ore rauco stagna cycni perstrepunt:
adsonat Terei puella subter umbram populi
ut putes amoris ore dici musicos,
et neges queri sororem de marito barbaro.

illa cantat, nos tacemus: quando ver venit meum?
quando fiam uti chelidon ut tacere desinam?
perdidi musam tacendo, nec me Apollo respicit:
sic Amyclas, cum tacerent, perdidit silentium.

Noisy, with harsh cries, swans now thrash the pools.
The girl of Tereus sings in the poplar shadow

176

So you would think a love song coming from her
And not a sister's complaint of a cruel spouse.

She is singing, we are silent: when will my spring come?
When may I be as the swallow that I may cease to be silent?
I lost my Muse by silence, Apollo does not look at me:
So the Amyclae, they were silent, silence lost them all.

Silence will not lose *us* all, though we may lose much: but we
too have heard (in Eliot's poems, as well as in other places) the
voices under the poplar shade of Philomela, the swallow, and
Procne, the nightingale,

The change of Philomel, by the barbarous king
So rudely forced; yet there the nightingale
Filled all the desert with inviolable voice
And still she cried, and still the world pursues,
'Jug Jug' to dirty ears.

Not all the ears have been dirty, and, in the desert of our time,
Eliot's voice has been inviolable; seeking, as I have been seeking all through this essay, for some final adequate compliment
to pay to him, I am driven back, as I feared I would be driven
back, on that 'language by itself' that I was seeking for – I pay
him back, as we are all forced to pay him back in the end, in
his own coin: his own incomparable words.

177

Michael Hamburger

T. S. Eliot

I

Almost it was too late, near closing-time
for Europe when he came to gather up
whatever petals wind and broom had spared
in the last garden; there it was he heard
the laughter of belated children leap
before the outraged keeper sent them home.

Then it was night; a sprawling town stretched out
sick limbs where temporary lovers walked,
while in the distance dying trumpeters
blared insult and self-pity at the stars.
He studied patience; and when next he looked
some kind of dawn quivered on dirty slate.

II

But in the heart's Antarctic, between sound
and silence, where the boundary of dreams
meets memory, pausing, at last he found
music and mastery for winter themes.

Garden and streets were gone, though twilight kept
both vaguely visible, the frozen air
recalled how once the children's mirth had leapt,
and how the trumpeters had known despair.

Marianne Moore

A Virtuoso of Make-Believe

The magazine, *Time*, has spoken of 'the ferocious fancy latent' in T. S. Eliot's 'cat poems'. It is tame praise, to substitute query for characterization and postulate triumphs which could not surpass fact; yet does not Mr Eliot appear to be, in discreet ways, a novelist? Observe in *The Naming of Cats*, would-be familiarity at an impasse; the manœuvre, 'O Cat'; the overture, Strassbourg Pie or potted grouse; the awaited denouement:

And so in time you reach your aim
And finally call him by his NAME.

'The doings of the Borgias,' Mr Eliot says, 'need to be told by a writer, not by a Dryasdust'; when he refers to a contemporary as having 'laid about him in uncompromising fashion', a poet who takes things hard, is lent the flavour of Dumas. He feels magic to be 'a natural human preoccupation'. One cannot have failed to note his interest in thrillers – 'supernatural thrillers', 'inverted thrillers', and 'flesh-creepers'. He ponders 'the maladies of contemporary society' and commends to the attention, pages 'which describe with frightful clarity the deterioration and damnation of a human soul'; then elsewhere with commensurate urgency devises a hero: 'Only the mind of a boy who has seen destruction come to the quiet families of an ordinary town could give a local habitation and a name to war's impersonal terror.' Raconteur-like indeed, the suggested effect of frustration where a writer is shown withheld from his task by the tyranny of circumstance – 'unemployed, starving, . . . thinking interminably of scenes for which he had a feeling but no pen.' Nor is the gusto feigned – note the comma after 'And' – with which mere romance is recalled to us: 'And, at night there is the ball. We see the glittering uniforms; . . . the Skorokhods, the Cossacks, the Court Arabs. Camellias and orange-trees stand in the centre of the supper-tables . . . we

179

look out on the ice floes of the Neva, until the ball ends brilliantly as it began. . . . Nostalgic and intoxicating . . . this evening's entertainment *à la Russe*.'

The intensities suggested by the foregoing excerpts from sources too varied to catalogue, point to any of several possibilities; a tale of sampans, pullaways and junks; a kerbside and inn-tale of 'suspense heightened till all the characters are drawn within its tense circle'; a 'classical haunting', or 'a modern dilemma expressing a permanent problem.'

Another query; since we have in the author of the Practical Cats, a virtuoso of make-believe, perhaps we have as well – my persistent suspicion – a master of the anonymous. May we not already have been carried past our destination on the railway, absorbed in a *roman à clef* by Mr Mistoffelees, the cat who could never be caught?

Brother George Every SSM

The Way of Rejections

Hence the soul cannot be possessed of the divine union,
until it has divested itself of the love of created beings.

St John of the Cross
quoted in the second epigraph to *Sweeney Agonistes*

It was, I think, in January, 1931 that in a friend's house on
the Devon coast I was handed a copy of *Ash Wednesday*. I
remember remembering as the bus jogged on through cold
country lanes, the contradictory phrases:

Calm and distressed
Torn and most whole

.

Terminate torment
Of love unsatisfied
The greater torment
Of love satisfied

I was then a novice in a religious community, learning slowly
and painfully the great gap between good desires and any kind
of joy in love and service. To put the emotions in order is far
harder than to arrive at a conviction that they ought to be
ordered. Here *Ash Wednesday* spoke directly to my condition.
The difficulty of being a Christian in the modern world is not
only intellectual, as most rationalists suppose, or moral, as
some believers think. Temptation often arises not so much
from objections to any particular doctrine, or resentment
against any obligation, as from a generalized feeling that nothing, certainly no religion, is worth so much concentration of
purpose. This infirmity of conviction is not confined to Chris-
tians. Yeats, it will be remembered, found it in 'the best'. It
may be that it arises from the dissipation of our imaginative
energies through so many frames of reference. In *Ash Wednes-*
day it is united with other forms of dryness and desolation.

Because I know that time is always time
And place is always and only place
And what is actual is actual only for one time
And only for one place

Because these wings are no longer wings to fly
But merely vans to beat the air
The air which is now thoroughly small and dry
Smaller and dryer than the will
Teach us to care and not to care
Teach us to sit still.

In the main tradition of Western Christian asceticism, represented for instance by St John of the Cross, not only temporal
comforts, privileges, and ambitions, but every spiritual consolation and assurance must be rejected, laid aside and proved
unnecessary, if the soul is to go forward upon the way. This
discipline is expounded in *Murder in the Cathedral*, where the
first three temptations are relatively easy to understand. The
fourth has been hard for the twentieth century and has perhaps suffered because Mr Martin Browne, who has so often
played the tempter's part, has seldom had a chance to consider
it simply as a problem of production. In one sense it is the only
temptation, the only one that touches Beckett personally. A
political come-back in alliance with the government or the
opposition is no more than a hypothetical possibility for
Thomas, or for his modern interpreter. To make himself into
a martyr, to rejoice in his escape from the world of strife and
chance and sin into 'the glittering jewelled shrine,' is a
genuine temptation to expression of thoughts that have in
fact possessed him until that moment. The answer is to be
found not only in the sermon, but in the whole of the long
chorus in which tempters, priests, and women join, from the
final speech of the fourth temptation to the end of part one.
This chorus is taken up again by the women in the middle of
part two, where the 'Puss-purr of leopard, footfall of padding
bear' turn to 'Scaly wings slanting, huge and ridiculous.'

Mastered by the animal powers of spirit,
Dominated by the lust of self-demolition,

By the final uttermost death of spirit,
By the final agony of waste and shame,
O Lord Archbishop, O Thomas Archbishop, forgive us,
Forgive us, pray for us that we may pray for you, out of our
shame.

These are the words of the chorus, of the Church, not as she
is in heaven, but as she is now on earth, straining, struggling,
suffering. Identification with the Church does not mean an
entry into a greater security, an additional illumination that
lifts the churchman above his brethren; but rather the recog-
nition of an action of God intertwined with the actions of men.
Our understanding of history acquires a new perspective that
makes it at the same time potentially simpler and immediately,
in the now and here, very much more complicated. So Thomas
says to the chorus,

Peace, and be at peace with your thoughts and visions;
These things had to come to you and you to accept them.
This is your share of the eternal burden,
The perpetual glory. This is one moment
But I know that another
Shall pierce you with a sudden painful joy
When the figure of God's purpose is made complete.

In the meantime, in this present life, 'Human kind cannot
bear very much reality.' Thomas himself has 'a tremor of
bliss, a wink of heaven, a whisper,' but no more.

Ash Wednesday is penitential poetry, *Murder in the
Cathedral* the passion of a martyr. On this semi-liturgical
background the small but significant elements of innovation
show up more plainly than in *The Four Quartets*, where the
poetic method is a new invention. But the same themes, with
the same variations in the treatment of those themes, can be
found in most of the other poems after *Gerontion*. It is time
to determine more precisely their significance for religious
thinking. The theme of learning at long last how to rejoice
in the will of God is familiar to all who are acquainted with
the tradition of Christian asceticism. In two respects Eliot's
formulation differs from that of earlier writers. The influence
of his old master, Professor Irving Babbitt, and of his early

183

studies in Indian literature, can be seen in the expression 'Make perfect your will' in *The Rock*, 'I have therefore only to make perfect my will' in *Murder in the Cathedral*. Babbitt's 'inner check' was an adjustment of the lower to the higher will within the human person, the discovery of a quality that is always there. I am not very well acquainted with the wisdom of the east, but I imagine that the Indian sage would claim that in finding his true self, he finds God. To the Christian God's service is perfect freedom, but this freedom is not normally discovered through the perfect exercise of free will.

However, we must not exaggerate the deviation. The immediate source of

> *And right action is freedom*
> *From past and future also*

is no doubt somewhere in Indian philosophy. A similar thought from a similar source was given an orthodox interpretation by no less a person than St. Thomas Aquinas, who quotes, 'the wise man masters the stars, as the astrologers themselves say.' St. Thomas held that

> *Most men follow their passions, that are motions of the sensible appetite, with which the celestial bodies may work together: few only are wise to resist passions of this kind. And therefore the astrologers can in many things predict truth, especially in public affairs, but not in personal, for nothing prevents any man resisting his passions by free will.* *

Modern scientific and sociological thinking has substituted biology, psychology and economics for the influence of the heavenly bodies. It is still true that 'We most of us seem to live according to circumstance,' as Downing says in *The Family Reunion*. The exceptions are unexpected. Downing himself is in no way obviously more intelligent or better than Charles, but he alone knows the nature of the Eumenides from the beginning of the play to the end. Without his part *The Family Reunion* might seem to teach salvation by sensitiveness or even intellectual ability (though Mary says 'I am not a wise person'). What distinguishes Downing, Mary, Agatha, and Harry is that measure of independence of judgment that will

Summa Theologica, Pars Prima, cxv. art. 4.

in the end enable them to choose their authority. This freedom has a greater moral significance in a world where public standards are weak. It is not to be thought of in contrast with grace, for the operation of grace is the condition of its exercise. 'The faith and the love and the hope are all in the waiting,' until 'the darkness shall be the light, and the stillness the dancing.'

A more important innovation in Eliot's account of the Christian discipline is his enlargement of the dark night of the soul to cover every kind of mental perplexity through changing scenes and frames of reference:

> *There is, it seems to us*
> *At best, only a limited value*
> *In the knowledge derived from experience.*
> *The knowledge imposes a pattern, and falsifies,*
> *For the pattern is new in every moment,*
> *And every moment is a new and shocking*
> *Valuation of all we have been.*

In mystical theology it often seems that dereliction has been so mapped by the masters of the spiritual life that the consternation of confronting nothing has ceased to exist. In Eliot's poetry scepticism returns to the heart of religion, as it does down a different road in the images of the Skeleton, the Accuser, the Questing Beast in the poetry of another Anglican, Charles Williams.

In *The Idea of a Christian Society* Eliot went so far as to propose an agnostic element – 'persons of exceptional ability who may be indifferent or disbelieving' – as a desirable ingredient in the *élite* of a Christian state. It is not easy to imagine such a proposal coming from a Communist, or from a Roman Catholic, who inherits from the Latin Middle Ages the tradition of days when every clerk was a cleric, with some responsibility for positive teaching. The idea is more readily acceptable to Anglicans, who have long relied on the sense of tradition in some of their clergy and laity to correct the liturgical and doctrinal idiosyncrasies of individual priests and even bishops; and therefore attach less importance to conformity with the letter of a formulary, and more to qualities

185

of balance and poise, a sense of history and a sense of proportion, in their assessment of theological orthodoxy. When the idea of orthodoxy is applied outside theology the word has a less doctrinaire sound in English than in the continental languages. The drift of Eliot's meaning in *After Strange Gods*, his 'primer of modern heresy,' and in a long note appended to his essay on Dante, may perhaps be illuminated by a consideration of his work as editor of *The Criterion*.

In *The Criterion* the same critical discussion continued before and after his conversion to a theological orthodoxy. Always it was concerned with the elimination of heresy, in the sense of one-sided conclusions by one-track minds in social, literary, and philosophical matters. At one time in the nineteen-thirties many of the younger contributors were attracted to Communism, but they continued to observe, in their work for *The Criterion*, a decent respect for the labours expended in the creation of a European tradition, and to many of them the place of Christianity in that tradition grew more personally significant as the years drew by. On the other hand the editor learnt from them a more radical attitude to social evils. His *Outline of Royalism* was never written, and *The Idea of a Christian Society*, which took its place, was probably several degrees nearer to the middle of the road in politics. The negative way has continued to eliminate extreme reactions from current heresies; and it was by a natural process of development, not by any exhaustion of his critical faculties, that Eliot arrived at a better opinion, first of Tennyson and then of Milton.

In the view that he has inherited from his religious tradition theological orthodoxy does not belong to any individual or to any particular church. Even the whole Church on earth at one and the same time is not infallible. In *The Rock* the figure of the Church Universal stands over against Saint Mellitus, Bishop Blomfield, and the chorus, who all in their own way have 'aimed at orthodoxy.' Saint Augustine's City of God 'that does all to the glory of God' may legitimately receive an even wider acceptation, that would put Arjuna among its citizens, with other saints, sages and statesmen, known and

186

unknown, who have in their own office and ministry obeyed
the will of God. Some future Dante may see Darwin and
Huxley with Virgil in Limbo among the 'masters of them
that know,' for all students of the natural sciences will inherit
their tradition, nor will they be able to absorb it all into a new
synthesis.

Eliot's reserve in communicating religious experience has
parallels in earlier Anglican poets, for instance Vaughan, and
George Herbert's

Church-bells beyond the stars heard, the soul's blood,
A land of spices, something understood.

But I think it has to do with his desire to remain as near as
possible to the plane of prose thinking where most of his
contemporaries live; for he has said* that 'the business of a
poet is to express the culture in which he lives, and to which
he belongs, not to express aspiration towards one that is not
yet incarnate.' This, I think, explains such an approximation
to the scientific method as

I can only say, there we have been; but I cannot say where.
And I cannot say, how long, for that is to place it in time.

Eliot has always been aware of the pressure of his own age,
with its own particular presuppositions, upon his personal consciousness. In the beginning of his poetry he thought of himself as a submarine animal:

I should have been a pair of ragged claws
Scuttling along the floors of silent seas.

And at the end of *The Rock* the Church herself lives submarine:

Our eyes look upward
And see the light that fractures through unquiet water.
We see the light but see not whence it comes.

He has taught us to look for light from outside our own age
and beyond this world. A friend has reminded me of a
memorable occasion when a group of people whose outlooks
were very various met for the discussion of some correspondence in a weekly newspaper where the Church had been

*In a lecture given in Paris in May, 1945, and printed in *The
Adelphi* for July-September.

criticized not, as so often happens, for her failure to be sufficiently helpful in some social or cultural direction, but for not fulfilling what her critics, external but not unsympathetic, conceived to be the function of a church. It was then that Eliot confessed how he once found people on their knees in a church outside the time of public worship, in an attitude of body and mind that was quite unfamiliar to the modern world as he knew it then. They were waiting upon God. That he himself has learnt to wait, 'to sit still,' seems to me the clue not only to his maturity as a poet in an age of crisis and distress, but to his mature attitude to kinds of poetry other than his own.

For in the end the negative way leads to its own elimination, not to 'emptiness, absence, the void,' but to the denial of the void, the ear open for 'hidden laughter.' In the final chorus of *Murder in the Cathedral* we are already in the way of the affirmations, interpreted to this age in the writings of Charles Williams:

They affirm Thee in living; all things affirm Thee in living; the bird in the air, both the hawk and the finch; the beast on the earth, both the wolf and the lamb; the worm in the soil and the worm in the belly . . .

Even in us the voices of seasons, the snuffle of winter, the song of spring, the drone of summer, the voices of beasts and of birds, praise Thee.

The romantic element has always been there in Eliot's poetry, from *La Figlia che Piange* – 'Weave, weave the sunlight in your hair.' In criticism it has been his task to bring us back to Dante, purged of the obtrusive images induced by the Gothic revival, that we might understand for the first time in our age the religious significance of romance and the romantic significance of all religion, primitive and mature. He came into the world dissected by Frazer and Freud ('These fragments I have shored against my ruins') and the fragments slowly formed themselves into a whole that could be seen, and being seen, could satisfy. But first of all every easy way must be rejected.

188

Anne Ridler

I Who am Here Dissembled

Certainly, as you said, a mug's game.
The poem, written, is lost: may earn a wage
But cannot grow, or comfort old age.
Saints move on the unbroken beam,
But poets look with a refractory eye
On decomposing light, and need to stray.
    The work is restless, restless to refuse;
    At last even the self dissembled dies.

But where the wretched bones were laid, the tree
    Softly rustled its leaves like a child clapping;
    And a bird sang out of the juniper: such a singing
Stilled the world and earned its glory's fee –
    To break the sorcery and to find relief –
    The gold chain of love and the millstone of grief.

Eugenio Montale

Eliot and Ourselves

I am glad indeed to be able to join in paying homage to Mr T. S. Eliot if not by a deep study of his work, which I could hardly undertake owing to lack of documentation, at least by 'bearing witness'. When I translated *A Song for Simeon* (Solaria 1929) and *La Figlia che Piange* (for the American number of *Circoli*, 1933) and headed them with one of the first notices to appear in Italy on the author of *The Waste Land*, I was even less of a specialist than I am to-day. It was Mario Praz who lent me those verses. They were in the Ariel Poems series – their first edition, I believe – minute volumes of only four pages with a short lyric and a post-cubist style illustration. Before that I had come across nothing of Eliot save one or two early lyrics of the so-called Laforgue period: *Portrait of a Lady* and *The Love Song of J. Alfred Prufrock*. These I had read in French translation. But even so the comparison between the earliest poems – which I had felt for rather than grasped through the unavoidable distortion of their foreign dress – and the Ariel Poems gave me the feeling of an arch thrown over two pillars, it pointed out a direction. It is the direction Georges Cattaui, one of the latest and subtlest of Eliot's interpreters, suggests in his essay (published by Egloff in Paris) when he uses the heading: *T. S. Eliot or The Return of the Mayflower*, meaning the rediscovery of Europe by an American of old stock. Later, helped in person by the *miglior fabbro* Ezra Pound, who contrived a similar return of his own, though his way was more eccentric (he was under the influence of Joyce and his more antiquarian or archeological sensibility was disguised with difficulty beneath an appearance of open-mindedness) I was able to take part in other stages of Eliot's return – from *The Waste Land*, which I got to know after the Ariel Poems, and *Ash Wednesday*, down to the recent *Quartets*, not omitting

190

the substantial interludes for the plays – the part of Eliot's
work the Italian reader finds hardest to judge. But, despite all
this, much of Eliot's writing – for he is a very penetrating
critic and essayist as well as poet – had to remain merely on
the library list, and now I fear it is too late for me to become
a real expert in Eliot studies.

But I cannot let this prevent me from paying my homage
to a poet whose career and significance seem to me exemplary.
There are some men one can meet every day without ever
being able to get on to terms of friendship with them: with
others one feels an immediate closeness as soon as one first
makes their acquaintance or just runs across them. Like
Valéry, T. S. Eliot belongs to this latter kind. The accent of his
poetry cannot be forgotten: one knows it again even after a
long lapse of cultivation. And as man and poet he requires no
special conditions from those who draw near, he is not subject
to the changes and all the crises we have become used to in
the poets of the 'thirties who followed him. (As it was too easy
and inconclusive to surpass him on the plane of fecundity it is
not without reason that a poet such as Auden has undertaken
Eliot's journey backwards, and is attempting to reconquer the
New World.)

Of course Eliot too has had his crisis. It led him from the
romantic nihilism of his youth (as far back as 1929 Eugéne
Jolas talked of his *métaphysique de la désillusion*) first to Charles
Maurras' ideas of 'order' and at last to the golden gardens of
Anglo-Catholicism. A revolutionary in poetry, though calling
himself classical, a conservative in politics and religion – here
too there is something for which we can thank Eliot. He has
never used the stages of his moral or religious development to
cover up any kind of ideological *escamotage* or the dangers of
potential literary decline. In other words his conversion was
not due to looking in a mirror.

If we observe closely we see how he has gradually made
contact with the world of his origins, and his reconquest
cannot be conciliated easily with the precise idea of a crisis or
conversion. Let us be literal, which is always revealing in
poetry, and stop to glance through the relatively slim volume

191

of his complete works up to 1939, as far as *Burnt Norton*. Where lie Eliot's experiences?

There, doubtless, you get a strong impression of French symbolism, the symbolism which, like impressionism in painting, has had a powerful but generalized influence all over Europe. Then you get that very Anglo-Saxon way of regarding our Italian *dolce stil nuovo* which Eliot has in common with Pound. Often enough it works itself out in inlaid work and the glittering game of quotations and recollections. Then, not least amongst Eliot's experiences, indeed playing a preponderating part, is the discovery of the great tradition of English metaphysical poetry. But above all else, and from the very outset, you feel Eliot's genuinely personal – it has no trace of Pindaric derivation – *sprung rhythm:* the sense of an interior and personal fount of music vibrating all possible harmonics lying below common words. Notice that he alone is not responsible for this discovery. But the lesson of the imagists, their sense of the prosodic *impromptu* now at last bears its fruit. It is certainly Eliot who has best harvested this fruit, as much in his objective lyrics as in the chamber music of the *Quartets*.

Of poets writing in English who have selected free or mixed forms as their means of expression Eliot is one of the few for whom the completion of a verse is not marked by the little typewriter bell or the intimidating *non possumus* of the last syllable of the iambic pentameter. There is nothing exterior about his vertical quality, nothing of what Monsieur Prud-homme believed to be the definition of written poetry – turning back on your traces rather than going ahead. There is an internal gravitation bringing the whole back to the centre – a gift Eliot already had as far back as *Prufrock*.

Some Englishmen who are otherwise of the best literary education find Eliot's European success 'exaggerated' and insinuate that his constant perfection should be judged with the measure of his lyrical productiveness, which in quantity is not torrential. Others make so bold as to note, though without going deeply into the comparison, that European judgments on Anglo-Saxon literature are anything but authoritative as is

192

shown by the example of Edgar Allan Poe who was so badly
reputed at home and reaped such glory abroad.*

But when we have put aside the infinity of differences, as
well as our belief that rigid distinctions between accursed and
elect in art are unjust and anti-historical, we still need to remember that Poe was helped in Europe through the services
of a translator of genius, Baudelaire, who gave him a definitive
form and his place in a milieu and a culture. Whereas up to
now (with a few and partial exceptions) Eliot has had the dis-
service of interpreters with good intentions but always at odds
with their inadequate means of expression, with language
which inevitably flattens the lightness out of his recitation.
The French – to take the best example, Gide's *Little Gidding* –
keep the nuances and the 'fading' of the original texts very
well, but are forced to water down a good deal owing to the
rational character of their language. And as for the Italians,
when they are not content with being modestly literal they are
forced to search for monosyllables, elisions and caesurae which
wrench and twist the plastic and expansive genius of our
language. And it seems reasonable to think that a German
Eliot would come out all inked over in the romantic manner,
as they say happened with Rilke's Valéry.

But this doesn't mean we need fear there is something
equivocal deep down about Eliot's recent reputation in Europe.
The fact is that Eliot, like Valéry before him, has contributed,
at least in Italy, to renewed contact with the high European
tradition which had been lost for many years. Eliot and Valéry
recalled Italian readers to a less superficial knowledge of their
patrimony in poetry and to a closer sense of their classical
spirit.

But are they classical poets? Certainly not for those who
think the classical moment is limited to expressing felicitously
the familiar and the obvious, or those who reject any participation of poetry as such in the current of history, or those who
don't believe that poetry is a laborious discovery every genera-

*When I wrote these lines I didn't expect Eliot's penetrating
comments on Poe's reputation in Europe, in the second of his Rome
conferences (December 12th, 1947).

tion makes with its own means. But everyone who refuses to give them some wretched place in the generic and trite categories of 'anti-decadentism' will see them as strong, vital and significant poets who cannot be reduced to terms of a school. Eliot and Valéry are diverse and even opposite as poets, for though both set out from Pascal's terror of the individual 'I' and its solitude, it was only to reach positions far distant from one another. One dissolved his original immobility in the Heraclitean flux: the other, through the experience of the mystery of the incarnation, reaped the unchanging Presence beneath the changing veil of phenomenal life. They are not gratuitous poets, facile sons of themselves, but artists who owe something to more than one other artist. And to-morrow too they will have a recognizable countenance if the men of to-morrow still look for poetry. Valid originality, as Eliot has warned us, is not originality which has no resemblance with anyone else: it is what is irreducible to similarities and is conditioned and guaranteed by them.

Poets of poetry, poets for poets, their example might indeed authorize the lack of moderation of some of their less gifted followers: but it will never justify the passiveness of a man who says 'no' to a whole epoch out of homage to a prejudice. Through them and a few others what changes we see in a landscape which, in the eyes of many of our critics, was from Leopardi onwards taken up with episodes of realist or grotesque-romantic poetry (Heine, a truncated Baudelaire, a few minor poets here and there . . .).*

Let us look back and remount the current even if when we follow the thread more than one great tradition of poetry disappears for a moment from our sight. Eliot, Valéry. Then a little further back two others: Yeats (older-style but rejuvenated by contact with the younger generation) and Apollinaire – they cannot be said to have exhausted their scope merely with the gift of their apparent spontaneity. And still further back the symbolists of the first generation, the *maudits* and their almost-contemporary Hopkins, and at

*Here and in several other places there are references to the critical writings of Beredetto Croce.

194

bottom – and not initiating the series – Emily Dickinson,
poised between the sublime and the 'nonsensical' . . . In less
than a hundred years what an inheritance of voices for the
world of to-morrow left by *a certain idea* of poetry (which
some think erroneous) – granted the world of to-day still
succeeds in begetting history.

Quick said the bird, find them, find them
Round the corner . . .

Through and for these voices and the suggestiveness of
their teaching, other voices (no matter where and when),

Other echoes
(Will) inhabit the garden . . .

Translated by Bernard Wall

E. Martin Browne

The Dramatic Verse of T. S. Eliot

When T. S. Eliot undertook to write for the stage, he knew
very clearly what he wanted to achieve. He had analysed, in
his critical work, the nature of dramatic poetry; he had appreciated, from seeing plays, the effect which an acted play
can make upon an audience; but he had had no experience of
how it reaches the stage, and no inside knowledge of how the
effect is created.

In this he suffered a disability common to English poets for
a long time. From the Restoration onwards, a gulf widened
between poets and theatre men. In the last century, only a
very few verse-plays were staged, and those were practically
all the work of versifiers rather than of poets. The giants of
poetry, when they wrote plays, produced unactable solemnities. Their successors in this century gained only a small and
specialized audience of poetry-lovers. The general public was
untouched and the stage-folk unattracted by a dramatic poetry
which bore little relation to the life or the speech of human
beings.

Eliot might seem an unlikely person to restore that relationship. This shy, slow-spoken man would not move easily
among the ebullient, ephemeral people of the theatre. He
might understand little of the theatre's audience, which
gathers not to hear poetry but to see a show. But the playwright needs to know how that audience reacts, and to what
stimulus applied by the actors: how little, how very little, he
can take for granted either of its knowledge or of its apprehension: yet how strong and swift can be its response to the
right evocation of pity, laughter, terror from its heart. Could
Eliot know these things?

He set out to learn. On the one hand, he studied the great
work of the past from this point of view. His dramatic writing
is firmly rooted in Greek tragedy, in Shakespeare and in the

196

Bible, with Chekov as a notable modern influence. On the other hand, he watched the stage, consulted with actors and producers, tried experiments. He is still learning, and will go on doing so.

Dramatic verse, the special subject of this essay, sets a particularly difficult problem. It has long been in disuse, and has been regarded with suspicion both by actors and audiences. The actor thinks it difficult to 'play.' In naturalistic drama, a subtle communication with his audience is easily established through a turn of the head or a half-spoken syllable. But in a verse play he must 'deliver' the lines: how can he make them sound like the speech of a real person? Not only are the technical demands of verse, in breathing, diction, gesture, exacting as well as unfamiliar: when they are fulfilled, the result, as he fears, may be a barrier against the audience. It is more difficult, so many playgoers feel, to 'suspend disbelief' in a character speaking verse.

To solve this problem, then, dramatic verse must have two things: a speech-rhythm which seems natural to actors and audience, and the power to express individual character. These in addition to what is required of all stage-dialogue, that it should speak with immediately apprehensible point and clarity.

Eliot began to wrestle with the first part of the problem in *The Rock*. He had written earlier two dramatic fragments of *Sweeney Agonistes*, whose experiments in jazz-rhythms for dialogue have since been tried on the stage with some success. But these were not written with performance in mind, while *The Rock* was commissioned for a large popular audience.

The verse in *The Rock* is limited to an impersonal Chorus, so characterization is not called for. But a contemporary speech-rhythm is essential, and two developments follow. First, the iambic foot of Shakespearean tradition is given up: the stress shifts to the beginning of the foot, in accordance with the change that has come over English speech. This trochaic-cum-dactyllic foot is of course no more rigidly adhered to than was the iambic in Shakespeare's later plays. The verse is infinitely varied, with many inverted feet: but the rhythm is strongly maintained.

The other change is a final freeing of the verse from the counting of syllables. The ten-syllable line of 'blank verse,' which was almost uniform in Shakespeare's early plays, came to vary from eight to fourteen syllables in his later ones: but still the ten-syllable basis was at the back of the mind of both writer and hearers. Eliot has broken this 'blank verse' tradition of syllables by going at once back and forward. He has gone back to the basis established by the mediæval poets, of a fixed number of *stresses* in the line without any fixed number of syllables. He has gone forward to meet the development of prose-rhythms by the inclusion of a very long, sweepingly rhythmic line having six or eight stresses, but still a part of the verse-structure. Thus a form of verse much more varied than any before is placed at the service of the theatre; and this Chorus of *The Rock*, which in its half-masks is so forbiddingly impersonal to look at, is able by its poet's voice to rouse great audiences to exaltation or to laughter, as they listen to the prophet's vision or to the jest shrewdly aimed at contemporary follies:

The Word of the LORD came unto me, saying:
O miserable cities of designing men,
O wretched generation of enlightened men,
Betrayed in the mazes of your ingenuities,
Sold by the proceeds of your proper inventions:
I have given you hands which you turn from worship,
I have given you speech, for endless palaver,
I have given you my Law, and you set up commissions,
I have given you lips, to express friendly sentiments,
I have given you hearts, for reciprocal distrust.
I have given you power of choice, and you only alternate
Between futile speculation and unconsidered action.
Many are engaged in writing books and printing them,
Many desire to see their names in print,
Many read nothing but the race reports.
Much is your reading, but not the Word of GOD,
Much is your building, but not the House of GOD.

198

Will you build me a house of plaster, with corrugated roofing,
To be filled with a litter of Sunday newspapers?
We thank Thee for the lights that we have kindled,
The light of altar and of sanctuary;
Small lights of those who meditate at midnight
And lights directed through the coloured panes of windows
And light reflected from the polished stone,
The gilded carven wood, the coloured fresco.
Our gaze is submarine, our eyes look upward
And see the light that fractures through unquiet water.
We see the light but see not whence it comes.
O Light Invisible, we glorify Thee!

With the next of his dramatic works, Eliot faced the second problem, that of characterization in verse. In his play for Canterbury this problem only arose to a limited extent, for he was writing for the semi-liturgical setting of a Chapter House, where a bare platform stage gave immediate indication that the details of individual character would be subordinated to the larger significance of the story. Nevertheless, *Murder in the Cathedral* is a play with a hero, and contains at least five historical personages whose names are known. Its Chorus no longer wear masks, but are Women of Canterbury, ordinary 'scrubbers and sweepers,' the most human interpretation of the Greek 'friends of the hero.' So for all these the verse has to be a medium for characterization.

In this play, Eliot makes the task easier for himself by using a variety of verse-forms, and also two stretches of prose, to suit the style of the different scenes. The most superficial level, that of the quarrels between Becket and the Knights, is rhymed doggerel:

This is the man who was the tradesman's son, the backstairs
brat who was born in Cheapside,
This is the man who crawled upon the King, swollen with
blood and swollen with pride,
Creeping out of the London dirt,
Crawling up like a louse on your shirt . . . '

This is purely external in feeling. More subtle, and sometimes rather crabbed, is a four-stress rhyming verse for the Tempters who dramatise the tortuous progress of Becket's inner struggle:

King commands, Chancellor richly rules,
This is a sentence not taught in the schools.
To put down the great, protect the poor,
Beneath the throne of God can man do more?
Disarm the ruffian, strengthen the laws,
Rule for the good of the better cause,
Dispensing justice make all even
Is thrive on earth and perhaps in heaven.

There is an easy, near-blank-verse for dialogue with the Priests and Women, rising at times to fine oratory:

Peace! and be at peace with your thoughts and visions.
These things had to come to you and you to accept them.
This is your share of the eternal burden,
The perpetual glory. This is one moment,
But know that another
Shall pierce you with a sudden, painful joy
When the figure of God's purpose is made complete.

And for the Chorus, a very varied series of forms, from the three-stress lines of the women's domestic talk:

Seven years we have lived quietly,
Succeeded in avoiding notice,
Living and partly living.
Sometimes the corn has failed us,
Sometimes the harvest is good . . .

to the long, complexes of pleading or of praise:

O Thomas, return. Archbishop, return, return to France.
Return. Quickly. Quietly. Leave us to perish in quiet . . .

In addition, Eliot has followed the precedent he established with his final Chorus in *The Rock* which is based on the *Gloria* of the Mass, and used the rhythms of two more Christian hymns as ground-bass of choral odes. Here is the one founded on *Dies Irae:*

More than footfall in the passage
More than shadow in the doorway
More than fury in the hall.

200

*The agents of hell disappear, the human, they shrink and
dissolve*
  Into dust on the wind, forgotten, unmemorable, only is here
  The white, flat face of Death, God's silent servant

This variety is perhaps the easy way out of the problem of
verse-form. It is readily acceptable to the contemporary mind,
with its tendency to constant flitting, its lack of repose and
concentration: so audiences are happy with it, and do not feel
dissatisfied at the lack of a unifying principle in the play's
rhythms. Much of the new dramatic poetry made by Eliot's
followers is on these lines. But for Eliot himself, this is only a
stepping-stone on the journey towards a more complete unity
of form. He has a hunger for that unity and will not rest till
he attains it. He must have a verse-form capable of enclosing
within itself all the moods and characters of the play.

Before leaving *Murder in the Cathedral* for its successor, in
which a long step towards that unity is taken, it is worth
noticing that the demands of characterization, limited though
they are in this play, are much more subtly fulfilled than may
at first be obvious. Take the Priests as examples. They are
numbered One, Two and Three; and at a first reading might
appear to differ in no more than their numbers. But try giving
a speech of Number One to Number Three, and you will
quickly find out that they are people of strongly marked
character, each of whose speeches belongs to the designated
speaker and no one else. Number One is elderly, worldly-wise,
with good manners, fond of his food:

  I saw him as Chancellor, flattered by the King,
  Liked and feared by courtiers in their overbearing fashion,
  Despised and despising, always isolated,
  Never one among them, always insecure. . .
  Please dine with us.
  Your men shall be looked after also.
  Dinner before business. Do you like roast pork?

Number Two is younger, aggressively loyal, efficient:

  I am the Archbishop's man: let us give the Archbishop wel-
come.

201

Do you not know that the good Archbishop
Is likely to arrive at any moment?
The crowds in the streets will be cheering and cheering.
You go on croaking like frogs in the treetops,
But frogs at least can be cooked and eaten.

and Number Three is the still, deep thinker who sees the end of things:

For good or ill, let the wheel turn.
The wheel has been still these seven years, and no good.
For ill or good, let the wheel turn.
For who knows the end of good or evil
Until the grinders cease
And the door shall be shut in the street,
And all the daughters of music shall be brought low.

It is he who at last pronounces the epitaph on the Knights:

Go, weak, sad men, lost, erring souls, homeless in earth or
heaven . . .

In the small circle of pain within the skull
You still shall tramp and tread one endless round
Of thought, to justify your action to yourselves,
Weaving a fiction which unravels as you weave,
Pacing forever in the hell of make-believe
Which never is belief . . .

The Family Reunion is a masterpiece, but not a successful play. It can never become as popular as has *Murder in the Cathedral*. Its audience tends to greet with sympathetic relief Aunt Violet's statement

I do not understand
A single thing that's happened.

and Harry is continually assuring his relations that

I would explain, but you would none of you believe it;
If you believed it, still you would not understand . . .

For his experience is one that cannot be conveyed in words: the poet has deliberately attempted the impossible. He has thereby laid himself open to the gibes of all those who do not believe that such an experience really happens, and to the fury of people who justifiably claim that events in a play must be

202

clear to the spectator and the story must have an end. But to
those who recognize the experience he writes of, Eliot has succeeded in conveying it in this play, so that some people regard
it as their most profoundly satisfying evening in the theatre.

From the point of view of this essay, the play's interest is
a narrower one, and its success is accepted. A verse-form has
been created capable of including every kind of contemporary
speech, from the banal conversation of a drawing-room at tea-
time to the revelations of the heart's depth and the terror of
eternal things. It is based on four main stresses to a line, with
a complete flexibility in the number of syllables: the rhythm
is strongly trochaic with many dactyls interspersed: there is a
definite cæsura, and the end of the line invariably has significance. The form, therefore, though appearing loose at first
reading, is in reality closely knit, and should impose its discipline naturally on a sensitive actor. This verse is dramatic in
the true sense, that the form of the verse heightens the tension
and sharpens the characterization. Take as an example of the
first, Harry's speech to Mary about the Eumenides just before
they appear, and observe the powerful effect of the end-pauses
and the pulsation of the rhythm:

When I remember them
They leave me alone: when I forget them
Only for an instant of inattention
They are roused again, the sleepless hunters
That will not let me sleep. At the moment before sleep
I always see their claws distended
Quietly, as if they had never stirred.

To illustrate the adaptability of the verse to character, take the
silly sentimental Aunt Ivy after Harry's first 'mad' revelation
of his supposed wife-murder:

But I understand –
I have heard of such cases before – that people in his con-
dition
Often betray the most immoderate resentment
At such a suggestion. They can be very cunning –
Their malady makes them so. They do not want to be cured
And they know what you're thinking.

203

These passages reveal the mastery of characterization which Eliot has by now acquired. He is able in this play to create individuals fully alive in their idiosyncracies and consistent in their thoughts and feelings: yet to bind them into the greater whole which reveals them as types of human nature. Humour is freely introduced, and a kindly but penetrating satire. Here again the verse serves him well, sharpening the edge of naturalistic conversation by the contrast between Ivy's dactyllic flutter and Violet's massed cohort of strong stresses, easing off again into Charles' smooth flow:

Ivy

Were I in Amy's position, I would go south in the winter.
I would follow the sun, not wait for the sun to come here.
I would go south in the winter, if I could afford it,
Not freeze, as I do, in Bayswater, by a gas-fire counting
shillings.

Violet

Go south! to the English circulating libraries,
To the military widows and the English chaplains,
To the chilly deck-chair and the strong cold tea –
The strong cold stewed bad Indian tea.

Charles

That's not Amy's style at all. We are country-bred people.
Amy has been too long used to our ways
Living with horses and dogs and guns
Ever to want to leave England in the winter.

The verse is also successful in allowing smooth and easy transition from mood to mood, thus overcoming the dangers of a play which mixes the commonplace with the profound, and achieving that unity of form which we saw to be lacking in *Murder in the Cathedral.* No better example could be given than the opening speech. Amy, sitting by the March evening's fire, passes from an order to the parlourmaid, through the querulous grumbling of an old woman, to a revelation of her soul's deepest fear, and back again:

Not yet! I will ring for you. It is still quite light.
I have nothing to do but watch the days draw out,
Now that I sit in the house from October to June,

And the swallow comes too soon and the spring will be over
And the cuckoo will be gone before I am out again.
O Sun, that was once so warm, O Light that was taken for
granted
When I was young and strong, and sun and light unsought
for
And the night unfeared and the day expected
And clocks could be trusted, to-morrow assured
And time would not stop in the dark!
Put on the lights. But leave the curtains undrawn.
Make up the fire. Will the spring never come? I am cold.

Already, by a single speech, the ear is attuned to the rhythms which beat throughout the play, and finds them natural, inevitable and right. But even this subtle verse-form will need relief, to avoid monotony and to differentiate certain passages from the rest. Keeping a strict discipline, Eliot has elected to differentiate two types of passage in this way, the Chorus of the four Uncles and Aunts, and the lines spoken in a mystical state.

The Choruses are formally like some in *Murder in the Cathedral*, beginning and ending with long, multi-stress lines and varied in the middle by a three-stress passage:

In an old house there is always listening, and more is heard
than is spoken.
And what is spoken remains in the room, waiting for the
future to hear it.
And whatever happens began in the past, and presses hard on
the future.
The agony in the curtained bedroom, whether of birth or of
dying,
Gathers in to itself all the voices of the past, and projects them
into the future.
The treble voices on the lawn
The mowing of hay in summer
The dogs and the old pony
The stumble and the wail of little pain
The chopping of wood in autumn
And the singing in the kitchen

205

And the steps at night in the corridor
The moment of sudden loathing
And the season of stifled sorrow
The whisper, the transparent deception
The keeping up of appearances
The making the best of a bad job
All twined and tangled together, all are recorded.

The mystical passages spoken by Agatha at the end of each part and after the disappearance of the Eumenides, are 'runes', and are cast into a two-stress verse which gives the effect of a spell being woven:

Round and round the circle
Completing the charm
So the knot be unknotted
The crossed be uncrossed
The crooked be made straight
And the curse be ended.

There are also two passages of lyric verse, mostly of three stresses, in which Harry shares, first with Mary and then with Agatha, a kind of trance. When they awake from these trances, the verse reflects the change by reverting to the normal, four-stress form used for conscious speech:

Mary

I believe the moment of birth
Is when we have knowledge of death
I believe the season of birth
Is the season of sacrifice
For the tree and the beast, and the fish
Thrashing itself upstream:
And what of the terrified spirit
Compelled to be reborn
To rise towards the violent sun
Wet wings into the rain cloud
Harefoot over the moon?

Harry

What have we been saying? I think I was saying
That it seemed as if I had been always here
And you were someone who had come from a long distance.

206

Whether I know what I am saying, or why I say it
That does not matter. You bring me news
Of a door that opens at the end of a corridor,
Sunlight and singing:

These variations of the form serve their purposes without detracting from the unity of the whole work. Indeed, they enhance it: for as we enjoy the variety, we feel that it is controlled by an overriding unity. *The Family Reunion* is a verse-play of a kind unknown on the English stage since the Restoration. The blending of lyric and dramatic elements into a single verse-organism is indeed more like Greek than English writing for the theatre. Yet this is, in form as well as in content, a work essentially contemporary, in which twentieth-century actors feel at home. Eliot's achievement is of a value far greater than that of a single play: it signalises the rebirth of English dramatic poetry.

Claude Edmonde Magny

A Double Note on T. S. Eliot
and James Joyce

Die Geschichte ist ein Epos im Geist Gottes gedichtet . . .
Schelling

The devotion which T. S. Eliot has always shown towards his friend Joyce is well known. I need no further proof than the two letters he addressed to *The Times* correcting the signally malicious Obituary Notice which that journal published on the death of the author of *Ulysses* and which, because they were refused by the columns for which they were intended, were published by *Horizon*. It is more interesting to discover between their works, so different from a formal point of view, a striking relationship in the content itself, and, as a consequence, unexpected analogies in the very technique.

One of Eliot's central preoccupations, which blazes out in *The Four Quartets* of which it forms the subject, but which was everywhere present in the earlier poems, is with Time. Without a doubt the drama of our modern consciousness lies in the split – growing ever wider since the Rennaissance – in the close relationship in which mediæval man stood to Eternity. The rationalism of the seventeenth century (which culminates in Malbranche's theory of the vision in God, the immediate apprehension of eternal verities by the human intelligence in the bosom of the uncreated Word), the eighteenth century's nostalgia for the paradisial innocence of the 'noble savage', the naive confidence which the nineteenth century held in the indefinite progress of humanity, are all so many myths designed to dress a wound which daily grows more gaping. It is not without significance that two of the *oeuvres* which have left the deepest impress on contemporary literature, should both have for their essential theme an obsessive longing for a return into the past which the heart desires, while reason knows it to be impossible.

208

Joyce's work is axed on a philosophy of history taken from Vico: it is clearly expressed in *Finnegan's Wake*, a cyclical poem whose last line links up exactly with the first, after the ballad evoked by the title: *Begin Again, Finnigan;* but this philosophy had already provided the inspiration for *Ulysses*, with its structure so meticulously traced from that of the *Odyssey*, which, although certainly a work of the past, is definitive and in fact eternal in that it can serve as a model for all future works. Right from *The Portrait of the Artist* Joyce is seen as essentially preoccupied with eliminating, through his description of it, the temporal succession of events from the world. His aim is to use his art to show us each thing in the very moment of its *epiphany*, that is to say, at the instant when, all its successive shapes melting into one, it passes as a living thing into eternity. * The real mould to which Stephen Dedalus feels himself drawn is to *'transmute the daily bread of experience into the radiant body of everliving life.'* The various technical devices which are so lavishly used in *Ulysses* (sometimes indiscriminately) are so many means of realizing, more or less directly, this transmutation: Gertie McDowell or Mrs Bloom will be stripped of their temporal attributes once the reader has been led to discover that their real names are Nausica and Penelope, and the discussion on *Hamlet* in the Public Library, where the cards are so adroitly shuffled, has no other object than to suggest to us the profound identity, in spite of the plurality of their historical incarnations, of the Father and the Son (as in the Trinity), the child and the man, of Stephen-Telemacus and Bloom-Ulysses. It is not Shakespeare himself who is Hamlet, but his son who died prematurely (as did Bloom's) and whose name the Prince of Denmark bears: it is not Shakespeare's mother who is the ageing sinful Queen, but the poet's wife, Ann Hathaway, who first seduced and then deceived him. It is not John Shakespeare's ghost who wanders through the night crying vengeance: it is the spirit of William Shakespeare who, to revenge himself wrote *Hamlet* (in hatred of his wife) and *King Lear* (in hatred of his brothers). In fact, Shakespeare is at the same time himself and the ghost of the

*cf. *Stephen Hero*, pps. 188-190.

father and the Prince, just as Joyce is equally Stephen and Bloom and, as in *Finnegan's Wake*, Shem and Shuan are Adam: 'When Rutlandbaconshouthamptonshakespeare or another poet of the same name in the comedy of errors wrote *Hamlet* he was not the father of his own son merely, but being no more a son, he was and felt himself the father of all his race, the father of his own grandfather, the father of his unborn grandson who, by the same token, never was born . . .'

The chief criticism which can be made of this technique is that it is indirect, and consequently, *negative* in the greater part of its results; it allows of an artificial elimination of time from the world, without, for all that, really transmuting the objects and the people into eternity. It is the same with the correspondence which, from *Dedalus* onwards, Joyce establishes between time and space,* whose interchangeability explains a curious connection which can be established between *Ulysses* and *Finnegan's Wake*. The two books are based on the same postulate: the possibility of the microcosm to mirror adequately the macrocosm, just as the Leibnitzian monad can reproduce the whole world in itself. *Ulysses*, which in substance is the account of a long voyage round the Mediterranean lasting for several years, is compressed into the framework of 'twenty-four hours in the town of Dublin'; while the history of the world which is related in *Finnegan's Wake* unfolds itself entirely, outside time, along the banks of the Liffey thus establishing between the map of the world and the map of 'Dublin and its environs' – hence in the spatial order – an identity of structure, analagous to that which in *Ulysses* connects – in the temporal order – the episodes of the homeric sage and the different moments of Mr Bloom's day.

Eliot does the same thing when in *The Waste Land* he moves his recording apparatus – the gaze of the blind prophet Tiresias – in time and in space, from the Thames of Elizabeth and Leicester to that of Sweeney and Mrs Porter, from London

*For example, when Stephen is walking along the river bank: '*Space*,' he says to himself, 'is the ineluctable modality of the visible,' the world of nebeneinander. Then, as he closes his eyes it seems to him that now he is walking only in time, which is 'the ineluctable modality of the audible,' the world of nacheinander.

Bridge to Dante's *Inferno*, and goes as far as to identify the sacred legend of the Graal with the pagan fertility myths, assimilating Attis-Balder, the Hanged-Man of the Tarot pack and the crucified God. Jessie Weston's book, to which the title and the notes refer, plays in this poem the part which Vico and the Odyssey played for Joyce. Just as at the end of *Sweeney Among the Nightingales* Eliot deliberately merges Oedipus and Agammemnon, in *The Waste Land* he intermingles (as Joyce will do in *Finnegan's Wake*) all the great legends of humanity, as if to lay bare the eternal symbols which the collective consciousness uses and has used: a juxtaposition at the heart of the same song which will be able to reveal the secret identification between the typist and Queen Elizabeth, between Mr Eugenides and Phlebas the Phœnician or between raped Philomele, the Pia of Dante and the Thames's third daughter. This device – the mythical transfiguration of contemporary people – is exactly the same as that used by Joyce: 'Just as the one-eyed merchant, seller of currants, melts into the Phœnician Sailor,' (we are told in the notes) 'and the latter is not wholly distinct from Ferdinand Prince of Naples, so all the women are one woman . . .' Thus Stephen Dedalus was Telemacus (or Hamlet) and Mrs Bloom is all women from Penelope to Cybele.

Even more important than the formal similarity between the technique of these two writers is the similarity in meaning. As is the whole of Joyce's work, so is Eliot's poetry (and even his criticism) dominated by the desire for an impossible return to the past, by *nostos*, the nostalgia for a past one knows can never recur. Ulysses is bound to disappointment on regaining Ithaca, just as Joyce would have certainly been disappointed if he had gone back to Ireland.* When he returns to the nuptial bed Bloom mentally abolishes the historical fact (here the adultery which his wife has just indulged in with Blazes Boylan, to say nothing of that which she contemplates

*Cf. Budgen, p. 231. In another place Budgen tells us that out of the whole book Joyce liked best the episode dealing with Ulysses' return, where Bloom, come back to the nuptial bed, mentally kills his wife's lovers, 'the ugly duckling of my book.' (Ibid. p. 264.)

with Stephen), whether past or future, by the kind of 'mathematical catechism' through which he resolves everything (including his wife's suitors and past and future lovers) into their constituent elements, and smiles (hypothetically) to think of the infinite series of which each man is but a middle term even while he believes himself to be the first. Similarly, from his earliest poems Eliot destroys the future by treating it as if it had already happened: thus all events are annihilated before they have even been accomplished: '*There will be time, there will be time . . .*' Mr Alfred Prufrock tells himself

And indeed there will be time
To wonder 'Do I dare?' and 'Do I dare?'

he goes on: but scarcely has the action been envisaged than it is already too late: everything is foreseen, everything is known,

For I have known them all already, known them all —
Have known the evenings, mornings, afternoons,
I have measured out my life with coffee spoons . . .
And I have known the eyes already, known them all . . .
And I have known the arms already, known them all . . .

Eliot was thirty-three when he wrote *Gerontion*, that epic of retrospection, where the whole of a life is weighed and found wanting. One would have said that he wanted to be old already, with all his life behind and not before him, as if living was something too tiring and anyhow useless. It is revealing that at the end of *Animula* the last line of the *Hail Mary* is quoted with the word *birth* substituted for *death:*

Pray for us now and at the hour of our birth

(and not *nunc et in hora mortis* as in the liturgy). There is in Eliot something of a true horror of birth, which is probably linked with his well-known aversion for the Spring, symbol of all deceitful resurrections (deceitful because temporal) which are symbolized in *April is the cruellest month,*

. . . this Birth was
Hard and bitter agony for us, like Death, our Death.

The Kings in the *Journey of the Magi* have the same refrain. And in *A Song for Simeon*, the old stylite begs God to be good and recall His servant to Himself: it is no longer, as with the hero of *Gerontion*, of his own life only that he is tired; now it is of all lives to come, of the futile perspective of the centuries ahead which his mind lays out before him:

I am tired with my own life and the lives of those after me,
I am dying in my own death and the deaths of those after me.

As with the prophet Tiresias, overwhelmed by having fore-suffered:

And I Tiresias have foresuffered all
Enacted all

as with the sibyl of *The Satyricon* who wanted nothing more than to die,* the burden of time has become intolerable to him.

For, in time, everything is done to wound the human soul: its mechanical aspect of a progression, an industrial belt which carries us inexorably forward, is no less intolerable than its apparent spurts and bounds: it traps us with false hopes, promising that one day something absolutely *new* will happen; but, odious as is stagnation, the coming of a real *event* would be more painful still:

We do not wish anything to happen

sings the choir at the beginning of *Murder in the Cathedral*. Destroying or saving, engulfing or falsely beguiling, Time, at each moment is our enemy.

At the period in which he was writing *The Waste Land*, Eliot took refuge (but unlike Joyce, only temporarily) in a timeless perspective: he was waiting for the real liberation, hard-won through the anguish of *Ash Wednesday*, and the ascent to Eternity whose stages are recorded in *The Four Quartets* for, once Time has been accepted, all the consequences of the Incarnation can be developed. *The Waste Land* is a poem as static as is *Ulysses* or *Finnegan's Wake*: in the end nothing has happened, and, as Pierre Leyris so rightly says: 'King Metiegne still sins behind the gasworks'.† The curse which lay over the waste land has not been lifted: the water which could have fertilized the soil or quenched the soul's thirst has served only to drown Phlebas the Phœnician, bearer of the

*Lines 190-193.

†The passage from *The Satyricon* to which I refer is well known and is quoted at the head of *The Waste Land*.

Graal. The Thunder's advice: *Give, Sympathize, Govern* is impossible to work out in practice, and Buddha as well as St Augustine 'those two representatives of Eastern and Western asceticism' as the note tells us, have been sent away back-to-back. Like the prophetess of Cumae nothing is left to us but to long with all our hearts for a death which will never come – because nothing will ever happen. Madame Sosostris, the wise woman said it: the Hanged Man (i.e. the crucified God) was not in the cards, but only death by drowning. (The waters of grace can only destroy those who will not allow themselves to be carried along by them). In *The Waste Land* as in *Ulysses* (Jesus Christ did not die for Bloom the Jew, either), we are in the bleak, even time before the Incarnation, before the unique, exceptional event took place, that which, moreover, the cards are unable to predict, because it is outside Time. Even if she hadn't had a cold and had been able to see what the one-eyed merchant carried on his back, Madame Sosostris would never have been able to foretell the uncreated word, the *logos* of the Gospel according to St John, making himself man and coming down among us, or rather, her cold and the limitation of her vision – as also doubtless the fact that the merchant was one-eyed – only express a fundamental incapacity. Man cannot transcend time. And yet the future already exists from now, just as the past remains eternally in the present.* The art of the Tarot (among others) is an immediate result of this, but it is an art threaded through with enigma. Everything has meaning in the game which the fortune-teller spreads out on the table, but no one can understand the meaning and profit by it. The 'character in the cards', symbol of the narrator (Eliot, Tiresias, or Man?) is the drowned Phœnician sailor identified through the quotation from Shakespeare with Ferdinand, Prince of Naples and bearer of grace, and through the notes, with Tiresias the seer who was not only blind but androgy-

*What might have been and what has been
Point to one end, which is always present.
Footfalls echo in the memory
Down the passage which we did not take
Towards the door we never opened
Into the rose garden.*

214

nous. There is also the *femme fatale*, Belladonna, lady of the reefs and dangerous passes, the illusory promise of salvation (she has not yet become Our Lady of the Rocks) with whom one makes love without love (Cleopatra, Pia, the typist, Mrs Porter, Elizabeth, etc*), the reef on which the mariner will founder, The Wheel (of birth), the Man with a Trident (Neptune, symbol of that that is troubling or disquieting), and, finally, the one-eyed merchant, who is the same as the Phœnician sailor; that which he carries on his back and which 'it is forbidden to see' is perhaps the double which, like Stetson,† we have all murdered and buried in the garden, we the *hypocrite lecteur, mon semblable, mon frère*, and who cannot be raised from the dead because the Son of Man has not yet died for us. Such a horoscope is indeed not to be treated carelessly: we understand the fortune-teller's insistence on carrying it personally to Madame Equitone, so rightly named.‡ *One must be so careful these days.* In Joyce dreams play exactly the same role of the uncomprehended, incomprehensible prophecy; Stephen's dream in *The Portrait of the Artist*, just as the dream in *Ulysses* – without forgetting the dream in *Finnegan's Wake* where H. C. Earwicker (Here Comes Everyman) sees the whole future of humanity – are used to eliminate time in making an eternal past of the future.

From this point the paths of the two writers diverge. This is not the place to analyse how Eliot, through *The Four Quartets* carries on his effort to integrate time and its multiplicity of dimensions into the spiritual life of man, so as to make possible a true access to eternity which no one can reach without having first come to terms with time. (This is the lesson of humility we learn from the Incarnation). Joyce, however, remained fixed in his endeavour (condemned in advance) to blot out history, and in this confusion between the intemporal and the eternal probably lies the reason for the failure of *Finnegan's Wake*, a work which is not so much indecipherable or even

*Cf. line 56. 'I see crowds of people, walking round in a ring.' And further on, the dead souls seen from high on London Bridge.
†Lines 70 et seq.
‡She for whom everything is of the same value, and for whom every moment of time is the equivalent of any other.

difficult (as was said somewhat hastily) as boring, because it indefatigably repeats one thing and one thing only from which, in the end, all human content is removed since, finally, its whole meaning is this '*And all that has been done has yet to be done and done again.*' Here, history is not even a nightmare as it was to Stephen, but a dream without substance or reality.

It remains to be explained that *The Waste Land* and *Ulysses* could have had – and still have – the same resonance. Eliot, working a quotation from Dante or Webster into the texture of his poem, and Joyce making a pastiche of Chaucer's style and that of a girls' magazine are doing no more than giving a momentary (and how much a literary) satisfaction to one of the oldest and most stubborn of man's desires: they dream, in fact, of doing nothing less – despite the exteriority of moments in time, and through them of the separate structures of cultures – than to remake a unity of the whole human race. The real hero of *The Waste Land* is Tiresias, that summary of all humanity, because as Ovid says, having tasted the pleasures of both sexes he contains within him the two natures, masculine and feminine. In *Ulysses*, man is certainly broken up into the trilogy Stephen, Bloom, Mrs Bloom: father, son and woman, but their ties are close enough to ensure their ultimate identification. In Mr Bloom's perambulations round Dublin, Joyce wanted, as did Eliot in *The Waste Land*, to write the saga of humanity, the epic of the collective consciousness (and so we have the differences in epoques, in countries, in sexes, in social background, in outlook), such as it could effectively be unfolded in an All-knowing mind, * *total* rather than omniscient. It is significant that Eliot used Frazer and Jessie Weston to establish an identification between myths whose content are apparently so different, whereas in France a Malraux, for example, has taken the lesson of Frobénius quite otherwise and

---

*Cf. the quotation at the head of this essay. 'History is an imaginary epic in the divine intellect' and the excellent definition which Stuart Gilbert makes of Joyce's undertaking: 'The structure of *Ulysses* (though to a less extent than that of *Work in Progress*) indicates that Joyce aspires to outsoar the category of time and see a simultaneous universe, to take, so to speak, a God's eye view of the cosmos.' (p. 355.)

216

uses ethnology for diametrically opposite ends. And the very particular satisfaction which *The Waste Land* and Joyce's novel give us comes from their power to fulfil for a moment that ever-frustrated dream of a kind of humanity-Moloch, a vast crucible in which all the collective mirages of humanity over thousands of years will be swallowed up and all differences between people effaced – of a huge statue inside which we would all be, identical one with the other, staring out of the same windows, seeing with the same eyes, so much so that each one of us would perceive exactly the same objects and the same universe as was perceived by all the others.

Translated by Sonia Brownell

Hugh Gordon Porteus

Resurrection in the Crypt

If you wish to be understood, Mr Eliot once remarked in the course of a broadcast, you must use the language of your audience, even if it be the jargon of Hollywood. I have not Mr Eliot's precise words at hand, but I do remember that they were chosen and delivered as from pulpit to pew; and I wondered at the time (long before the institution of the Third Programme) how many of his potential listeners had his attention. To the demotic sensibility, verbal precision and detachment seem offensively antisocial. More common than objections to Mr Eliot's manner – ('pedantic', 'liturgical') – have been objections to the matter ('obscure') of his work. Any obscurity in Mr Eliot's work is due to the fact that he is a master of paradox: he is even fond of describing himself as orthodox, for example. But he is never *poetically* obscure. Only people who do not like poetry, or who do not understand verse, will deny that Mr Eliot's poems are poetically lucid. In his introduction to the Selected Poems of Miss Marianne Moore, Mr Eliot has observed significantly that 'we have all to choose whatever subject matter allows us the most powerful and the most secret release; and that is a personal affair.' Thus Mr Eliot has evolved, and made manifest in his work, a personal mythology as potent as, and more patent than, that of Blake. Certain recurrent motifs have the appearance of obsessive images; obsessive in that clearly they besiege, but do not delude, their author. The events to which these images refer back do not matter, though they are responsible for the passionate intensity, as well as for the rigid impersonality, characteristic of Mr Eliot's utterance. What matters is the architecture of the images into valid poetic structures. The conversion of intensely private matter into matter of wide public interest is the great triumph of Mr Eliot's genius.

The number of people interested in the exploration of *les*

frontières de l'esprit may always be limited, but it is not limited by geography. Mr Eliot's researches on these frontiers have been noted and developed in places as widely separated as Greece and China. Recent English translations of the poems of Mr Pien Chih-Lin and Mr George Seferis have provided an opportunity of seeing just how widespread Mr Eliot's influence is. These two poets, the translators of Mr Eliot's verse into Chinese and Greek respectively, reveal a profound understanding of its underlying meanings. English readers for whom Mr Eliot's poetry is all Greek, or all Chinese, may ponder this.

Perhaps no living writer *means more* than Mr T. S. Eliot. One could of course elaborate this statement in various ways. He has already meant more, he is likely to mean more still, than can be demonstrated by mincing his words through the Cambridge sausage machine: an instrument that is not to be despised.

Some fifteen years ago I suggested that Mr Eliot weighed his words as for an urgent cable addressed to posterity but liable to interception by the *Zeitgeist*. It is difficult to avoid rationalizing in some preposterous way an early enthusiasm: it is gratifying to be able to confirm later the rightness of one's instinct. Most people have had the experience with Shakespeare, that he means more at later stages of development. It is not only in this sense, I suggest, that Mr Eliot means more: at different levels, and on different planes, new meanings emerge from further readings. It would be proper to object that such interpretations are simply private; and Mr Eliot has sometimes had occasion to disown meanings that have been read into his work by certain readers. The impressive fact remains that many lines of Mr Eliot's poetry are susceptible of more meaning than Mr Eliot consciously intended, that new facets of meaning revealed do not contradict but actually reinforce the literal face value. I take this as a proof that the poetic process was at the crucible stage unconscious and drew on the resources hinted at in the more recent investigations of Jung. But the poetic process was not terminated at that point, as it would be by a surrealist. Order was brought to bear upon the material. And it is by *order* that Mr Eliot is likely to mean more in the future. But it is not order alone, either. The poetry of Mr Empson, for example, is far more complicated, more cleverly fabricated, very often, than the poetry of Mr Eliot in a similar genre. Perhaps the one clinching test of living writing, whether it be poetry or prose, is that one not only wishes to read it again, but that one does re-read it, with fresh pleasure and with added profit. As Mr Pound has put it: 'Literature is news that *stays* news'. Mr Eliot's writing is likely to stay news longer than Mr Pound's not because it is so much superior, or so much inferior, to the writing of the poet he has called *il miglior fabbro*, but simply because, for the general reader, it is more legibly ordered. What Guinicelli actually said to Dante about Arnaut was that the latter *fu miglior fabbro del parlar materno;* and in that estimate the operative word is surely *fu*. This is merely one aspect of that strange encounter, so fraught with many a curious implication, which seems to have been generally overlooked.

Quantitatively a great deal more has been written about Mr Eliot's work than he has ever risked writing himself, though the attentive reader will discover that his work explains itself quite adequately when it is viewed as a whole: the criticism illuminates the poetry, the poetry illustrates the prose, and both illuminate life. But Mr Eliot's significance is very much more than just literary. He has been and will continue to be an increasingly influential figure because he keeps ahead of the current of ideas, making the news that stays put; in contrast to the intellectual journalist – who extracts the other sort of news out of the current of events. Mr Eliot took no part in the Spanish Civil War, it is true. But he did not lock himself in an Ivory Tower like Mr Yeats, or retire to an island like Mr Auden. His relation to his time, particularly to the 'twenties and 'thirties, and to his own contemporaries, particularly to Mr Pound, Mr Wyndham Lewis, and Mr Joyce, it is important not to underestimate. This is something that his academic commentators have shirked. It would almost seem that these four writers are alone in recognizing that they do, in spite of themselves, form a quartet.

This quartet – Eliot, Lewis, Joyce and Pound – fertilized

220

the intellectual life of the first quarter of this century in a profound manner. They may well come to be seen as the last quartet of that sort, in the way that Dostoievsky, Tolstoy, Chehov and Turgeniev made a last quartet in Russia. And this 'last quartet' of first-order creative minds, so fiercely critical of everyone, and especially of its own members, had nothing in common with the usual log-rolling cliques, like that sodality of the W.C. district, the Bloomsburies. They agreed to differ in much more than their specialist interests, but were nevertheless aligned in a sort of tacit comity upon certain fundamentals, over and above the fashionable pink liberal mobs. If they created fashions, it was as a by-product. They did not follow fashions. All four were artists of vision and conviction, and their work bears witness to their consistent character. Any reorientations have been simply changes of emphasis.

In this quartet Wyndham Lewis was the animator, with his restless curiosity, his inexhaustible fund of inventiveness, and his volcanic energy. Eliot and Pound contributed to Lewis's periodical, *Blast*, in 1914–16. Joyce joined them later, and all four can be seen holding together *The Little Review* in 1917. It is extremely instructive to consult these back numbers. Eliot's contributions, such as the four *Preludes*, are not revolutionary in any way: their pictorial counterpart would be Sickert's Camden Town street scenes and squalid Mornington Crescent interiors – solid local craftsmanship with a discreet french polish.

Nevertheless, of these four figures, Mr Eliot and Mr Lewis seem in retrospect to have been most closely involved with one another. Even their differences link them; for in many ways their talents are complementary. It is true that Mr Eliot and any one of the three will form a pair, because each has something in common with Mr Eliot. Mr Eliot with his tolerant and contemplative outlook was best fitted to comprehend them; and of course he has printed them all, in his capacity as editor or as publisher. When it is considered how great has been the contribution of each to the development of English prose and verse, it is worth remarking that all four have been almost more at home on the Continent than in England. All endured

221

ong spells of exile. All abominated the bastard forms of internationalism but became good Europeans. Mr Eliot and Mr Lewis have also consistently defended the detached critical intelligence from the plagues rampant in the intellectual world. It is almost too obvious to observe that it is among the intelligentsia that you find the real enemies of Intelligence and of those values which should be the proper care of the functionary M. Benda has defined as a *clerc*.

Impelled to scrutinize the implications of intellectual movements that are spiritually barren, Mr Eliot has never allowed himself to be deceived by contemporary politics. Since he has always been a redoubtable critic of liberal doctrine, he has not fallen for the routine anti-liberalist baits which await those whose only objection to liberalism is that it is 'not practical politics'. His criticism of socialism and conservatism, his hostility to fascism and communism, have been motivated by other considerations than self interest. Those whose views on Mr Eliot's political attitude are confined to misunderstanding his often misquoted pronouncements in the preface to his volume *For Lancelot Andrewes* – now out of print – may be invited to search a little deeper, as well as a little further, into Mr Eliot's uncollected papers and into his more recent writings. He has not hesitated to lend his support to several temporarily unpopular movements; but he has never identified himself with a lost cause; and his caution has never been mere timidity. Mr Eliot understands the *tao* of Laotze and the Confucian *chung yung:* that Middle Way which is (in his own words) 'a way of mediation, but never, in those matters which permanently matter, a way of compromise'.

The terrifying detachment and cultivated impersonality of much of Mr Eliot's work gives him already in his lifetime a quality of remoteness that cries out to be redressed. He has done much to encourage his readers to picture him as a sort of masked academical and historical figure. Thus Miss Laura Riding has written that 'unless we are deceived by his modesty, he would be content to be a Bishop, or to be Professor Saintsbury.' I cannot help seeing him, myself, as a sort of Chinese sage. It would not do to press the comparison too far, but there are many respects in which he closely resembles the celestial moralist and anthologist, Confucius. His emphasis on authority, orthodoxy, tradition, formality, etc, has been very similarly misunderstood. For example, in contrast to popular misconceptions of such doctrine, Mr Eliot has himself insisted that 'tradition cannot mean standing still'; just as Confucius warned: 'Let a man of to-day hark back to the ways of antiquity, and disaster will take him'. Then again, Confucius diffidently described himself as 'no innovator, but a transmitter'; adding that 'at sixty, his ear was inclined to the reception of the truth'.

About the utterance of Confucius when he is pontificating is there not sometimes something almost pompous and priggish? For example (and quoting at random) there is what he said in response to the inquiries of Tzu Lu: 'An enlightened person is earnest, urgent, and bland; with friends, earnest and urgent; with brethren, bland.' Happily Confucius is not a merely legendary figure, like the fabulous Lao Tze, who after a lifetime of anonymity suddenly vanished westwards on a blue pony. The friends and brethren of Confucius were sufficiently enlightened to record not only the odds and ends of the Master's ponderous solemnities, but also his offhand gossip, his endearing human foibles, the ridiculous detail of his daily habits and all those common touches in great men which help to make the whole world kin. Thus we read in the *Analects* such delightful and delicately *malicieux* revelations as that 'even in his underclothing, the Master wore nothing of a red or reddish tint'. Such disclosures rather enhance than injure our respect for a dignified celebrity. It is for this reason that among others I think we cannot have too many snapshots of Mr Eliot in undress.

Another reason why we should cherish any accessible glimpses of the personal and informal in Mr Eliot is that he – alone of the 'last Quartet' – so very carefully expunges all traces of personality from his never quite informal work. Mr Lewis is often extremely formal in his serious prose and verse, and more austere still in his painting; but he employs a highly informal and personal style for his pamphleteering. Mr Pound bawls, minces or guffaws 'to the life' in almost every line he writes. And Joyce scarcely for an instant stopped dramatizing himself, drawing his dædal portrait in a mirror and recording his thoughts and conversations. To the extent that all art has its autobiographical aspect, it is possible to discern a little fragmentary self-portraiture in Mr Eliot's work. *Portrait of a Lady* shows the young Boston dandy, or the budding *jemen-foutiste*, peering over a feminine shoulder into the mirror. And it is surely unnecessary to stress that Sweeney and Prufrock, and such characters as Harry in *The Family Reunion*, embody evident traits of their author. And even in his essays on Dante, or Andrewes, or Baudelaire, clearly Mr Eliot reveals a good deal of himself. But often what emerges is a portrait of Mr Eliot's *alter ego*. The *opposite of himself* is a constant apparition in the work of all articulate artists: the Egyptian *ka* or double whose materialization accounts for the frequent startling contrast between art and artist. But in Mr Eliot's self-portraits – from the Learesque caricature onwards – Ego and Id play bo-peep to any extent; and always there is the attempt at self-effacement – a sort of cheating, as Montaigne observed in defence of the unretouched asperities of his Gascon descriptions. What is impressive is the overriding consistency of style and doctrine that remains in Eliot when all that is detectable as 'personal' has been exorcized. We suspect a very powerful dæmon underneath the deceptively impassive surface, and seek vainly for vestiges of it by holding the page upside down against the light and reading between the lines. There is nothing there but the quiet assurance of an urgent message dispatched, for some reason, by the Absolute.

Amalendu Bose

T. S. Eliot and Bengali Poetry

The powerful influence of T.S. Eliot on Bengali writers became manifest in the early 'thirties. In the pages of the progressive Bengali literary periodicals of the time, Eliot's name was frequently mentioned; his works were reviewed, sometimes with striking acumen; his views on literature were carefully discussed; some of his poems were done into Bengali (notably *The Journey of the Magi* by Rabindranath Tagore and *The Hollow Men* by Bishnu Dey); a spate of Eliotesque verse began to appear.

Young Bengali writers responded to Eliot's works for much the same reasons as did young British writers. They found in Eliot a liberating force from the pervading sentimentality and conventional poeticism of contemporary literature. They found in him a new awareness; a penetrating insight into the corroding boredom, the lack of purpose and direction, the omnipresent sense of spiritual disintegration that distinguished post-war life in Europe. True, the external factors that bred *The Waste Land* spirit were different for European and Bengali writers. Nevertheless, the deepening frustration engendered by a series of political crises, the squalor and complexity of life in a huge modern industrial city like Calcutta (and Calcutta is the nerve-centre of Bengali life), the rapid break-up of the age-old social order – all these brought to the intellectual Bengali bourgeoisie an acute sense of things coming to a dead end. Above all, there was the feeling that the western European pattern of civilization on which the English-educated Bengali had built his faith, was on the verge of collapse. Familiar with trends of modern European thought, the Bengali intellectual found in Eliot's early poetry and Huxley's novels a reflection of his own mental processes. The contemporary sense of disequilibrium and incertitude sounded in Eliot's early verse up to *The Hollow Men*, had its distant but unmistakable re-

225

verberations in the poems of young Bengali writers of the
'thirties. With Bishnu Dey, 'dreams have turned into a cactus
bush'; Buddhadeva Bose would forget the 'cactus-forest in our
life'; Samar Sen writes:

> *No peace*
> *The sun of plenty scatters a nightmare of poverty through*
> *the slum.*
> *Old time*
> *Has brought through life's decay, the pain of age.*
> *The silent vulture of nightmare*
> *Flaps above the sodden body at midnight,*
> *And the tuberculous lust burns on through barren days.*
> *Therefore I muse upon the complete history of my ruin*
> *Unnerved, like the blind Dhritarashtra,*
> *And wail in futile delirium;*
> *We have no escape, no chance of victory.*
> *The educated mind, impotent, suffers the putrefaction of*
> *decay,*
> *Searches always at the root of all futility*
> *Under the curse of sex-starved Urbashi.*

('The Intellectual')*

With Eliot, the young Bengali intellectuals had observed 'the
immense panorama of futility and anarchy which is contemporary history,' but no more than Eliot did they stay long in
the dead alley of a divided consciousness. From futility and
mere mockery they have sought to proceed towards a whole
view of life. Some, into whose minds the penetration of the
Western way of thinking is deep, who are aware of the inter-
mittent current of materialism in Indian thought and are profoundly impressed by the Russian experiment, tend towards
dialectical materialism. Some others have probably believed
that the paralysis of civilization manifest in the western world
relates to no more than the post-Renaissance pattern of civilization in Europe, and that if the traditional Indian conception
and practice of a moral, rather than a legal state and society,

---

*This poem and others mentioned below occur in *Modern
Bengali Poems*, edited by D. Chatterjee and translated mainly by
Martin Kirkman; Signet Press, Calcutta, 1945.

despite its suppression and prostration for a considerable period, be readjusted in the context of modern science and economics, it may ensure an equitable, happy, stable and worthy society for India. The call of Gandhi and Tagore is not to be brushed aside.

It is not my suggestion that our poets are sharply divided into two camps – they are too individualistic to be so, and we observe continual intersection and intermingling of thought-currents; not that our poets, whatever their ideologies, have reached any haven of immutable beliefs – they are still moving ahead. I do not at all propose to consider in this essay the several views of life that jostle in recent Bengali poetry. What is relevant here is that young Bengali poets have been stimulated to a profound sense of the age although their rejection of Eliot's latter-day view of life may be witnessed in, for example, Bishnu Dey's reviews of *The Rock*, *Murder in the Cathedral*, *Four Quartets*, and Sudhindranath Datta's essay on 'Eliot and Tradition'. 'Our civilization,' writes Eliot, 'as it exists at present . . . comprehends great variety and complexity, and this variety and complexity, playing upon a refined sensibility, must produce various and complex results.' The expression of the awareness of this variety and complexity may not unlikely produce a bewildering and obscurantist effect. 'The problem for the artist,' as Matthiessen has said, 'is to discover some unified pattern in this variety; and yet, if he believes as Eliot does that poetry should embody a man's reaction to his whole experience, also to present the full sense of its complexity.' That some Bengali poets have confronted this problem honestly and, to a large degree, successfully, is attested by such poems as Sudhindranath Datta's *Search*, Bishnu Dey's *The Rider*, Samar Sen's *New Year Resolution*, Manindra Roy's *The One-Eyed*. As in Eliot, the multilateral inspiration of modern Bengali poetic experience is at once intellectual and emotional, based equally on life and literature. Poets like Datta and Dey are well-versed in modern learning; the latter's essay 'In this changing universe' is an admirable survey of modern thought. Their minds accommodate ideas of recent psychology and anthropology along with the knowledge of their ancestral

227

philosophy. Perhaps one sometimes gets an impression of esot-
ericism and pedantry in their early poems, but because they
do not, in Eliot's words, 'confuse the material and the use
which the author makes of it' but succeed in unifying their
experiences of life and literature and finding an 'emotional
equivalent of thought', their poetry, at its best, presents a
fusion of thought and emotion not reached in Bengali poetry
outside Tagore. At its best too, this poetry finds an 'objective
correlative' to the emotion in some dramatically contrived
situation or character; a brilliant instance of such contrivance
can be found in Amiya Chakravarti's *Chetan Shankra*.

But this fusion of thought and emotion in the context of
contemporary sensibility and intellectual specialization requires an original technique of expression, and it is Eliot's
original technique that has left an enduring impress on recent
Bengali poetry. To others too, the Bengali poets are indebted:
to Ezra Pound, Hopkins, Wilfrid Owen, the French Symbolists, but the indebtedness to Eliot is consistent and haunting.
To-day the benumbed sensibility of the reader must be shocked
into alertness by a certain quality of surprise in the poem;
moreover, where there is a rapid association of thoughts in
the verse arresting images are necessary to give a clue to the
total texture. Mainly from Eliot, our poets have learnt the
juxtaposition of imagery derived eclectically from various
sources; the use of hard, concentrated and therefore precise
images; linked nuances; the sequence of the beautiful and the
unlovely, the conventionally pretty and the rudely realistic;
mocking comments in parentheses; sudden allusions to well-
known lines and phrases, chiefly from Tagore. Fragmentary
imagery, truncated syntax and broken rhythm, presenting a
discontinuity on the surface and corresponding to a punctuated
movement of thought, the split-up sections of a poem, are
unified into a dominating pattern by the sheer integrity and
intensity of the emotional perception.

And then there is the matter of prose rhythm. Partly to
attain to an athletic rhythm and partly to get away from the
almost inescapable spell of Tagore's rhythm whose astonishing
genius has contrived a thousand different melodies out of the

228

old basic metrical schemes, the young Bengali poet has perforce resorted to prose-rhythm. To-day Samar Sen usually, and
Amiya Chakravarti often (not to mention a score of lesser
poets), express themselves in the medium of prose-rhythm,
and it is notable that Buddhadeva Bose, Jibanananda Das,
Sudhindranath Datta and Bishnu Dey who are masters of
verse metrics do not underrate the value of prose-rhythm. The
process of emancipating Bengali verse from the shackles of
mechanical regular metre had certainly started long before
Eliot's influence began to make itself felt. Moreover, to write
verse in prose-rhythm is very much more difficult than to
write it in metre, and this is especially true of a language like
Bengali in which the tradition of prose literature is comparatively poor, while on the other hand the plenitude of vowel
sounds and rhymes makes metrical writing much easier than
prose writing. In his essay 'The liberation of rhythm and
Rabindranath,' Datta maintains that the resolution of the
dichotomy between verse and prose which every authentic
poet attempts to accomplish has at long last reached success in
Tagore; Datta ends his essay with the significant query,
whether what has been a salvation to Tagore may not turn
out to be a curse to others. Primarily their study of Eliot's
poetry convinced the Bengali poets of the æsthetic value of a
conversational prose rhythm in the treatment of material –
such material as their modern urban environment offers them
abundantly – but once they had learnt this lesson, for the
actual manipulation of prose rhythm, these poets had to read
Tagore's later poetry. Tagore's spell remains inescapable still.

Since 1930, the archetypal influences on Bengali poetry are
those of Eliot and Tagore (his later poetry); and it is a nice
question as to whose influence cuts deeper. Clearly the time
for a full evaluation is not yet. One has the feeling that the
amazing later poetry of Tagore, however inevitably it may
have evolved from the earlier, was possible because of the
stimulus it received from Eliot's poetry. At any rate, of the
stimulating and liberating action of Eliot's poetry on the works
of younger Bengali poets there can be no doubt. And yet there
is need for caution when one speaks of influences. I have not

the faintest intention of suggesting that influences tell the whole story of recent Bengali poetry. Young Bengali poets have too much creative vitality in them to be mere imitators: indeed, in their reviews of recent English and Bengali poetry, Bishnu Dey, Sudhindranath Datta and Buddhadeva Bose strike a consistently critical note. 'One of the surest tests,' writes Eliot, 'is the way in which a poet borrows. Immature poets imitate; mature poets steal; bad poets deface what they take, and good poets make it into something better, or at least something different. The good poet welds his theft into a whole of feeling which is unique, utterly different from that from which it is torn; the bad poet throws it into something which has no cohesion. A good poet will usually borrow from authors remote in time, or alien in language, or diverse in interest.' It is in this manner that our poets have 'borrowed' from Eliot, and if by the authenticity of their poetic devotion they have amply repaid their debt and have moved away from the creditor, surely no one will be happier than the creditor himself.

Norman Nicholson

Words and Imagery

I remember very clearly when first I met the poetry of
Mr T. S. Eliot. One hot summer day in 1934 when I was 20, a
friend called for me to go to the cricket field where I spent
most of my afternoons at that time, for I was convalescing from
a long illness. He was carrying the collected volume of Mr
Eliot's poems (the volume that begins with *Prufrock* and ends
with *The Hollow Men*) which had been added to the local
library at our request. I must have heard of Mr Eliot before
this, but only enough to think of him as a most advanced
modern poet, and my idea of a modern poet was of one who
splashed words on the page like a child splashes ink on blotting
paper. I remember that I took the book, glanced at a page or
two, and said, surprised, 'Why, some of it rhymes!' Then we
went over to the cricket field, where we sat in the shade of the
elderberry hedge, reading the poems with bewildered,
hilarious fervour, like that of a drunk man converted at a
Salvation Army street mission. Later we were called upon to
umpire a tennis match, and we stood at opposite ends of the
net, shouting to each other across the court:

The young are red and pustular
Clutching piaculative pence.

For weeks after that I went about with my head a froth of
words and imagery. I read every book mentioned in the notes
to *The Waste Land* and laid bare one meaning below another
like a woman peeling an onion (though I was not to meet that
simile for another year or so). Recently I learned from a friend
that I had grabbed his arm in the street and said 'Read *The
Waste Land*: It's the greatest poem in the English language.'
If the incident is true (I can't remember it myself), then my
remark was quite without exaggeration, for it *was* the
greatest poem I had read up to that time. Indeed, it was the
only poem I had read, for not until then did I learn how to

read poetry at all, not until then had I any conception of the peculiar shock and sensation of poetry, of the feel of the growth and greenness of words. I had been like a man casually plucking handfulls of grass and not looking what he was doing; now, by accident, I had got hold of a nettle and I looked.

Such personal reactions, however, are neither sufficiently perceptive nor sufficiently significant to be of interest to anyone, were it not that I think that they represent the reactions of a whole generation of readers. For many, of course, the impression went very much deeper, but others can deal more competently than I can with Mr Eliot's profound influence on those who have followed him. All I want to do now is to point out that this influence is not confined to intellectual circles; it has touched the lives and thoughts of many who have only half-understood the poetry and many who have not even read it. Perhaps I can make clearer what I mean if I draw a parallel with the Impressionist painters and their successors. The work of these, in spite of the popularity of recent exhibitions, can have been seen only by a small proportion of the people, yet, because of its influence on poster artists, industrial designers and so on, it has given to a whole generation and more a new conception of colour and a new way of looking at pictures and at the countryside. In the same way the influence of Mr Eliot has reached an enormous public, filtering down through the work of hundreds of poets, novelists, dramatists, radio-script-writers, journalists and even advertising agents. I have spotted it also in films, dance lyrics, sermons and blurbs. The revival of liturgical drama in the Church of England, for instance, is undoubtedly due to the success of *Murder in the Cathedral*, which may also have been responsible for the fashion in choral speaking.

Unimportant as these examples may be, I think they demonstrate that the influence of Mr Eliot is greater in range as well as in depth than that of any other contemporary poet. And what are the main characteristics of what I might call this surface influence? The first is that of language. When I read those poems in the cricket field it was the language which excited me first of all. Immense new possibilities were opened, and the dictionary became a box of fireworks, every one of them ready to flame and sparkle when it was touched off. It was not just that Mr Eliot had burst through the seams of a worn-out and shabby diction – this had been done before. Wordsworth had done the same thing for his generation by relating poetic diction to common speech. Moreover Wordsworth succeeded better than anyone before or since because he had a wonderful sense for those words which are so essential, so basic to the language and the emotions, that they scarcely change their significance from age to age. If you examine the poems like the *Matthew* and the *Lucy* series you will find that hardly a word he uses has become debased in meaning. Mr Eliot, however, related poetry not so much to common speech (though he made some experiments in that line in his dramatic works and monologues) but to that great commerce of language from which the modern reader draws his vocabulary – slang, journalism, literature and every other possible source. The result was that in these earlier poems he did not so much create a poetic diction as make it possible for other poets to create theirs.

The second characteristic is that of imagery. Let us look once again at my cricket field. It was a small but pleasant place, where, in 1934, many young men would be practising or lounging about for there was much unemployment in the town. Behind the elder hedge were the allotments and an orchard; on the north side, a school of dark slate, already falling to pieces; on the east, the railway sidings where, on Saturday afternoons, half the engines of the Furness Railway would congregate, the smoke blowing across the pitch and into the batsmen's eyes. Beyond, you could see the town, the slagbanks and the ironworks; out of sight, but not far away, were the iron ore mines, now almost worked out, miles of derelict land where nature was already fighting back. Above the railway, on a hill, stood a sandstone church, built in the 1880's out of the profits of the ironworks, rather bleak, not unhandsome but far too large for its average congregation. Over all this, like a smoky mist which came out of the sea, hung neglect, decay and despair. Here was the rotting edge of a civilization, the withered outer leaves. But on the fourth side of the field, across a fence of barbed wire and old iron bedsteads, were the meadows, where buttercups and grasses swirled over gently bumping ground for a couple of miles to the sea, and from thence there was nothing between you and the Isle of Man. That was our world in the 1930's. It was the world in which we all lived though the contrasts were plainer here in Cumberland than in many parts of England. And it was Mr Eliot more than anyone else who made us see it whole, who made us aware of the meadow behind the muckheap, who pointed out the significance of the delapidated school and the empty church on the hill. It was not a very hopeful picture that he made of it, but, at 20 years of age, we did not bother much about hope . . . indeed, we found despair quite exhiliarating. What mattered was that suddenly everything in our world had its meaning. The most disparate events and objects took a new relation to each other, becoming allegorical while still remaining themselves. From then onwards it was possible to move about and hear the everyday landscape and everyday lives giving forth liturgies and elegies of purpose and pity. The corrupt, calamitous, comic age, which so many were trying to explain in terms of economics, biology, anthropology, psycho-analysis, or even British Israelitism, was suddenly seen to have a significance in itself. The modern world came into focus for the first time.

234

Ruthven Todd

A Garland for Mr Eliot

Strictly contrived, the principles declare
That death is not averse to pleasantry;
The green mummy turned to gold must share
A small portion of the Inferno's immortality:

Also observed, the country village where
The good men flourished in their solitude –
'Good' meaning more than canticle or prayer:
Further, the soldiers marcelled in parade.

Provided excuse for poetry: words would snare
The late drinkers shambling from the pub,
And Tiresias' unexpectant eye upon the stair,
Golden rod, New England's rocks, or scuttling crab.

The curious obsessions formed the mind, aware
Of the sad ways man made towards their aim,
Even the gestures his hero could not dare
Became the impulse which created him.

John Heath-Stubbs

We Have Heard the Key Turn

Time present and time past
Are both perhaps present in time future,
And time future contained in time past.
If all time is eternally present
All time is unredeemable.

T. S. Eliot: *Burnt Norton.*

It is important to realize that no major poet can reject or
deny the validity of an earlier experience in the light of a
later one – even though he may believe that later experience
to be the fuller and more mature. The charming, Italianate
pastoral humanist, who was the youthful Milton, can still be
detected in the great Puritan epics of his later years. That
close interweaving of sensual and intellectual passion which
marks the love poems of Jack Donne, the brilliant young
Elizabethan man-about-town, is still there, but lifted to a
higher plane, in the mystical verse and prose of the Jacobean
Dean of St Paul's. The æsthetic preoccupations which give to
much of the early poetry of Yeats its langorous and dream-
like air, are not really any the less present in the realistic,
austere and bitter poems of his last phase. The work of each of
these poets is to be approached as a unity, and attentive critical
study will show it to be so. It is not that we read into their
early work hints of their later development; rather, we must
always consider their latest work, the matured fruit of many
years of the most intense imaginative living, in the context of
the initial moment of experience which their first poems
record.

This same unity is, I believe, to be found in the work of
T. S. Eliot; but I am aware that to many critics this has seemed
not to be the case. Some, accepting the religious experience of
his later work, would, it seems, prefer to regard the earlier

236

poems as no more than the expression of bitterness and
sterility. But to others this same development has appeared as
an averting of the eyes from the realities of the modern world,
and a taking refuge in mysticism, and within the walls of an
institutional Church. The late Demetrios Capetanakis – who
was one of the most profound and sensitive of modern critics –
seems to have hinted at this when he wrote: 'Although T. S.
Eliot's poetry is based on the tradition of the English poets
who tried to make man real by compelling him to face
nothingness, in its latest phase it has become too detached
to be disturbing or compelling in any way.' Nevertheless,
I believe that both these attitudes to Eliot's poetry are false.
To be the poet only of sterility, bitterness and despair, or
the purely contemplative mystic who has lost touch with
humanity – these are, perhaps, the two temptations which
have beset Eliot's path as a poet. But the reality of his poetry,
the essential consistency of his development, is the measure of
his successful resistance to these temptations. The early poetry
ceased to be purely a poetry of sterility as soon as the possibility of redemption became apparent in it – and this was
perhaps earlier than even Eliot himself was conscious of at the
time. But the abyss – the 'making men more real by compelling them to face nothingness' – is still present in the later
work, though integrated with the positive religious attitude
which Eliot has now embraced.

It is my purpose in the present note to suggest this con-
tinuity in the development of Eliot's work, with special reference to the earlier poems, beginning with the *Prufrock*
volume of 1917. The debt of these early poems to Jules
Laforgue has often been pointed out, but there is already an
essential difference between the world of Laforgue, who died
in 1887, and that of the youthful Eliot. Laforgue is the poet
of the misery and boredom of the refined nineteenth century
bourgeois society; this boredom is as monotonous and mean-
ingless as the scales practised, through the long afternoons, by
the frustrated virgin girls of the well-to-do suburbs:

Tu t'en vas et tu nous laisses,
Tu nous laisses et tu t'en vas,

237

Défaire et refaire ses tresses,
Broder d'éternels canevas.

One might almost say that whereas Eliot knows he is living in a dying civilization, for Laforgue – much more horribly – there is no reason why it should ever end. In the *Prufrock* poems we are presented with the figure of a young man, a young American – the tedium of New England society, from which he has escaped, is sketched in *The Boston Evening Transcript*, *Aunt Helen* and *Cousin Nancy*. This young American finds himself in an aristocratic, European world whose weariness and over-sophistication have infected him also. It is the world of Henry James, and also of Proust. Henry James, like Eliot, was an American expatriate, and Proust, as a Jew, was always something of an outsider in the Parisian society whose rottenness at once fascinated and horrified him. Yet Prufrock, lingering in the drawing-room where:

. . . *the women come and go*
Talking of Michelangelo

can envisage his escape, through a moment, on the plane of physical sex, of assertion of his own unique individuality. That act of assertion he dare not undertake, tormented by the consciousness of his own emotional inadequacy, and, above all, by the intellectual knowledge which outruns experience and renders real living impossible:

And would it have been worth it, after all,
Would it have been worth while,
After the sunsets and the dooryards and the sprinkled streets,
After the novels, after the teacups, after the skirts that trail along the floor –
And this, and so much more?

It was only later in the course of Eliot's development, and in relation to a higher and quite other experience, that the moment was to become real. It was transformed into

The awful daring of a moment's surrender.

And finally becomes

The moment in the rose garden,
The moment in the arbour where the rain beat,
The moment in the draughty church at smokefall.

It is the moment which is outside time, yet which requires times as the condition of its realization.

All the cunning and over-refinement of the old civilization are personified in the central figure of *Portrait of a Lady*. She is evidently an elderly woman, with what is vulgarly called a 'past', who is attempting, not indeed the seduction of the youthful speaker of the poem, but the assertion over him of some more subtle emotional claim, whose precise nature he cannot divine, and hence fears all the more. She says:

'I have been wondering frequently of late
(But our beginnings never know our ends!)
Why we have not developed into friends.'
I feel like one who smiles, and turning shall remark
Suddenly, his expression in a glass.
My self-possession gutters; we are really in the dark.

It is surely, however veiled, a mother-relationship that the Lady seeks to establish. Her cunning foreshadows that of Lady Monchensey, the Clytemnestra of *The Family Reunion*. But in that play the Erinnyes which Harry's rebellion against the possessive claims of his mother let loose upon him were to turn out to be the ministers of grace, and in the final tragedy there is the possibility of reconciliation. Only through such a reconciliation could the Lady of the *Portrait*, with her private ritual:

And four wax candles in the darkened room,
Four rings of light upon the ceiling overhead,
An atmosphere of Juliet's tomb

be replaced by, or transfigured as, that other Lady:

Lady of silences
Calm and distressed
Torn and most whole
Rose of memory
Rose of forgetfulness
Exhausted and life-giving
Worried reposeful.

For here she is the Church whose subtle and at first hardly definable emotional claim Eliot had learned, in humility, to concede.

239

One is tempted to wonder how much the world of *Prufrock* and the *Portrait of a Lady* is a real world and not a dream-world – the young American's romantic conception of what European society should be like. At any rate it seems remote from the reality of *Rhapsody on a Windy Night*, where the protagonist is walking home through London in the small hours because, presumably, he has missed his last 'bus and has not the price of a taxi-fare. But it is the harsh reality of the world between the wars that predominates in the *Poems* of 1920. Here, the Lady of the *Portrait* has become that symbol of corruption and lust diseased, the Princess Volupine, with her 'meagre, blue-nailed, phthisic hand, or her ritual has changed to that of

> . . . *Madame de Tornquist, in the dark room*
> *Sifting the candles*

– a sinister ceremony, suggestive of a Black Mass, performed by one who has deliberately shut herself in from the stream of history. But the dominant figure of these poems is that of Sweeney. It is his monstrous form that 'guards the horned gate,' and he enacts a sordid parody of the tragic fate of Agamemnon. Sweeney stands for the mediocrity of our civilization, *l'homme moyen sensuel*. Mr Van Wyck Brooks, in his *New England Indian Summer*, plausibly suggests that the name Sweeney connotes the Irish Catholics who have largely taken possession of modern Boston, disrupting its traditional Puritan culture, and who hence provide, for Eliot the New Englander, a fitting symbol for the intrusive vulgarity of twentieth century bourgeois life.

In these poems surely we may detect

> *The laceration*
> *Of laughter at what ceases to amuse.*

There is a harshness and bitterness not to be found in the earlier poems, and a contemptuous hatred of Sweeney. Later, in *Sweeney Agonistes*, Eliot was to see Sweeney also as hunted by the Erinnyes, and hence no less susceptible of forgiveness than the tragic Harry of *The Family Reunion*. But at present his poetry was sweeping him towards the inferno of *The Waste Land*. The Waste Land is not only the stricken

240

country of the Grail myths, it is also an infernal city, like Dante's City of Dis, and all the cities of the world:

Jerusalem Athens Alexandria
Vienna London

seen under an unreal and infernal aspect. The City, in poetry,
is the natural symbol of human life lived in a complex of
relations between individuals. But here all these relations
have been disrupted, and replaced by their shadows. Love and
its fruition are absent, but there is the neurotic mutual torment of the rich couple, the joyless copulation of the clerk and
the typist, the woman in the public house scene who seeks
abortion through fear and poverty, and the suggestion of
perversion in Mr Eugenides' invitation to a week-end at the
Metropole. Religion is absent, but is represented by its
shadow, magic; Madame Sosostris, the famous clairvoyante,
warns against that Death by Water that should, in reality be
the means of rebirth.

All the women in *The Waste Land* are one, and the Lady
achieves her most terrifying metamorphosis as the woman who

. . . Drew her long black hair out tight
And fiddled whisper music on those strings
And bats with baby faces in the violet light
Whistled, and beat their wings
And crawled head downward down a blackened wall.

Yet her appearance is a prelude to the description of the Chapel
Perilous, which is, or might be, a place of initiation. For when
we have reached the heart of this poem we have heard the key

Turn in the door once and turn once only
We think of the key, each in his prison
Thinking of a key, each confirms a prison.

It is not said which way the key turned, still less that release
was effected. But once the existence of the prison is made really
known, there is always the hope and the possibility of release.

The *Four Quartets* are the record of four pilgrimages,
whose purpose is the rediscovery of and reconciliation with the
past. They lead to a deserted house in New England, where
there is a secret garden with a lily-pond, and leaves concealing
unborn children, like the dream-children of Kipling's *They;*

241

to a village in Somerset which once gave birth to the poet's own forefathers (here, and not in the cosmopolitan drawing room where the Lady sat serving tea to friends, could the reconciliation with the old civilization be effected); to a cape by the sea, on which stands a shrine of the Virgin Mother of God; and, finally, to a place in the heart of England and history 'where prayer has been valid.'

Valid, one asks, for what? The experiment of Nicholas Ferrar, who attempted to establish at Little Gidding a religious community life, was, historically speaking, a total failure. Puritan opposition forced him and his family to flee to the Continent, never to return. The place is remembered for the visit of a broken king in the hour of his defeat, in a war in which both sides ultimately suffered defeat – not only the king, but also the poet 'who died blind and quiet.' Milton once stood for much against which Eliot was in reaction – Puritanism in religion, and a certain tradition of rhetoric in English verse; that at this point he, too, is forgiven seems to me to be deeply significant.

It is only in the acceptance of total defeat that this final reconciliation, with Time, and with the will of God expressing itself through the purgatory of history, is possible. Only now can we listen to the voice of the Lady Julian, the fourteenth century anchoress of Norwich, to whom, lying, as it seemed, at the very threshold of death, her Lord revealed that 'Sin is behovely, but all shall be well, and all manner of thing shall be well.' In the light of what had gone before in Eliot's experience it seems to me that this is most truly 'becoming more real by facing nothingness.' It is through this courage that the poet who, in the person of *Prufrock*, once cried, with bitter irony:

But though I have wept and fasted, wept and prayed,

Though I have seen my head (grown slightly bald) brought in upon a platter,

I am no prophet – and there's no great matter;

has, whether they willed it or not, or knew what they were doing, led two generations of his fellows into the wilderness, to fast and pray indeed.

Vernon Watkins

To T. S. Eliot

Hurried and late, my praise comes for your calm,
Unhurried verse. The valedictory fame
Of men was tested by your candle-flame.
An age drew near; you waited with your palm.
Turning, you saw the evening light embalm
Civilization caught in its own shame
An hour before the great procession came:
Olives and stones, the people and the palm.

A witness there, you grieved for that disease
Crossing the broken myth of ancient man.
You drew, in praising the four mysteries,
Profoundest joy, born of profoundest pain.
'All here encountered I shall know again . . . '
    'If I am steadfast, one will bring the keys . . . '

T. S. Eliot and Eugenio Montale

Parallels in history, though apt to be misleading, offer a tempting playground for speculation. Should the principle of Plutarch's *Lives* be applied to literature, as indeed it has been done every now and then, we might walk as through a gallery of portraits arranged in groups according to more or less evident affinities, and wonder at the mystery of the growth of the human tree, which causes similar flowers to blossom at the same time in distant and apparently unrelated branches. Hölderlin, Keats and Foscolo, temperamentally unlike each other as they were, present to us in flawless verse the same aspiration to a classical dreamland, to a beauty loaded with ethical meaning, a beauty which is truth. The parallel extends to the fate of their more ambitious works: *Hyperion, Le Grazie*, are unfinished poems, Hölderlin's inspiration was cut short by madness. In our century, in the period between the two wars, two poets have arisen in the Anglo-Saxon world and in Italy, whose outlooks show remarkable affinities which can only partially be accounted for through the same cultural influences. *The Waste Land* and *Ossi di seppia* conjure up the same vision of a barren, disconsolate world, of a desperate aridity searching every cranny of the rocks for a drop of water:

> *If there were the sound of water only*
> *Not the cicada*
> *And dry grass singing*
> *But sound of water over a rock*
> *Where the hermit-thrush sings in the pine trees.*

The barren landscape, symbolical of a state of the soul, which plays such a part in Eliot's verse, is also the landscape of Montale's poetry, of the following early lines, for instance:

> *Meriggiare pallido e assorto*
> *presso un rovente muro d'orto,*

244

ascoltare tra i pruni e gli sterpi
schiocchi di merli, frusci di serpi

Osservare tra frondi il palpitare
lontano di scaglie di mare
mentre si levano tremuli scricchi
di cicale dai calvi picchi.

E andando nel sole che abbaglia
sentire con triste meraviglia
com'e tutta la vita e il suo travaglio
in questo seguitare una muraglia
che ha in cima cocci aguzzi di bottiglia. *

Eliot had possibly in mind some barren district of America, but
Montale's barren land can be more easily identified: it is his
native land, the Cinque Terre near La Spezia, whose spirit
permeates his first volume of verse, and offers an exact counterpart of the poet's inner landscape: the Cinque Terre,
whose wretched inhabitants wage a constant war against the
elements, save every grain of fertile soil from disastrous land-
slides, and grow scanty vinyards among cruel rocks; the Cinque
Terre, whose rare pine-trees are distorted into fantastic shapes
of dishevelled despair by the prevailing winds: a narrow strip
of waste land in one of the most enchanting regions of the
world, the Riviera. There is nothing there so grand in scale

*I give here a translation I made twenty years ago, but the sound
of the last stanza would be better conveyed by a type of assonance first
used in modern English poetry by Owen, later adopted by Auden:

To rest at noon, pale and entranced,
in the shade of a burning orchard wall,
to listen, among thorns and brakes,
to the whistling of thrushes, to the rustling of snakes

To gaze through the leaves, downhill,
at the glitter of scales in the sea,
while tremulous rises the shrill
of cicadas on the barren cliffs.
And walking in the dazzling day
to feel with a sad dismay
how life and its toil are all
like this skirting along a wall
that bristles with sharp bottle-shards.

as in the American deserts; similarly it might be maintained that also the vision of the Italian poet is not endowed with the wide range of that of the author of *The Waste Land:* Montale's world is a small world reflected in a convex mirror to the vast sheet of glass presented in the English poem which marks one of the important dates in the history of contemporary literature. But allowing for proportions, the message of the Italian poet who compares life to walking along a wall bristling with bottle-shards, and the message of the Anglo-American poet who plods through cataclysmatic landscapes whose grandeur verges on Dante's Inferno, are substantially the same.

When in 1928 I submitted to Eliot my translation of Montale's *Arsenio** he must have recognized in the poem the accent of a kindred inspiration. And when about the same time I lent to Montale in Florence *A Song for Simeon* and *La Figlia che Piange* in the Ariel Poems, the Italian poet was so much impressed that he felt the desire to make the two poems his own by translating them.† For a long time the figures of the two poets were associated in my mind: I saw a family likeness in their outward appearance of sallow, prematurely aged men, slow, unemphatic in their manners, seemingly incapable of strenuous physical effort, reserved and concentrated in an inner vision, unworldly, like priests of an unhallowed religion. Eliot was then evolving towards a more positive creed, finding in Dante the model of the perfect poet, and in his verse the secret of the correlative objective. It is remarkable that Montale, who had known Dante from his early youth, should nevertheless have developed a formula very close to the correlative objective through his reading of Eliot's verse. For in the thirties Montale, growing fully aware of Eliot's power, without loss of originality enriched his own technique with devices strongly reminiscent of Eliot.

Covert allusions to personal experiences, which, puzzling to the reader as they are, diffuse an intimate atmosphere in a poem, so that one seems to share them in a dream-like fashion,

---

*Published in *The Criterion*, VII, 4 (June 1928).
†See Montale: *Eliot e noi*, in *L'Immagine*, I, 5 (Nov-Dec 1947).

as if with a little effort one might remember them as parts of one's own past, and still that effort will not be undertaken, since the lyrical import of the experience is already transfused into the verse; quotations often in a foreign language embedded in the texture of a poem, which receives illumination from them; notes throwing light on the text, though often in a non-committal way: these are traits of Eliot's technique which Montale seems to have mastered in his second volume of verse, *Le occasioni* (1939). Thus in many of his later poems (for instance *Ballata in una clinica*) Montale's imagery avails itself of precise details of an experience (objects, often alluded to only in their essential feature) through which he finds the emotional equivalent of thought. Thus in *Sotto la pioggia* (in *Le occasioni*) a phrase of St Teresa, 'Por amor de la fiebre,' and the tune of a gramophone record, 'Adios muchachos,' have the same function in the economy of Montale's verse as quotations from Provençal poets or Dante, or from the popular Australian ballad 'Mrs Porter and her daughter' in Eliot's poems. And the tone of notes such as: 'Riguardo alla leggenda evocata cfr. Eduardo Posada, *El Dorado*, etc' to *Costa San Giorgio* (in *Le occasioni*), reminds one of the references to Frazer and Miss Weston in *The Waste Land*. The personality of both poets does not obtrude itself on the reader: to Eliot the lasting poem is not the result of the pouring forth of personal emotion, but of externalizing the emotions in a pattern, thus giving them a universal stature: he does not write in his own person, but projects his own experiences into characters such as Prufrock or Gerontion. Montale avoids speaking in the first person, resorts to indirect expression of his own feeling to such a degree, that some have actually spoken of an absence of feeling in him; he transposes his own state into symbols generally suggested by the landscape, whose aspects tend to become fixed in the eternity of an instant. Eliot aims at writing poetry which should be essentially poetry with nothing poetic about it; to get beyond poetry, as Beethoven, in his later works, strove to get beyond music; the same avoidance of the obviously 'poetic,' the same lucid, firm, almost prosaic intonation in Montale, whose first volume of verse by its well-chosen title *Ossi di seppia* (cuttle-fish bones) seemed to convey the idea of a neat, arid, shining object and also of a stray thing which has been washed ashore by the storm. 'Not an absence of music, but a new sense of it, which does not reject cacophony and dissonance, a music which, according to Eliot, is the function of the whole poem, not of isolated lines.'*

Though Montale has, then, certainly learned a few things from Eliot, there was, as I have said, an initial affinity between the two poets, which imparts to their verse the same character of subdued translucency, of beauty and tenderness laboriously distilled from the crucible of sorrow, of a lyric power bursting out of the very aridity in which it is shut. The flavour of their poems I do not know how to convey better than with Leopardi's image of the 'scented broom, content with desert places':

Qui su l'arida schiena
del formidabil monte

tuoi cespi solitari intorno spargi,
odorata ginestra
contenta dei deserti.

*These are words of Giovanni Macchia in his essay *Sulla poesia italiana contemporanea* in the volume *Studi*, Napoli, 1947. The quotation from Eliot is from his lecture *La musique de la poésie* in the volume *Ecrivains américains d'aujourd'hui*, Geneva, Editions du Continent, 1944.

Richard March

A Journey to the Centre of the Earth

On Saturday afternoons when Mr Stetson left the office he
would sometimes take a walk through the deserted City
streets. A wistful air of peacefulness pervades the silent passages and alleyways that wind maze-like between and through
the office blocks.

A little while ago (he cannot exactly remember the occasion) it was drizzling when Mr Stetson hurried past the
Mansion House and up King William Street. The gentle rain
had softened the harsh spring light and hung like a veil over
the buildings and across the purple pavements.

It was unusually quiet that afternoon, a little eerie. The
blackened buildings, the occasional passer-by, the dray man
with his shaggy horse and cart, all had a spectral look, and
vanished noiselessly into the mist.

Mr Stetson passed the Monument with its crown of spikes
blurred by the rain, and turned into Lower Thames Street
where the fish market was closed and deserted. In between
the warehouses he saw the freighters moored to the quays.
The tide was running out. A double line of barges towed by a
black and yellow tug nosed slowly up stream. The bargemen
called to each other in their weird and melancholy sing-song.
He walked on more rapidly, as though it were really necessary
to reach some destination, although he had long convinced
himself that his progress was purposeless and circumambula-
tory, the expression of a spiritual tergiversation. Mr Stetson
soon got tired but continued his walk, for what else was there
to do? The smell of the river, the sight of the ships and the
wharfside gave him a wonderful sensation of liberation, and
filled his mind with exotic memories, as though he remembered exciting adventures from another place and time. They
caused his heart to beat more rapidly, tormented as he was
by the anxiety of the moment that is poised so perilously be-

249

fore the void, and that is certain any minute to disintegrate into nothingness. In this terrible moment, thought Mr Stetson, which is like a precipice, breaking off abruptly into the yawn of nothing, there is no compromise or relief save that which every mortal creature has of belonging in the world. And personality, in which all possibilities have their origin and destiny, takes comfort in the man of flesh and bone, who thinks and drinks, and eats, and sleeps, and dies. Yes, the man who dies.

With this gnawing anguish in his heart, then, to which was added the fear of being followed by a stranger who might dare look into his soul and challenge his right of way, Mr Stetson walked on more quickly along the cobbled street which was covered with large pools full of mud and garbage. Seized with panic, he broke into a run past the shuttered warehouses, and plunged forward through the rain that hung before him like a net of spawn.

Where should he go? Mr Stetson felt he had been walking for hours. He was worn out. Without noticing much where he was going, he turned into a narrow passage flanked by prim little houses. It was quite empty, and had such a comforting and restful air that he shuffled along its pavements with a sense of relief.

The rain had stopped. A humid neutral light flowed up the street, and over the grey stone houses with geranium pots in the windows. It gave to the soft Spring evening a feeling of quiet assurance. His footsteps echoed on the stones. He felt calmer and his anxiety no longer oppressed him so sharply. Mr Stetson felt almost as though a faltering hope, if only in the shape of an immense interrogation mark, had once more cast its shadow on the world.

To his astonishment he noticed that in the middle of this alley there was a little shop, a book shop, with a stall in front beneath a tattered awning. The window and the stall were crammed with antique and weather worn volumes. As he idled at the stall, sampling the familiar assortment, he began to recover his composure. It seemed to him that he had entered a haven of safety, a refuge from the pursuing terrors.

Among the rows of shabby books, he caught sight of a title stamped boldly in faded gold, which read: *A Journey to the Centre of the Earth*. Jules Verne, magic name! He took up the volume and turned the faded pages, while the excitement, the thrill of far-off days when he had first read the book, began to stir in him again. The absurd engravings depicting the adventures of the eccentric German Professor and his be-wildered nephew exerted the same enchantment on his imagination as they had done long ago.

'A very rare volume,' said a deep, drawling voice at his side.

Mr Stetson looked up with a start. Just beyond the awning, and in front of a board nailed to the wall, bearing the name of the shop, stood a tall, grave, youngish-looking man in a bowler hat. He wore a stiff white collar, and a striped suit that gave the impression of being somewhat too small for him. His manner was agreeable and suave. His speech, if a little halting, was carefully articulated. His whole personality made a strong but not easily definable impression on Mr Stetson. He seemed a trifle foreign, perhaps, in this setting.

'You are the proprietor?' he asked.

The tall youngish man in the meticulously pressed striped suit looked steadily at him for a minute out of very blue eyes, in which there seemed to linger a suggestion of melancholy, and then replied, in his measured voice, enunciating the words very distinctly, but with a curious air of hesitation:

'That is so, well, ah . . . in a manner of speaking.'

Mr Stetson was nonplussed. He had a queer feeling as though he had met this stranger somewhere before. He seemed so friendly and reassuring, that he soon found himself talking about the merits of his favourite author, that is, the favourite author of his boyhood days. The bookshop proprietor agreed. No one else save a Victorian enthusiast like Jules Verne could have conjured such fabulous enchantment from the materials of a world that nourished within itself all the elements of the diabolical.

'But that particular book is not for sale. The fact is I am still studying it myself.'

'Indeed you are!' Mr Stetson exclaimed in astonishment.

251

He looked intently at the bookshop proprietor's sallow face which seemed vaguely familiar to him. The youngish man in the bowler hat evidently thought so too, for he remarked drily:

'I believe we have met before somewhere. It must have been a long time ago, on board ship, if I remember right, during the War.'

Mr Stetson puckered his brow.

'In Italy, towards the end of the Civil Wars, perhaps. That is certainly a long time ago. I often hardly know whether my memories are those of real experiences, or of things I have read about and imagined.

'The reality of time is certainly difficult to determine. But you had an interest in gardening, I remember. We passed the time very often discussing your experiments in horticulture.'

Mr Stetson, as though he felt disinclined to pursue these reminiscences observed somewhat testily, that at any rate there was more sense in that nowadays, than in reading fanciful tales of impossible journeys. 'Why?' asked the youngish man in the striped suit and dove-coloured spats who wore such a fatigued and despondent air, in a shocked voice. 'I don't consider such a journey at all impossible. There is indeed an obligation on people to undertake some such expedition.'

Mr Stetson waved the suggestion aside indignantly. 'You cannot undertake an expedition to the centre of the earth! It has no centre!' The journey would be purposeless he went on to explain. It would not have a destination. It would be unending.

The proprietor gave a sardonic laugh, and invited him to step inside. There were few customers at this hour, he explained, so they might as well take their ease and have a chat.

'There is yet time,' he said, 'time for you, I hope, and for me.'

'Not for me,' Mr Stetson said. 'For me the hands of the clock are always moving towards the final stroke.'

The proprietor smiled wryly, and led the way through the shop, between the rows of tattered books, and out at the back into a small paved courtyard.

252

In spite of his air of lassitude and indecision, his companion inspired in Mr Stetson a feeling of confidence. His physical presence helped wonderfully to soothe his previous anxieties. He had almost lost the nervous fatigue of the long tramp through the City streets. His host's manner was kindly and persuasive, almost avuncular in fact, in spite of his hesitations. They strolled round the little courtyard which was laid out like a sunken garden, with cactus in boxes round the sides, and large geranium pots in the middle. At the further end was a wall with a wooden door from which the paint was flaking away in patches.

'Now this romance of Jules Verne's,' Mr Stetson began. 'I can well understand your attachment to it. In an atmosphere like this it is possible to recapture the exuberant day dreams of our fathers.'

Mr Stetson glanced at his companion who was frowning. He had a habit of drawing his eyebrows together so that two deep grooves showed above the bridge of his prominent nose. This gave him an expression of extraordinary concentration. His eyes were large and blue, but their light seemed to be turned on an inward scene, so that they remained somewhat enigmatical. He thrust his head (this large bloodless head crowned with a bowler hat) forward as he spoke, like a preacher in a pulpit explaining to his flock the subtler casuistries of their sinful lives. But Mr Stetson didn't notice this just then. As they strolled slowly round the drab little garden, his host described, very vividly, the descent down the crater of Mount Sneffels, and the dark tortuous route that had once led to the centre of the earth. The author had reinforced his story with the most exact scientific calculations that always turned out to be miraculously correct.

His host went on to observe that the significance of such calculations was apt to be very different from what those who made them had intended. The celebrated discoveries have only led to the conclusion that the Universe is without a Creator. The scientist is driven on by a mystical, irrational urge to discover the so-called laws of the universe, penetrate deeper into their mysteries. It is not only a question of dis-

253

covery and revelation, but also of the will to dominate and to control. The scientists' unconscious intention seems to be to replace the Creator. There is the paradox.

But as he grows more successful and powerful, it is slowly borne in on modern man, that the mystery that still confronts him remains mysterious and impenetrable. Furthermore, it had now lost some of its value for the spirit. It had been stripped of the myth and the magic which formerly gave it content and meaning. The world as portrayed by science is a tawdry jig-saw puzzle. And we have gradually realized that this world without any foundation, this creation without a creator, must be absolutely senseless. The absence of God has become a reality. Only disillusion results from this dreadful realization.

Mr Stetson glanced at him with indignation.

It is better, his host continued, to start again. It is better to descend into the depths and find a centre somewhere in the world. The centre is God. God dwells at the very heart of the world.

But these regions of the central sea, objected Mr Stetson, are dull. One might arrive there at the point of the eternal, where all Time is one, but it's a boring neighbourhood, a region without drama, or conflict, and above all, without tragedy.

That was precisely the purpose of the search, his companion explained, that the present lose its importance, and the past and the future be experienced as interchangeable values.

Past and Future inhered in the regions of the eternal and the eternal after all, was in oneself. To submit oneself to the revelation, at the centre of the earth, required a degree of humility and restraint which gave a peculiar twist to the experience of the actual.

In the gathering dusk, Mr Stetson glanced uncomprehendingly at his companion whose face was tired and drawn. Though a very ordinary gentleman who lived in a villa in Golders Green, and habitually carried a black brief-case with his initials stamped on it, in gold, he felt disturbed. We are in a world without foundations, he kept on repeating. And we

254

are still able to communicate with one another. Walking blindly along the precipice which separates us from Nothingness, we still communicate with one another and reveal to ourselves the potentialities contained in the living moment. In this tension we created the reality that is our insoluble life. It is a world of the banal, the sordid, and the trivial; still, we are at home in it.

His companion did not seem to be listening to what he was saying. They walked slowly round and round, their footsteps echoing on the flagged stones of the sunken garden.

The worst of the contemporary world, the bookshop proprietor remarked at last, was the disappearance of the human being. So few people seemed to be upset about it, this tragedy of the disappearance of the human being in our world. What use was all this fuss about reordering society, or rearranging the machines in a more efficient way, in a world without human beings? The only course now was to insist again on the humanity of Man, and this implied a search for his relationship to God. Thus might what was eternal in his soul be redeemed. The revelation of eternal life could be found in the authority of the Word. It was a question of preparing the mind for its reception.

It was quite dark now. Mr Stetson could no longer see the garden or the house, and was again agitated by a certain nervousness, the sensation of being pursued, which had accompanied him during his walk through the City streets. The bookseller suddenly stopped his leisurely ambulation in front of the wooden door at the farther end of the garden. It was closed, and it struck him as peculiar that there did not appear to be any gardens or houses adjoining the other side of the wall. Perhaps the door led on to an area of vacant lots, such as one saw on the outskirts of big cities. Perhaps the brown and oily waters of London River gurgled beyond the wall on its broadening course past Greenwich Reach and the Isle of Dogs.

Mr Stetson had a queer sensation that the door might reveal something unexpected and amazing. He suspected that his companion spent his leisure hours contemplating this prospect which provided an answer to a terrible problem that

255

disturbed his peace of mind.

'What is on the other side of this door?' Mr Stetson inquired. It seemed as though his companion, in his hesitating way, had some deliberate purpose in leading him to this spot.

'What would you wish there to be?' the other replied with the faintest suggestion of irony in his voice. Mr Stetson could not believe that there was anything at all beyond the door, only nothingness, the dark, the void. Beyond that thresh-hold gaped the edge of the world without foundation or centre, a world from which the idea of the Maker had died away.

They stood before the closed door and groped for the key, while their hearts struggled in the grip of a terrible anxiety. The issues were tragic and without solution, but the painful role exalted them.

In the darkness Mr Stetson could no longer distinguish the features of his companion, though he stood very close to him. He saw him fumbling in his pocket for the key. That took a long time, and when at last he found it, he muttered that he had forgotten the position of the lock. Mr Stetson was seized again by a violent fit of agitation as he watched these proceedings.

'This is the danger point, the final challenge,' he said, in distress.

'Do we dare and do we dare?' his companion asked.

'The final challenge must be accepted,' Mr Stetson exclaimed.

The door opened softly, and mysteriously, since neither of them could have explained how the key had worked in the lock. For Mr Stetson, existence broke off just at this point, and he sensed with a feeling of vertigo, which it was impossible to suppress, the presence of the void, the icy breath of Nothing. They stood on the brink that was ever crumbling beneath their feet. In this final moment which is every moment, he thought, we can recollect ourselves, and reach again into the inner personality, we taste once more the source of Being.

'Pass through,' his companion invited sepulchrally. And to Mr Stetson's astonishment he saw that the door had opened as if by magic. The gloom on the other side seemed even denser.

A sharp wind blew through the gap and they shivered.

His companion's form bent forward slightly, took a long step, and ignoring all obstructions passed over the thresh-hold. Mr Stetson braced himself and followed. Here, at the frontier point, into which their destiny was now compressed, the suspense was all but unbearable.

To his relief the deep quiet voice sounded in the darkness from an indeterminate spot close by. But now it carried an almost defiant note.

'At this point many a one has failed,' it said. 'Here there is neither rest nor movement. Here the past and the future are gathered.'

'Excuse me,' Stetson stuttered. 'I find the darkness very oppressive. I can't see anything at all. We may be at the bottom of a very deep pit; for ought I know, in the bowels of the earth from which there's no escape.'

'Perhaps we are, but we can descend lower still,' the bookseller answered, but his voice sounded faint.

'This wall of darkness is impenetrable,' Stetson groaned. 'If you don't mind, I'll light a match.' He put his hand in his pocket and pulled out a box of matches.

'You mustn't do that,' warned the voice. 'It's no great distance now to the centre of the earth. The atmosphere down here is full of sulphur and dangerous gases. There will be a terrible explosion if you strike a match. We will be blown to pieces.'

But Stetson was beyond caring.

'Do you suppose,' he cried frenziedly, 'that I am frightened by the prospect of destruction!'

He took out a match, and held it threateningly to the box. His hand shook with fear, and somehow he could not believe that his companion would dare him to strike it.

'Very well, go on then, if you must,' said the voice.

A sly and mocking note in it very nearly caused Mr Stetson's nerve to fail. He was uncomfortably aware that the situation contained an element of the absurd. And in his anguish he was almost on the point of putting back the match into the box, when a sudden and ungovernable exultation

257

surged through him, a leap of the will beyond the confines of reasonableness or logic. A convulsive movement agitated his hands, the sound of the striking match rent the darkness, and a thin blue and yellow flame quivered before their eyes. For an instant it shed a spectral ring of light around them, and Mr Stetson saw that his companion with the pale drawn face beneath his bowler hat, still stood close by his side. Was this the last, the ultimate moment?

As they waited in the silence and the darkness, the centre of their loneliness, and watched for the match to burn itself out, Mr Stetson became aware that instead of the shattering thunderclap that he had expected, the light had suddenly increased. The flame spat and spluttered and seemed to leap out of his hand. Its radiance was blinding like a magnesium flare. The heat was intense and Mr Stetson was very much alarmed. Surely we must be in hell, he thought, and looked to his companion who now, to his astonishment, had shed his wearied and woe-begone air, and led the way forward with agility and skill as though he really knew where they were going. His expression, which at first had been irresolute, now struck Stetson as purposeful and energetic.

With this sudden infusion of energy into his ambiguous companion the atmosphere appeared to grow less suffocating. All the same, he wondered, as he clutched his hands, when would they ever succeed in escaping from this terrible nightmare? Was this a moment in time and of time, a moment dissecting the world of time? They seemed to be walking on air, they were scorched by a sulphurous river; at one moment Stetson had the impression that they floated among a squadron of galleys and triremes and that the din of battle reverberated in their ears, the clamour of contending armies sounding in the distance. And then again Mr Stetson felt as though he were mounting an infinite stairway on his hands and knees. He felt as though he was drowned and that his body was being dragged along the ocean floor by the tides. But all the time, the youngish man in the bowler hat and the natty striped suiting, steadfastly remained at his side. And furthermore, Mr Stetson became aware of the fact that his companion was

258

singing to himself. The words and the melody sounded strange, but Mr Stetson had to acknowledge that his host had a very fine resonant voice, and sang wonderfully indeed.

'Light, light,' sang the bookseller with the exhausted smile, 'the visible reminder of Invisible Light.' And Mr Stetson noticed to his intense relief that day had broken, another silvery, indeterminate, rain-washed city day.

'Thank God!' said Mr Stetson.

With a gasp he realized that he was entirely alone, and sitting on the edge of his bed at home, in the villa at Golders Green. The window was open, and a pale light slid down the housetops. Mr Stetson clutched his head in dismay. He had a bad headache. He scarcely dared remember what had happened to him since he left the office. He could still hear a strange and haunting voice singing in the distance, and that reassured him a little. He rose unsteadily, struggled to his wash-stand and poured himself out a glass of water. His throat felt very dry. I really must be more careful in future, he thought to himself, and he glanced out of the window to see whether that new crop he had planted in the garden, showed any signs of sprouting. To his annoyance he noticed that his neighbour's puppy had got through the fence again and was scratching about among his beds. I'll fix that tike one day, he muttered angrily, as he began to strop his razor.